FOOD AND POVERTY

The Political Economy of Confrontation

RADHA SINHA

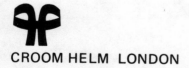

CROOM HELM LONDON

First published 1976
© 1976 by Radha Sinha

Croom Helm Ltd
2-10 St John's Road, London SW 11

ISBN 0-85664-697-0

Printed in Great Britain
by Biddles Ltd, Guildford, Surrey

CONTENTS

LIST OF TABLES

PREFACE

The origin of this book goes back to a summer evening in Delhi when my host had persuaded me to join him at a wedding reception. It was being held in a five-star hotel and there were several hundred guests attending. What appalled me most was the elaborate scale on which the whole thing was arranged, at a time when Maharashtra was in the grip of a severe famine and people were dying of starvation. Still more disturbing was the presence of a significant number of high-ranking bureaucrats and political leaders, the very same ones who claimed to be committed to eliminating poverty, inequality and hunger from the face of India.

This contrast between the world of 'professing' and the world of 'practice' has been forcefully demonstrated in frequent, elaborately organised huge international conferences, meetings and symposia on the problems of poverty and hunger. One of the conspicuous examples was the richness of the cuisine served to the delegates to the Rome Food Conference in 1974 which was deliberating on the ways and means to combat mass starvation around the world.

World leaders, who in their public pronouncements promise the millenium, become mean and vicious at the negotiating table. All this is done in the 'national' interest, though in practice this often turns out to be a sectional interest promoted by particular lobbies. Besides, in politics, short-term interests often supersede the long-term interests of the country. For these reasons issues of poverty and food, particularly concerning people of distant lands, have never been a major vote-catching issue in the richer countries.

However, the time has come when brushing aside the issues of trade and aid as peripheral problems for the richer countries may go against their long-term interests. Therefore the problem of world poverty and hunger has to be seen as a growing crisis of confidence between the richer and the poorer countries which, if not tackled in due time, will threaten the very life-style of the people in richer countries by increasing the risk of confrontation between them.

Seen in this light, aid and trade concessions are no longer simply moral issues, a question of salving one's own conscience; they become vital for the very existence of a stable society for future generations in developed and developing countries alike. A failure to defuse the issues at the earliest opportunity will certainly force the developing countries to resort to more desperate measures. The tragedy is that with the growing crisis in the developing countries, the leadership in these countries may tend to apportion more and more blame for their distress on the misdeeds of the richer countries. This would lead to a greater hardening of attitudes on both sides. It is important, therefore, that the richer countries pay serious attention to ameliorating the genuine grievances of the poorer countries; the imaginary grievances can then be easily exposed.

The genuine grievances are numerous. The richer countries have given enough cause for bitterness and frustration among the developing countries. If this book is able to reflect some of the bitterness and frustrations of the developing countries, my efforts will not have gone in vain.

The amelioration of genuine grievances would certainly require reorganisation of world trading and investment policies. In the short run, this may hurt the domestic economies of the developed countries. Therefore these governments will have to explain to their own people the long-term implications of alternative policies. Here the voluntary organisations and aid lobbies can play their part in creating an awareness of the issues. In fact, these organisations and lobbies themselves have opted for the line of least resistance and ignored the long-term aspects of the problem for short-term gains. It is easier for such organisations to 'educate' the public opinion but they have invariably not done so. One major role that voluntary organisations and aid lobbies can play is to get together with consumer lobbies, etc., to draw the attention of consumers to the high prices for various goods being paid due to restrictive trade policies. Similarly, attention could be drawn towards the fallacious arguments being put forward for maintaining enormous military machines to keep armament industries in high profits.

Because of my Asian background this book draws heavily on conditions prevailing there. To a considerable extent this is justifiable because the majority of the very poor live in the more densely populated countries of Asia. To be sure, no one solution is necessarily appropriate for all the different types of developing countries — be they in Asia, Africa or Latin America. My main aim has been to highlight the implications of the 'liberal' or 'democratic' solutions advocated by the 'Western' elites. It is often not realised that such solutions may have huge social costs. It is not being argued that the alternative solutions are always preferable to the 'liberal' solutions. Often they may not be. But in discarding them, care needs to be taken that this is done on rational grounds.

In any case, the ultimate choice between alternatives rests with the elites of the developing countries who have to find their own solutions, often by trial and error. They must, however, remember that systems cannot be wholly transplanted; and that the process of finding an appropriate solution is a really painful one. Above all, the elites of the developing countries who readily blame the richer countries for continuing injustices towards them, cannot afford to ignore the issues of a fairer distribution of resources and political power at home. By evading the issue or by changing the rules of the game to suit their convenience, they may be sowing the seeds of their own destruction.

I have received considerable sympathy and support from many colleagues and friends in the course of the preparation of this book. I am deeply indebted to Mark Elvin, Lawrence Smith, Mike Tribe, George Houston, Norman Clark, Philip Thomforde, André Biro, Kurt Lewenhak and Sister Merlyn D'Sa for reading the draft and making valuable suggestions. I am particularly grateful to Gerry Mueller, Alan Whitworth and Gautam Pingle for helping me in the various stages of the completion of the book.

It is not easy for me to express my gratitude to my colleagues and friends in various divisions of the Food and Agricultural Organisation who have directly or indirectly helped in the shaping of my views on the world food problem during my long association with that Organisation. I am particularly indebted to my colleagues in the Statistics Division of the Organisation for their unfailing help.

It goes without saying that none of the people mentioned above are in any way responsible for the views expressed in the book, nor for any errors and omissions that remain.

Finally, I am grateful to my secretary, Miss Frances Stevenson, who tolerated my excessive demands on her time during the preparation of the manuscript.

Radha Sinha

Glasgow, Scotland
March 1976

LIST OF ABBREVIATIONS

ACP	African, Caribbean and Pacific countries
CAP	Common Agricultural Policy of the EEC
DAC	Development Assistance Committee
EEC	European Economic Community
FAO	Food and Agricultural Organisation of the United Nations
GATT	General Agreement on Tariffs and Trade
GNP	Gross National Product
GSP	Generalised System of Preferences
IBRD	International Bank for Reconstruction and Development
IDA	International Development Association
IFC	International Finance Corporation
ILO	International Labour Organisation of the United Nations
IMF	International Monetary Fund
IWP	(FAO) Provisional Indicative World Plan for Agricultural Development
LDC	Less-Developed Country
ODA	Official Development Assistance
OECD	Organisation for Economic Cooperation and Development
OPEC	Organisation of Petroleum Exporting Countries
SDR	Special Drawing Rights
UN	United Nations
UNCTAD	United Nations Conference on Trade and Development
UNICEF	United Nations Children's Emergency Fund
UNIDO	United Nations Industrial Development Organisation
USDA	United States Department of Agriculture
WFP	World Food Programme
WHO	World Health Organisation of the United Nations

No man is an *Island*, intire of it selfe; every man is a
peece of the *continent*, a part of the *maine*; . . .
any mans *death* diminishes *me*, because I am involved in
Mankinde; And therefore never send to know for whom the
bell tolls; It tolls for *thee* . . .

John Donne

INTRODUCTION

> . . . for hundreds of millions of these subsistence farmers, life is neither satisfying nor decent. Hunger and malnutrition menace their families. Illiteracy forecloses their futures. Disease and death visit their villages too often, stay too long, and return too soon.
>
> . . . What these men want are jobs for their survival, food for their families, and a future for their children. They want the simple satisfaction of working toward something better — an end to misery and a beginning of hope . . .
>
> . . . We are talking about hundreds of millions of desperately poor people throughout the whole of the developing world. We are talking about 40 per cent of entire populations. Development is simply not reaching them in any decisive degree. Their countries are growing in gross economic terms, but their individual lives are stagnating in human terms.
>
> Robert S. McNamara[1]

These excerpts from an address by the President of the World Bank symbolise the growing international concern for the 'poor', the malnourished and the unemployed whose numbers are increasing to alarming proportions. It is increasingly being realised that nutritional deficiencies are largely a function of poverty and unemployment. Attempts to accelerate the overall rate of growth of an economy, or simply to increase agricultural output do not necessarily improve the conditions of the poor. Recent experience in several countries suggests that the selective approach to agricultural development, in which scarce resources (such as chemical fertiliser, pesticides, water and extension services) are concentrated on the people, farms and regions best able to take advantage of modern technology, rarely works to the advantage of the poor. For a variety of reasons it is the richer farmers who usually benefit most from agricultural policies in most developing countries. For reasons of economy and prestige they prefer to buy tractors and other agricultural machinery rather than use traditional labour-intensive techniques, even though this may result in greater unemployment among an already underemployed labour force. Thus the people who suffer most from hunger are further deprived of the means of feeding themselves.

If the 'market' continues to be the main arbiter of how the available food is distributed both within and between countries, then the lack of sufficient purchasing power will remain the chief obstacle in the way of feeding the poor adequately. Even if the state interferes with the market through price-controls and rationing, the bureaucratic machinery which supplements or replaces private enterprise is apt to inherit its value-system. Those who have no jobs, with no purchasing power to back their demands, continue to be jobless and unable to buy food even if there is an abundance of it.

In a primarily subsistence economy, landlessness or the ownership of inadequate land may affect the poor in much the same way as lack of paid employment in a highly monetised economy. In countries with low population densities the redistribution of land, if politically feasible, and the settlement of new lands may go a long way towards providing additional employment. In densely populated countries, however, the redistribution of land with a view to creating peasant proprietorship may produce holdings too small to be viable. Thus joint farming is often the only answer. Voluntary cooperative farming, if it survives long enough, always runs the risk of turning into a rich man's oligarchy. Therefore, broadly equal economic and political status for each member is a necessary precondition for the success of a co-operative enterprise. Any programme of land reform, at least in the very densely populated countries, probably has to begin by abolishing private property in land.

In an international context, national purchasing power is largely determined by export earnings. Developing countries have a considerable need for foreign exchange to import agricultural inputs and technical know-how in order to increase domestic production, or to import grains to feed the hungry millions, not to mention industrial and manufactured imports. To think of a major breakthrough in agricultural production in the developing countries without major reforms in the world trading system is to put the cart before the horse. Any major reform of the world trading system (or any scheme for a more equitable sharing of natural resources between countries) is as strongly opposed, or as resolutely circumvented by the richer countries as are proposals for land redistribution or the nationalisation of mines and industrial enterprises by the rich within the poorer countries. Much the same goes for the sharing of international political power. The major international organisations, though not originally intended as such, have developed into oligarchies serving to rationalise perpetuation of the political power of the richer countries *vis-à-vis* the poorer countries;

those agencies with any effective power continue to be dominated by the rich countries. The realities of the world power structure are such that whatever the overt policies of the international agencies they will tend to remain marginal to the real interests of the developing countries. The comments of A. H. Boerma, the former Director-General of the Food and Agriculture Organisation (FAO), are instructive:

> . . . civilisation has a profound moral obligation to provide food for those who are hungry and in need . . . when governments, for national political reasons, side-tracked the very first attempt[2] to translate this international moral force into practical terms, one of the essential, if unwritten, principles on which the Organisation has been founded was seriously weakened. As a result FAO has never again felt itself able to put forward any great practical scheme at the same high level of bold, global vision which might have made a major impact on the world food situation that is still a disgrace to the twentieth century.[3]

The role of these agencies will continue to be restricted mainly to collecting information, financing ameliorative schemes, research projects, and organising conferences and symposia, much of which is of only academic interest. The problem of the very poor is so immense that nothing the international organisations, with their limited resources, can do is likely to make any significant difference. Whether they can make a major contribution towards providing moral and intellectual leadership with regard to world poverty, and whether they can create an appropriate climate for major national and international social, economic and political changes is doubtful. Apart from their statutory inability to interfere with the domestic policies of member governments these organisations, particularly the World Bank and the International Monetary Fund, are committed to the international maintenance of private enterprise and 'the market'. They therefore find it difficult to advocate (or even reconcile themselves to) any alternative that may undermine the *status quo*. This is reflected in the fact that to date there has been very little attempt by the UN agencies to undertake any serious research on socialist economic systems, despite the fact that the majority of member governments profess to believe in some form of socialism.

The aim of this book is to show that at both the national and international level there is a reluctance to take a realistic view of the alternatives available in the fight against poverty, unemployment and malnutrition. Policies commonly advocated are either palliatives or suffer from misplaced emphasis. For example, population control, often put foward by the richer countries as a panacea for development problems, may not have much to offer *on its own* to many developing countries. On the other hand, the continuation of present rates of population growth will certainly put an intolerable burden on many developing countries. Even at significantly reduced rates of growth of population the *absolute* increase in the labour force in the next couple of decades will be large enough to tax all the ingenuity of governments and planners if they intend to provide some meaningful employment for the poor. It is highly probable that many poor countries will be unable to provide such increased employment opportunities under the existing framework of the market, the conventional price mechanism and private property. In the final analysis, any major eradication of poverty will not be possible until the imbalances in the distribution of world resources are corrected by appropriate trade and investment policies. The pace of change in this direction has been highly unsatisfactory and, unless some imaginative and constructive leadership emerges in the 'West', the growing discontent in the developing countries will both greatly increase the risk of confrontation between the richer and poorer countries, leading to economic chaos in the world, and hasten the 'slide' of the poorer countries into 'communism' — a highly unpalatable prospect for the 'West'. McNamara's warning,[4] though referring to internal income inequalities, could equally apply to international inequities.

More equitable income distribution is absolutely imperative if the development process is to proceed in any meaningful manner. Policies whose effect is to favor the rich at the expense of the poor are not only manifestly unjust, but in the end are economically self-defeating. They push frustrations to the point of violence, and turn economic advance into a costly collapse of social stability.

1 NATURE OF THE WORLD FOOD PROBLEM

The popular conception of the world food problem as a race between population growth and food supply is too simplistic. It also diverts attention from more relevant issues. In its simplest form the argument is that increases in food production in the developing countries have either been outstripped by unprecedented rates of population growth or, at best, have barely kept pace with them. It is also believed that the carrying capacity of the spaceship Earth has nearly been reached; little potential for increasing production exists. The inevitable conclusion is that many developing countries will be frequented by catastrophic famines in the very near future. As a result of widespread crop failures in the early seventies such alarming prophecies have become more common.

Admittedly, the incidence of hunger and malnutrition[1] is relatively high in densely populated countries, but as will be shown later, this is related not so much to population growth as to the unequal access to land, and other sources of wealth and income in these countries.[2]

In a study of the world food problem, prepared by the FAO for the World Population Conference (1974), it has been shown (see Table 1) that at the world level the rate of growth of food production substantially exceeded population growth throughout the 1950s and 1960s.[3] In both decades, population grew at around 2 per cent per annum, while food production in the 1950s increased annually by about 3.1 per cent, slowing down to 2.7 per cent per annum in the 1960s.[4] The rate of increase of food production was much the same in both the developed and developing countries. However, population increases in the developed countries continued at around 1 per cent per annum as against 2.5 per cent per annum in the developing countries.[5] This high rate of growth of population in the developing countries was mainly the result of the successful introduction and growing acceptability of modern medicine, and the application of new ideas in public health and sanitation.

Thus the unprecedented rate of population growth which has been experienced by the developing world is itself partly a sign of the success of developmental efforts and not of failure. Undoubtedly, huge increases in population over short periods have created serious problems for some densely populated countries, particularly in their efforts to accelerate

Table 1. Annual rates of growth of population and food production

| | 1952-62 | | 1962-72 | |
	Population	Food Production	Population	Food Production
		(per cent)		
Regions				
North America	1.8	1.9	1.2	2.4 (2.2)
Western Europe	0.8	2.9	0.8	2.2 (2.3)
Eastern Europe & USSR	1.5	4.5	1.0	3.5
Oceania	2.2	3.1	2.0	2.7 (3.0)
Other Developed Countries	1.3	5.0	1.3	3.5
Developed Regions	**1.3**	**3.1**	**1.0**	**2.7**
Africa	2.2	2.2	2.5	2.7 (2.4)
Latin America	2.8	3.2	2.9	3.1 (2.8)
Near East	2.6	3.4	2.8	3.0 (3.2)
Far East	2.3	3.1	2.5	2.7 (2.5)
Asian Centrally Planned Countries	1.8	3.2	1.9	2.6 (2.7)
Developing Regions	**2.4**	**3.1**	**2.5**	**2.7**
World	2.0	3.1	1.9	2.7

Based on FAO (1975), *Population, Food Supply and Agricultural Development*, Table 1, p. 2. The figures in brackets represent the growth rates between 1962 and 1974 for regions where the inclusion of 1973 and 1974 changes the trend rate of growth. Since the early 1970s were years of poor harvests in various parts of the world, the overall rates of growth of food production between 1962-74 barely kept pace with population growth in the Far East and, in fact, were slightly lower than population growth in Africa and Latin America.

the pace of economic development; the safety valve of migration, which was commonly available (and still is, though on a more limited scale) to the European countries in their early stages of development, is not available to them. But in many countries population densities are still low and an increase in numbers may often assist such countries in fully developing their resources. After all, the development of North and South America, South Africa, and Australasia owes a great deal to population increase.

It is undeniable, however, that some countries, particularly Asian countries such as China, India and Bangladesh, have serious population problems. Nor would their problems really be greatly ameliorated if possibilities of migration were open to them; even at a much reduced rate of growth the annual additions to total population would be staggering. The leaders of these countries are well aware of the seriousness of the problem.[6] India was one of the first countries in the world to adopt population control as an official policy although, largely for social and psychological reasons, it has not achieved any appreciable success. China, in spite of its anti-Malthusian Marxist thinking, has now adopted population limitation as a major part of its development policy. There are already some hopeful signs. In several developing countries the age at marriage, particularly for girls, has gone up. There has also been some fertility decline among mothers in the younger age groups; and there have been some changes in attitude to family size. These tendencies will certainly gain momentum with the increasing education and employment of women.

There is a definite double standard in the development literature on issues of population and food. While the 'unprecedented' rates of population growth have been underlined *ad nauseam*, the similarly unprecedented rates of growth of food production in developing countries have rarely received even a casual mention. FAO figures indicate that between 1961 and 1974 at least 31 out of 101 developing countries attained a rate of growth of food production of over 3.5 per cent per annum, a rate attained by only 5 developed countries (out of 34) during the same period, while in another 26 developing countries food production increased by between 2.6 and 3.5 per cent per annum. In terms of historical experience such growth rates are unmatched. Even the much-talked-of high rates of growth of agricultural output in Japan after the Meiji Restoration in 1868 did not exceed 2 per cent per annum. There is still some controversy as to whether the actual rate was much more than 1 per cent but earlier estimates of a 3 per cent growth rate have now been scaled down to 2 per cent.[7]

During the last two decades (1952-72) food production failed to keep pace with population growth in over a third of the developing countries. However, these countries account for only 14 per cent of the total population of the developing countries. Besides, many of these countries are producers of petroleum (e.g. Iraq and Indonesia) or cash crops such as sugar (e.g. Mauritius). Under the circumstances, the increasing incidence of hunger and malnutrition in developing countries cannot be explained wholly in terms of the failure of agriculture to keep pace with population growth.

Increasing imports of food

Of course, increased agricultural production and the consequent increase in incomes in the rural areas has led to an increased demand for retaining domestically produced food and this, in turn, has resulted in a slow rate of growth of the marketed food surplus transferred to the urban areas, and at a time when urban income and population have been growing faster than in rural areas. Consequently, there has been an increasing demand for imports of food,[8] particularly food grains, in several developing countries. However the developed countries import much more food and are more dependent on food imports[9] than the developing countries. Japan, the United Kingdom, Italy and West Germany are the largest importers of food grains; between 1970 and 1974 their net imports of cereals amounted to 37 million tons per annum, with their combined population of only 300 million people. As against this, the two largest developing countries, China and India, with almost 1,300 million people imported only about 9 million tons even though this period was one of poor harvests for both countries. During the same period, on average the food deficit richer countries imported (net) 48 million tons of cereals annually as against only 29 million tons imported by the developing countries. The fact that the food importing developed countries import much more on a *per capita* basis and are far more dependent on imports than the developing countries has escaped public notice mainly because countries are generally classified into two groups, developed and developing; and not food surplus and food deficit countries.

Current availability of food

According to recent UN estimates *per capita* food availability at the world level in 1969-71 (average) was at least 4 per cent more than the requirement (see Table 2), despite the fact that some major grain surplus countries, the USA, Canada, and Australia,[10] were subsidising their farmers to leave some of their land uncultivated. The total area of this land in 1970 was around 40 million hectares. Since on average the developed countries were producing 3 tons of cereal per hectare, the land withdrawn from cultivation could have represented a loss of as much as 120 million tons, equivalent to 10 per cent of the total world output of cereals.

The average energy intake in the developed countries during 1969-71 was 23 per cent more than the requirement,[11] while that in the developing countries was 5 per cent less than the requirement. The deficiency in the Far East (including the centrally planned economies)

Table 2. Average energy and protein supply,* by region (1969-71)

Region	Energy (K cals per capita per day)	Protein (gr. per capita per day)	Energy as % of requirement*
North America	3,320	105.2	126
Western Europe	3,130	93.7	123
Eastern Europe & USSR	3,260	99.3	127
Oceania	3,260	108.1	123
Other developed market economies	2,550	79.1	108
Total developed countries	**3,150**	**96.4**	**123**
Africa	2,190	58.4	94
Latin America	2,530	65.0	105
Near East	2,500	69.3	102
Far East	2,080	50.7	94
Asian Centrally Planned Countries	2,170	60.4	92
Total developing countries	**2,200**	**57.4**	**95**
World	2,480	69.0	104

Source: UN World Food Conference (1974), *Assessment of The World Food Situation* (mimeo.), Table 9, p. 58 (henceforth *Assessment*).

* The figures relate to protein and energy content of the food available at the retail level after making allowance for storage and marketing losses and waste.

and Africa varied between 6 and 8 per cent. On a world level the protein situation was more satisfactory than is usually thought. According to the currently prevailing views on nutrition 40 to 50 grammes of protein *per capita* per day is quite adequate for an adult. On this standard the developed regions have been eating twice as much (or even more) than they require. Even the developing regions seem to have enough protein on average levels of intake. But in those cases where the intake of energy is less than the requirement, some of the protein is used up in meeting the energy gap.[12] As such it is not easy to say whether the intake of protein in these countries is adequate, even though the figures may indicate this.

Thus it is not an overall shortage at the global level that accounts for

the widespread hunger and malnutrition. A recent US Department of
Agriculture Report[13] has suggested that if only 2 per cent of the
average annual world cereal production during the last decade were
assured to the malnourished in addition to what they already get,
much of the malnutrition in the world would be eliminated. Thus the
amount of grain needed to eliminate the worst aspects of malnutrition
would not be more than twice the quantities moved under various
food aid programmes during the 1960s.[14] Therefore the explanation
for the persistence of widespread hunger and malnutrition lies largely
in the fact that the poor (countries or people), for lack of purchasing
power, are unable to meet their basic human needs, while the rich
continue to carve up the lion's share of the world's food resources. The
average person in a developed country consumes nearly three times as
much sugar, more than four times as much meat, fats and oils, and
about six times as much milk and eggs as the average person in a
developing country.[15] Such disparities are not so obvious if the average
calorie intake of the rich and poor countries is compared. As can be
seen from Table 2 the average daily calorie intake in the developed
regions in 1969-71 was around 3,150 as against only 2,200 in the
developing regions. The respective intakes of protein were 96 and 57
grammes. Both the energy and protein intakes in the developed regions
were well in excess of requirements. However, such aggregates do not
provide a meaningful comparison of the qualitative differences in the
levels of food consumption between rich and poor countries. Over two-
thirds of the protein consumed by the richer countries comes from
animal sources, while it is plant foods which supply three-quarters or
more of the protein in the diets of the populations of the poor countries. This is reflected in the fact that the average cereal consumption
(taken directly, as well as animal feed for production of meat etc.) of
a person from the developing countries is nearly half a kilo per day; for
the developed countries as a whole it is three times as much. However,
for the USA and Canada it is a little more than five times as much.[16]

A lot of cereal production in the developed regions is used for the
production of meat, milk and eggs. The amount of grain used for
animal feed alone in the richer countries is around 370 million tons
per annum, which is roughly equal to the total amount of cereal consumed by China and India together.[17] Although most nutritionists
have been suggesting that animal products are not essential for a healthy
diet (though they may be desirable within certain limits) increasing
attention is being paid to the expansion of the livestock sector, not
only in developed countries, but also in some developing countries,

sometimes supported by international agencies such as the World Bank, involving a considerable diversion of grains to animal feed, and at a time when increasing numbers of people are being added to the millions already underfed. In poorer countries cereals must receive precedence because in situations 'when intakes of both energy and protein are grossly inadequate, the provision of protein concentrates or protein-rich food of animal origin may be a costly and inefficient way of improving the diets, since energy can generally be provided more cheaply than protein of good quality'.[18]

There is a growing recognition of the 'unfairness' in the present use of world resources between countries and it is being suggested that the richer countries should accept a voluntary 'cut' in their levels of consumption of food and other scarce resources.[19] A trend towards reduced consumption of animal fats for medical reasons is already underway. Between 1940 and 1971 the average American has reduced his consumption of butter from 17 lb. per annum to only 5 lb., while there has been an increase in the consumption of margarine from 2 to 11 lb. Lard has already been replaced by vegetable shortenings. Non-dairy whipped toppings and 'whiteners' are already replacing those of dairy origin.[20] Similarly, attempts are being made to substitute high-quality vegetable protein for animal protein.

It is still uncertain whether voluntary efforts directed towards reduced consumption of animal products will ever attain more than a marginal significance. Even if they do, it is difficult to visualise resources released by such efforts becoming easily accessible to the needy without a radical rethinking on the issue of a more equitable distribution of world resources between countries and within countries and without a major restructuring of the world economy. The economic and political power of the rich within most poorer countries will continue to thwart any radical redistribution of wealth and power; in much the same way the major world powers will probably continue to undermine any internationalisation which runs counter to their self-interest. It is too much of a dream to expect that the rich countries will 'apply at the world level that same moral responsibility, that same sharing of wealth, that same standard of justice and compassion without which our own national societies would surely fall apart'.[21]

The vulnerable groups

In view of the inadequacy of available statistics[22] on food requirements as well as on the levels and pattern of food consumption it is not always easy to estimate the total number of people suffering from malnutrition. A rather conservative UN estimate places it at around 460 million,[23] excluding the Asian centrally planned economies. Up to a third of the Asian population receives inadequate supplies of food. The corresponding figures for Africa, the Near East and Latin America are 25, 18 and 13 per cent respectively.

Of course, some malnutrition arises as a result of lack of education, faulty methods of cooking food, and social and religious prejudices against certain foods; but the main cause of malnutrition is poverty. The people who fall in the lowest income groups are normally the landless labourers, the unemployed, underemployed and small-holders (either owners or tenants). The urban unemployed and under-employed, and the new migrants would also fall into this group. All these groups suffer from lack of paid work either in the rural or urban areas. Landless labourers are probably the worst sufferers because the employment open to them is largely seasonal, during the sowing and harvesting seasons. This applies also to the small-holders; both owner-operators and tenants have to supplement their meagre incomes by working on larger farms as wage labour. A substantial number of land-less labourers and small farmers are forced by circumstances – lack of jobs, loss of land as a result of non-payment of debts or simply eviction by landlords – to migrate to the towns and cities in search of jobs. Continuous migration not only tends to swell the number of urban unemployed in almost all developing countries but also exacerbates the already critical problems of slums. The rapidity with which the urban population is growing presents a frightening prospect for most developing countries. In fact, in spite of the major land redistribution in China under the Communist regime, this tendency to move to urban areas has continued, though the problem of urban slums etc. has been kept within manageable proportions not only by making rural life more attractive and meaningful in the framework of the Peoples' Rural Communes but also by means of drastic methods of control over the mobility of the people, and on several occasions by the compulsory repatriation of people to their villages.

Sometimes industrial workers and the lower middle class also suffer from hunger and malnutrition, particularly as a result of infla-tion. The nutritional status of the organised factory worker in some developing countries is somewhat better than that of the low-paid white-collar employee because trade unions often succeed in getting concessional food for their members as a part of the wage deal. These facilities are not always available to the middle class, who may also suffer from nutritional deficiencies as a result of a conscious effort to diversify their diets towards animal products and other 'quality' foods such as vegetables, fruits, etc. There is a greater awareness among this group not only of the need for diversification to achieve a balanced diet, but also that these foods are status symbols. For lack of adequate income, a varied diet must be obtained largely at the cost of a reduced grain (and therefore calorie) intake.

Within these groups it is the women and children who suffer most. When there is a shortage of food it makes good economic sense for the women to feed the men — the earners in the family — and suffer self-deprivation. But at the same time most developing societies are (at least implicitly) based on the supremacy of men and the 'chauvinist' male frequently does not really care whether the female members and the children in the family have enough to eat. A survey conducted by the National Institute of Nutrition (Hyderabad) found that the average daily calorie intake of pregnant and lactating women was as low as 1,400 against the average Indian requirement of over 2,200.[24]

The worst sufferers are invariably the young children, particularly those who are weaned at an early age, either because a malnourished mother cannot breast feed her child adequately or because she is caught in one more sequence of pregnancy and childbirth.[25] The incidence of deficiency diseases is further increased by children's inability to digest bulky foods like rice or starchy roots in adequate quantities. Frequently, they lose their appetites due to infection.[26] A recent household survey in Sri Lanka indicated that the incidence of malnutrition is higher in households with several children than in smaller households. It was found that nearly half of the households having 4 or 5 children had an average daily *per capita* calorie intake of less than 1,800, while only 18 per cent of households with one child or no child had such a low intake.[27] It seems highly likely that the majority of children in larger families are suffering from nutritional deficiencies. It goes without saying that children from poor families would suffer more from malnutrition than children from richer families. The Hyderabad survey indicated that both in terms of calories and protein a child in a rich family received almost twice as much food as a child in a poor family.[28]

Medical and anthropometric evidence suggests a close link between malnutrition and infant mortality. Experts feel that malnutrition generally starts having an effect on mortality just after an infant is weaned. One to four year mortality rates tend to decline steadily as the calorie intake rises. Many of those who survive often have a stunted physical growth; whether or not nutritionally inadequate diets slow down

the development of a child's brain and intelligence remains unproven.[29]
According to the FAO[30] one half of child deaths can be attributed to
malnutrition. The total number of children suffering from malnutrition
is estimated at 200 million.[31] A recent UNICEF Report suggests that
over 10 million children are in great danger of dying and, even if
aid were available, some 3 million children would still die. Another 90
million children are in such a frail state of health that they will not be
able to withstand serious illness.[32]

What causes famine deaths?

Famines have been very much in the news in recent years. Two major
famines (Bihar and Maharashtra) in India within the last ten years and
the continuing crises in the Sahelian Zone (the countries south of the
Sahara) and in Ethiopia have given a new impetus to the Neo-Malthu-
sians who see such tragedies in terms of the failure of food production
to keep pace with population growth. This explanation is not always
valid. Even in countries where the rate of increase in food production
is greater than population growth, shortages may arise because of serious
droughts, floods or other natural disasters (locust, frost, etc.). The
uncertainties resulting from variations in climatic conditions are inherent in agriculture, and richer countries are not exempt. For instance,
between 1952-72 the instability of cereal production was much higher
in North America, Eastern Europe and the USSR, and Oceania, than in
the Far East.[33] In the case of North America and Oceania official
policies were also partly responsible for fluctuations in cereal production. The instability of output was much higher in Eastern Europe and
the USSR than in the West. This instability may partly result from
state interference in agriculture.

If the surpluses from good years could be saved to meet the deficits
in bad years, the disastrous consequences of crop failures could be
considerably reduced. Here there is a fundamental difference between
the conditions in rich and poor countries. In the latter large numbers
of farmers, as indicated earlier, live on the margin of subsistence; even
in good years, by the time they have paid their rent and the interest on
past loans (invariably at high rates of interest) they have little income left
for day-to-day living expenses. It is hardly likely that they could keep
stocks, to any significant extent, for bad years. Richer peasants and
traders do perform this function of building up stocks in years of
good harvest and releasing them for sale after poor harvests. It is part
of the normal functions of traders to spread the supply evenly between
different time periods and different regions. However, in countries

where there is a tendency for shortages to become acute in years of serious crop failures, the rich producers and traders frequently start hoarding food (grains) for speculative gains, which often exacerbates the distress.

What hits the poor people most is the lack of employment opportunities in years of deficient rainfall. Landless labourers and the small operators who have to work on wage-farms for their livelihood find their employment opportunities shrinking because the wage-farms, in the absence of an adequate water supply, try to economise on water by concentrating cultivation on smaller areas of land. This reduction in employment comes at a time when the small operator's output from his own farm has either vanished or has been drastically reduced. In the meantime the shortage of food pushes up its price beyond the means of the poor. The state, even if reliable information is reaching the capital, is often reluctant to acknowledge the existence of famine conditions since this acknowledgement tarnishes the 'image' of a country. In many countries, for lack of adequate communications, news from distant regions takes a long time to reach the capital. Even when the existence of famine is conceded, there may not be sufficient surpluses available for transfer to the stricken areas. Poor transport facilities are frequently incapable of handling a sudden increase in freight traffic even if sufficient food is made available. This happened in India, during the Bihar famine, when grain shipments could not be unloaded at the ports because of inadequate berthing facilities. The fair distribution of food may be further handicapped by inefficient and corrupt administrative machinery.

This interrelationship between poverty and lack of employment opportunities on the one hand and famine deaths on the other is well known. In 1878 the British appointed a Famine Commission to enquire into the causes of the frequent famines in India, which in the second half of the nineteenth century killed over 20 million people. The Commission reported that

. . . a main cause of the disastrous consequences of Indian famines, and one of the greatest difficulties in the way of providing relief in an effectual shape is to be found in the fact that the great mass of the people directly depend on agriculture, and that there is no other industry from which any considerable part of the population derives its support.

At the root of much of the poverty of the people of India, and the risks to which they are exposed in seasons of scarcity, lies the

unfortunate circumstance that agriculture forms almost the sole
occupation of the mass of the population, and that *no remedy for
present evils can be complete which does not include the introduction of a diversity of occupations, through which the surplus
population may be drawn from agricultural pursuits and led to find
the means of subsistence in manufactures or some such employ-
ments.*[34]

The importance of employment creation in eliminating famine deaths
can be easily demonstrated by the recent experience of the People's
Republic of China. Droughts and floods have of course continued to
occur in China in much the same way as in India or any other developing country in the region, but such natural calamities no longer lead to
massive destitution and loss of life. One of the main reasons for this
Chinese success is their ability to distribute the limited employment
opportunities, and hence also food, equitably. This has meant that
even during years of drought a basic minimum amount of food is
available to everyone. If there is a decline in total grain output, the
reduction is shared evenly in China, whereas in India the incidence of
drought falls largely on the landless labour and the urban poor.

Any attempt simply to increase food production will do little to
eliminate hunger and malnutrition unless it goes hand in hand with
employment creation and a more equitable distribution of food and
other resources between countries and between people. Essentially,
any attack on the world food problem has to be on three fronts
simultaneously. It involves (i) an increase in the *per capita* availability
of food at both global and country levels, which requires measures for
increasing agricultural production on the one hand and population
planning, particularly in the densely populated countries, on the other,
(ii) a more equitable distribution of income and wealth (land) within a
country so that the poor can produce or buy adequate food, which
involves programmes such as land reform and employment creation,
and finally, (iii) a more equitable distribution of world resources
between rich and poor countries, involving trade and aid issues.

2 INCREASING FOOD PRODUCTION

The view that the potential of the Earth to feed its increasing population has nearly been reached is seriously open to question. Of course, the Earth's surface is finite; therefore it cannot sustain a rapidly rising population indefinitely. But all the evidence suggests that for the foreseeable future there will continue to be un- and under-utilised potential. According to a US Government source,[1] out of nearly 3,190 million hectares of potentially arable land 1,406 million hectares, i.e. only about 44 per cent,[2] are currently under cultivation (Table 3).

Table 3. Potentially[3] cultivable land by region

Regions	Area in million hectares	Ratio of cultivated land to potentially cultivable land (%)
Africa	733	22
Asia	628	83
Australia/New Zealand	154	2
Europe	174	88
North America	465	51
South America	680	11
USSR	356	65
Total	3,190	44

Source: The White House (1967), *The World Food Problem: A Report of the President's Science Advisory Committee*, Tables 7-9, p. 434. Original figures were million acres.

However, much of the additional cultivable land falls in Africa, South and North America, Oceania and the USSR. The most densely populated countries of Europe and Asia[4] are left with only marginal scope for bringing new areas under cultivation and are likely to become increasingly dependent on foreign supplies of food.

Irrigation

With proper water management — irrigation and drainage — it would be possible not only to increase cropping intensities but also to make greater use of modern inputs such as chemical fertilisers and hybrid seeds, thereby substantially increasing per hectare yields in developing as well as in some developed countries. Per hectare yields of the USA, the USSR, Australia and Canada are still much lower than those of the Western European countries (see Table 4). The average per hectare yield of wheat in the USA is barely half of those of several Western European countries, and is even lower than those of Egypt and Mexico, two developing countries.

Table 4. Per hectare yield of selected crops (1972) (in kg.)

Countries	Wheat	Paddy	Barley	Maize	Sugar cane
Egypt	3,102	5,334	2,816	3,747	96,053
Canada	1,680	—	2,229	4,985	—
Mexico	2,721	2,639	1,171	1,148	60,714
USA	2,196	5,250	2,347	6,084	92,563
India	1,382	1,616	1,028	865	47,716
Denmark	4,378	—	3,965	—	—
France	4,579	—	3,899	4,580	—
UK	4,224	—	4,039	—	—
Australia	900	—	806	2,744	—
USSR	1,467	—	1,348	2,450	—
Japan	—	5,847	2,678	2,900	—
Korean Rep.	—	—	2,311	1,412	—
World average	1,628	2,251	1,793	2,785	

Source: FAO (1973), *Production Year Book*.

Admittedly, such crude comparisons of per hectare yields ignore differences in climate, topographical factors and the relative importance of particular crops in different countries' agriculture and therefore are not very meaningful except as broad approximations. Nevertheless, they seem to indicate that even with existing agricultural technology there is tremendous scope for increasing per hectare yields.

So far only about 201 million hectares or nearly one-seventh of the world total cultivated area is under irrigation.[5] But this proportion varies considerably between different countries. On the one hand, in Egypt the entire cultivated area is under irrigation, whilst in India the proportion is as low as 17 per cent, even though India has the second highest acreage under irrigation with nearly 28 million hectares. This is exceeded only by China where the area under irrigation is probably around 50 million hectares.[6] The top five countries in terms of irrigated area — the People's Republic of China, India, the USA, Pakistan and the USSR — together possess nearly 70 per cent of the total irrigated area of the world.[7] Even within these countries irrigation facilities, partly for geographical reasons, are unevenly distributed. For instance, much of the irrigation in India is concentrated in the North and North West, while a major part of Central and South-West India falls in a dry zone where rain is very scanty and irrigation facilities are few. Similarly, in China the major part of the North-West is rather arid. In such areas ground water is not always easily accessible.

Given the low proportion of cultivated land currently under irrigation, it is quite possible that large areas of land could be brought under irrigation without much difficulty in the foreseeable future. The potentially irrigable area is estimated at between 260 million[8] and 470 million[9] hectares. Whether this potential will be fully realised will depend not only on the availability of technical and financial resources for the construction of irrigation projects, but also on their adequate maintenance. In the case of large irrigation projects, particularly those which utilise surface flows of water, inadequate attention to drainage may lead to problems of waterlogging and salinity. The optimum utilisation of the irrigation potential may also be hampered by the inappropriate pricing of water, and a lack of communication between the irrigation departments or water authorities on the one hand and the farmers on the other. Lack of other complementary inputs such as chemical fertilisers, etc. may be an additional obstacle to the realisation of the full potential of such irrigation projects.

Chemicals

So far, the usage of modern inputs such as chemical fertilisers and pesticides has been rather low in most developing countries (see Table 5). On average the developed countries use four and a half times as much chemical fertiliser per hectare as the developing countries. The use of chemical fertilisers is highest in Western Europe, and lowest in Africa. However, there are wide differences in the use of chemical fertilisers among countries within the same region. For instance in Africa in 1972/73 consumption of fertiliser $(N + P + K)$[10] per hectare of arable land varied from 155 kg. in Egypt to almost negligible quantities in several countries; in Asia the highest consumption was 387 kg. in Japan, closely followed by the Republic of Korea. However, the highest world figure is that of the Netherlands with 717 kg.

Table 5. Use of fertiliser by regions (1972/73)

Regions	Kg. of NPK per hectare of arable land
Western Europe	192
North America	73
Oceania	36
Eastern Europe and the USSR	72
Other developed market economies	157
Developed Regions	90
Latin America	30
Far East	20
Near East	18
Africa	5
Asian centrally planned countries	40
Developing Regions	20
World	53

Source: FAO (1974), *Annual Fertiliser Review*. The totals for developed and developing regions here include the centrally planned economies.

Canadian consumption of chemical fertilisers at 24 kg., Australia with 25 kg. and the USSR with 49 kg. are comparable to many developing countries. Even the USA figure of 85 kg. is barely half that of Egypt. Thus if there were no serious limitation on the increased production of chemical fertilisers and if it could be ensured that the poorer countries were able to obtain them at reasonable prices — a doubtful proposition in the face of rising oil prices — there would be tremendous potential for increasing their use.

Similarly, the production and availability of food could be greatly increased through better control of pests and crop diseases. It is estimated that an average of 35 per cent of potential yields in developing countries are lost due to defective or inadequate control measures.[11] In India alone, pests, plant diseases and parasites cause a pre-harvest loss of at least 15-20 per cent of cereals production, and 25 per cent of pulses, oilseeds, fruits and vegetables production; and there are further losses resulting from rat and weed infestation.[12] Such losses are quite high even in developed countries. Cramer[13] suggests that 25 to 30 per cent of the potential value of crops is lost in Europe, North America and other developed countries, including the centrally planned economies, due to infestation. The total world loss is estimated by Cramer at about a third of the potential value of crops.

In West Africa post-harvest losses in storage and transport are estimated at 25 per cent of the volume of food produced.[14] In the USA storage losses for the main cereals range from 4 to 7.5 per cent, while in India, they are 5 to 8 per cent.[15] If an average figure of 6 per cent is assumed then nearly 20 million tons of cereals are lost annually in these two countries alone. If this rate of 6 per cent is applied to the world as a whole the total loss of cereals in storage would come to a staggering figure of 75 million tons which is three times the quantity theoretically required to alleviate world malnutrition.[16] Although the attitudes in developing countries towards pest control are changing rapidly, the use of pesticides etc. remains relatively low. For instance, by 1965, only 2 per cent of the total cultivated area in India was treated with pesticides as against 30 per cent in Korea.[17] However, even in some developed countries the use of insecticides is not very high. In the USA in 1966 only 57 per cent of the area under corn was treated with herbicides, and only 33 per cent with insecticides.[18] Only about a third of the crop acreage was being treated with 'selective' herbicides. In Europe the figure was as high as 85 per cent.

Seed

Even before the advent of high yielding varieties, improved seeds were estimated to have resulted in nearly a 10 per cent increase in cereal yields per unit of land. With the emergence of high-yielding varieties several-fold increases in yield became possible provided that adequate doses of complementary inputs were provided. However, the supplies of high yielding varieties are still limited. For example, the actual supplies of quality seeds in Asia in 1966-7 represented only 10 per cent of the estimated requirement for rice, 42 per cent for wheat, 4 per cent for pulses and 2 per cent for coarse grains.[19] A recent FAO survey of 97 countries (27 in Africa, 20 in Latin America, 20 in Europe, 14 in Asia, 12 in the Near East, 2 in Oceania and 2 in North America) indicates that in 82 countries the potential for the widespread introduction of improved varieties is considerable but that seed supply is inadequate. The realisation of the full potential of improved seeds requires an adequate system of distribution and the availability of complementary inputs. Furthermore, since there is always a risk of degeneration of the genetic qualities of the new seeds, there will be a continuing need for quality control and the development of new varieties.

There is no doubt that enormous potential exists for increasing agricultural production, both by bringing new areas under cultivation and by increasing per hectare yields through improved water management and the increased use of modern inputs such as chemical fertilisers, pesticides and high yielding varieties of seed.[20] In addition, much could be done to reduce losses in storage and transportation.

Furthermore, there are enormous possibilities for developing both deep-sea and freshwater fisheries. Even in densely populated countries, particularly in the monsoon countries, vast amounts of water are available in ponds, natural and man-made lakes and reservoirs in which fish farming can be developed without encroaching upon any farmland. Freshwater fishing, so far a fairly neglected field, requires much less financial investment and sophisticated technical skill than deep-sea fishing which requires huge investments in trawlers and skilled manpower; it also provides opportunities for creating additional employment for the small operator, and a source of additional income for the subsistence farmer.

Yet another possibility is that of developing industrially manufactured synthetic food which could be produced from chemical synthesis and mass culture of micro-organisms. The prospects for such developments in the field of food science and technology look promising but it is almost certain that mass production of synthetic foods would largely be limited to the developed countries. Those developing countries which suffer from a chronic shortage of foreign exchange are unlikely to be able to import synthetic foods. Besides, many such foods would be produced largely by capital intensive chemical plants, so their potential for creating employment would certainly be limited. Therefore, even if some developing countries were to import plants to manufacture synthetic foods domestically, in the absence of any significant additions to employment, such foods would not be available to the very poor.[21]

This applies equally to the fortification of cereals with lysine in order to improve the quality of protein in them. As seen earlier, much of the protein is wasted in a situation where the calorie intake is inadequate. In such cases the fortification of cereals, which does not increase the calorie content, is naturally wasteful.[22] Besides, fortified cereals are often more expensive than ordinary cereals. The very poor who cannot afford adequate quantities of cereals and pulses will certainly be unable to take advantage of fortified cereals. Thus, at least for the foreseeable future, the production of 'nutrition directed' food will be much less important than the increased production of the kinds of food currently consumed.[23]

However, translating this potential into reality would require huge investments of financial resources and energy as well as human skills. Some illustrative examples of the costs involved in various aspects of agricultural development are in order here. For instance the cost of land development may be as high as $2,500 per hectare depending on the condition of the land, and the costs of clearing and providing irrigation and drainage, housing, roads and other infrastructure.[24] Costs can be much lower if land development is largely based on mobilising 'surplus' labour. The cost of land clearing, even within the same region, may vary widely depending on the topography and vegetation. For instance, the cost of clearing in Brazil is reported to be around $15 per hectare while in Venezuela it is between $500 and $900 per hectare.[25]

Irrigation costs are extremely variable depending on the size and complexity of the irrigation project. The White House Study included a list of land and water development projects and the costs involved, both in total and per hectare.[26] Examples from Colombia for irrigation projects in areas not previously settled, ranged between $200 and $3,100 per hectare with an average of $1,150. In the large Nagarjunsagar project in India (which was to serve an area presently cultivated but not irrigated) costs were reported to be around $370 per hectare. The cost of providing additional irrigation in areas which already possess some irrigation facilities is also quite high. The cost of the first large (0.4 million hectares) ground water development scheme in Pakistan, including the costs of well construction, electrification and surface drainage, worked out at around $100 per hectare. If the costs of providing fertiliser plants, education and extension services had been included the total cost would have been doubled. The cost of flood control for Bangladesh (then East Pakistan) was estimated at $210 per hectare. The White House Study indicated that in the Indian sub-continent and South-East and South-West Asia alone the cost of irrigating all the potentially irrigable land (around 80 million hectares) would be nearly $80 billion.

Most developing countries cannot themselves meet the enormous costs involved in realising the full potential for increased food production. Some of them would need technical assistance for land improvement schemes and for the construction of irrigation and drainage projects. A rough idea of the foreign financial support that would be required can be obtained from the documents prepared by the UN for the Rome Food Conference (1974). In order to achieve the overall objective of pushing up the average annual growth rate of food production from 2.6 per cent in the preceding twelve years to at least 3.6 per cent per year in the next twelve years,[27] an increase in the flow of external resources into agriculture in the developing countries from the current level of US $1.5 billion to at least $5 billion per annum in the five years between 1975 and 1980, would be required.[28] The proposed allocation of this sum among various uses is given in Table 6. The Rome Conference was well aware of the immensity of this task and called for a major initiative.

It is doubtful whether such international support can ever be mounted, particularly in the current aid climate.[29] Even if the foreign resources were made available, it is doubtful whether the developing countries would be able to raise domestically adequate complementary resources, let alone evolve appropriate institutions and value systems so as to ensure that the fruits of development are equitably shared between the rich and the poor, thus guaranteeing social justice to all sections of the community without unnecessarily impairing incentives. And can the transition from 'traditional' to 'modern' farming be attained without creating ecological imbalances? Some of these issues form the subject matter of the following chapters.

Table 6. Estimated foreign assistance required for agricultural development in developing countries (in billion US $)

Items	1975-80 Annual amount required	Total
Land and water development	2.5	12.5
Import of fertilisers	0.5	2.5
New fertiliser plants*	0.2 (1.3)	1.0 (5.5)
Credit, marketing, storage and processing facilities	1.2	6.0
Agricultural research	0.6	3.0
Total	5.0	25.0

Source: UN World Food Conference (1974), *Proposals*.

* It was assumed that much of the new fertiliser producing capacity will be created in the oil producing countries. Obviously no external finance will be needed. The figures for total investment in new fertiliser plants are given within brackets.

3 CHOICE OF TECHNIQUE: WALKING ON TWO LEGS

As seen earlier, in countries suffering from a high incidence of nutritional deficiency, the objectives of food policy must include both increased food production and the creation of more employment, particularly in the rural areas. Policies aimed solely at increasing the production and supply of food guarantee, at best, the availability of food. Unless the poorer sections of the community have sufficient purchasing power they will fail to obtain a fair share of this available food except when it is provided as 'charity'. Few self-respecting persons in any country like to be 'on the dole', so the creation of employment opportunities for the unemployed and underemployed is a prerequisite for the solution of the problem of hunger and malnutrition. If policies aimed at increasing agricultural output lead to a net displacement of labour by machinery, then the dual objectives of food policy may turn out to be mutually exclusive. In planning for increased output, a further consideration has to be kept in mind: the use of some modern inputs and techniques that can bring about significant short- or medium-term gains in production, may, if used indiscriminately, have adverse effects on soil structure and bring about the impairment of natural resources. In such cases, there is a real conflict of interest between present and future generations. Any food policy, particularly in the choice of technology, has to aim at reconciling these conflicting interests.

Traditional versus modern farming

The commonly used terms 'traditional' and 'modern' farming are not easy to define. The word 'traditional' has often been used to describe all types of farming extending from 'shifting cultivation' to the advanced forms of crop rotation (involving the use of leguminous crops), and from farming practices which depend on sophisticated water management to those which make hardly any use of artificial means of water supply. Even less imaginative is the practice of branding all types of farming in developing countries as 'primitive'. It cannot be denied that some agricultural practices in developing countries are faulty but there is considerable historical evidence that farming practices in several developing countries such as Egypt, China, India, and Japan were not very far behind those of European agriculture for much of the nineteenth century.

As early as the 1890s, a British agricultural scientist, J. A. Voelcker, who was invited by the Government of India to suggest ways to improve Indian agriculture, stressed that:

> On one point there can be no question, viz., that the ideas generally entertained in England, and often given expression to even in India, that Indian agriculture is, as a whole, primitive and backward, and that little has been done to try and remedy it, are altogether erroneous . . . taking everything together, and more especially considering the conditions under which Indian crops are grown, they are wonderfully good. At his best the Indian *raiyat* or cultivator is quite as good as, and, in some respects, the superior of, the average British farmer; whilst at his worst it can only be said that this state is brought about largely by an absence of facilities for improvement which is probably unequalled in any other country, and that the *raiyat* will struggle on patiently and uncomplainingly in the face of difficulties in a way that nobody else would . . . what does, however, prevent them from growing larger crops is the limited facilities to which they have access, such as the supply of water and manure. But, to take the ordinary acts of husbandry, nowhere would one find better instances of keeping land scrupulously clean from weeds, of ingenuity in device of water-raising appliances, of knowledge of soils and their capabilities, as well as of the exact time to sow and reap, as one would in Indian agriculture, and this not at its best alone, but at its ordinary level. It is wonderful, too, how much is known of rotation, the system of 'mixed crops' and of fallowing. Certain it is that I, at least, have never seen a more perfect picture of careful cultivation, combined with hard labour, perseverence, and fertility of resource, than I have seen at many of the halting places in my tour.[1]

Much of this would probably apply also to agricultural practices in Egypt, China, Japan, Korea, and Java, in the late nineteenth century. There is also a great deal of evidence of state involvement in bringing about agricultural improvements. For instance, evidence of direct government involvement in spreading and advancing knowledge about improved agricultural practices in China dates back to the Sung times (AD 950-1350). Historians suggest that in less advanced areas officials had pictures painted on government office walls showing the peasants how to farm. They also had books printed and proclamations put out.

Efforts were made to popularise and supply pumping equipment (e.g. treadle pumps) in areas still unfamiliar with it.[2]

Numerous examples could be given to illustrate the high levels of agricultural technology employed in Asian countries, where the majority of the population of the developing countries still live. In spite of this, the label 'primitive' is still commonly applied to the farming systems of the developing countries. In fact, economists and social scientists from the developing countries frequently use such terms themselves. It is interesting to compare Voelcker's remarks on Indian agriculture with the following:

> Ploughing is generally superficial, fields uncovered, fertilization and manuring uncommon, and seed selection rare. Crop rotation and mixed cropping are practised in certain areas based on past experience. While mixed cropping is fairly widespread, crop rotation is not so.[3]

Such a text-book description of Indian agriculture betrays the ignorance of the urban elite whose only experience of Indian agriculture and village life has been through text-books often written by foreigners. In their anxiety to be accepted as equals by the international elite they tend to decry or disown anything 'traditional'. There is nothing new in this attitude. Developed countries, in their early stages of development, have often undergone similar experiences. One of the extreme examples of this was Japan for a limited period after the Meiji Restoration.

In search of modernity, important ancient monuments were demolished. Official zeal for westernisation led to the construction of a pretentious social hall in 1883 where the members of the 'elite society gathered and mixed with the foreign diplomatic corps in a conscious effort calculated to develop social graces through dancing, card games, and other pastimes indulged in by ladies and gentlemen in the best traditions of Occidental Society'.[4] This fetish of modernisation even extended to the advocacy of 'intermarriage with Occidentals as a sure means of improving the racial stock of the Japanese'.[5] This was seriously considered by leading Japanese statesmen and a letter was sent to Herbert Spencer seeking his scientific advice on the subject.

This search for 'respectability' and the mental laziness evinced in branding the indigenous techniques as 'primitive' has led to a somewhat indiscriminate recommendation for the adoption of modern agricultural technology. This tendency has received a further impetus from the genuinely serious problem of providing more and more food for rapidly growing populations.

While indigenous techniques, with sophisticated crop rotations and other cultural practices, have been able to preserve the soil structure and much of the fertility over a long period of time, and thereby cope with high population densities, there is a distinct possibility that soil fertility has by now reached an equilibrium state in which significant increases in output cannot be obtained without providing additional sources of plant nutrient. Under pre-modern conditions, the supply of plant nutrients depends largely on human and animal waste, refuse and farm, kitchen and town rubbish. The supply of much of this can be raised only to a limited extent. High-quality fertilisers such as green manures and oilseed cakes, compete for land with food crops. There-fore, for any sustained increase in agricultural production, reliance has to be placed on modern technology and plant nutrients, which can be increased at a sufficiently high rate without putting additional pressure on the land, which is in short supply in densely populated countries. Fish meal and chemical fertiliser fit this category of nutrients.

The use of chemical fertilisers in areas of assured water supply is one of the easiest means of increasing food production. It has certainly helped many developing countries to obtain substantial increases in agricultural output in recent years. However, the indiscriminate use of chemical fertiliser may have some adverse effects on soil structure, particularly if it leads to the replacement of a system of crop rotation by monoculture, the disappearance of livestock, or the elimination of ley farming[6] and farmyard manure. A few years ago the British Agri-cultural Advisory Council[7] was asked by the Minister of Agriculture to 'advise whether, and, if so, the extent to which, present practices are having adverse effects on soil fertility and soil structure'.[8] Although the enquiry relates to the United Kingdom, in view of the complexity of the problem the Report of the Council, published in 1970, stresses not only the need for avoiding vague and sweeping generalisations[9] but also throws significant light on the problems likely to be faced by other countries which opt for 'modern' farming.

The report stresses that it would be wrong to suppose that all-arable[10] rotations are universally harmful. If adequate drainage is pro-vided, yields can be maintained and increased even with all-arable rotations in areas of low rainfall and an easy-working soil. The soils which are unlikely to be damaged by such farming practices include well-drained sandy loams, light and medium well-structured loams and well-structured calcareous clays. But soils with a high fine sand, silt, or

clay or light sandy soils with inherently low organic matter tend to
suffer structural deterioration under such farming practices, particularly
in areas where rainfall exceeds 30 inches. Because of the adoption of a
tight cropping sequence, many operations are carried out under conditions that tend to damage the soil. Good soil management, particularly
with a view to avoiding structural problems arising from the use of
modern agricultural machinery, requires advanced drainage techniques.
Wet and plastic soils are frequently damaged by the wheels of heavy
machinery. Waterlogging and salinisation have caused problems for
many developing countries. In Pakistan, for example, the area affected
is estimated at over 5 million acres or about a fifth of the total gross
sown area. These problems can be aggravated by the extension of
canal irrigation and the construction of major multi-purpose river
schemes if sufficient attention is not paid to planting forests in the
catchment areas and dredging silt at regular intervals from reservoirs
and canals.

The Report of the Advisory Council underlined the fact that modern
methods of farming 'necessitate much greater attention to what is
happening below the topsoil, which in turn means knowledge of the
composition of the subsoil itself. This knowledge is by no means
always on the farm. Its absence is leading to surprises and mistakes
which are often quite unnecessary and, more serious, to the taking
of risks which cannot be justified.'[11] If this is the verdict on British
farmers, one can easily speculate on the kinds of damage that can be
done to the soil in developing countries as a result of the indiscriminate
use of modern agricultural technology, in the absence of adequate
dissemination of scientific information and technical advice.

The economic calculus of gain and loss which concentrates its attention on maximising gains over a short period of a year or a crop season
may often divert attention from the importance of the maintenance
and improvement of soil structure. It is not always recognised that the
effects of the soil on one year's cropping persist and influence the
quality and yield of subsequent crops. It is therefore essential that the
link between the past and present is recognised in methods of economic
analysis.[12] It would be wrong not to measure any major cropping
change against its long-term implications for soil structure, management
requirements and yields. Comparisons of the profitability of 'traditional' and 'modern' agricultural technology will not be complete
until the long-term implications of different technologies for future
soil fertility and soil structure are taken into account.

The risks of environmental pollution resulting from the excessive use of fertilisers and pesticides which have been experienced in the developed countries, though genuine in the long run, do not yet pose a serious problem for the developing countries. Even for cereals, the present per hectare use of such inputs is very small in most developing countries and the prospects for a rapid increase in their usage are not very bright, particularly in view of the oil crisis. However, the run-off from areas treated with massive doses of fertiliser or insecticide may affect surface and underground water supplies and thereby the terrestrial environment and aquatic life in streams, rivers, ponds and lakes through poisoning and eutrophication.[13]

The controversy about 'traditional' versus 'modern' farming has tended, at least for the present, to centre mainly around the question of whether or not 'modern' farming is labour displacing and/or socially unjust. Modern agricultural technology involves the use of inputs such as chemical fertilisers, pesticides, and agricultural machinery which are generally produced by a country's industrial sector or are imported from outside. The employment creating capacity of these industries is limited; whilst a few people in the rural areas may be engaged in the distribution of fertiliser or agricultural machinery, the production of these inputs is largely an urban affair. In cases where there is a very high level of use of agricultural machinery, particularly tractors and combine harvesters, there is a genuine risk of labour displacement. Developing countries with surplus labour are aware of this problem and the use of heavy tractors is generally limited to breaking up new soil and to land reclamation. However, in areas where the farming season is short and there is a shortage of labour in the peak agricultural season, it has been found that the wider use of tractors and other agricultural machinery sometimes enables farmers to grow two crops instead of one.[14] When this is the case, the increased use of machinery increases labour utilisation.

The wisdom of using irrigation machinery such as diesel pumps and tube-wells run by electricity is less open to question. By providing a regular supply of water the use of such machines enables more than one crop to be grown each year so that the labour requirement is not only increased but is more evenly spread over the year. In the case of tube-wells the holes can be bored much deeper than for ordinary wells making them less liable to failure in times of drought. Moreover, tube-wells are often run independently of human and animal labour. The efficacy of ordinary wells is considerably reduced during droughts, not only because the water may dry up but also because both animals and men become much weaker — for lack of adequate nutrition — and so are less able to draw water. Some of these problems were more clearly recognised by British civil servants in India, in the nineteenth century than they are by many modern development economists. For example, in his evidence before the Indian Famine Commission in 1881, the Deputy Commissioner of the Punjab said:

> Well cultivation may be said broadly to be never independent of aid by rain or by other means. It is not an absolute assurance against famine — it is only an insurance against its milder forms . . . The well cattle depend for their winter fodder largely on the Kharif harvest. All aid from rain failing, they are thrown for support entirely on the produce of water raised by their labour. At the same time, the winter rains failing, that labour becomes unusually continuous and severe. On the other hand it becomes a question of increasing perplexity to the well owner how he is to feed both his cattle and his own family. There is also this additional trouble, that the drought has made both air and soil so dry that the water does far less irrigating duty than usual. In the end, if the drought really lasts a year . . . it is perfectly certain that a vast number of well cattle will have died of hunger and fatigue . . . that the area before irrigated by wells will have greatly contracted . . .[15]

In addition, recent experience in China and India suggests that in areas where the density of tube-wells has increased beyond a certain level, the average supply of water from individual tube-wells has declined significantly. In some coastal areas in Gujarat (India) the tube-wells have now reached a depth of 1,000 feet and in some parts are now drawing up saline water. Obviously, in coming years these regions may have to rely increasingly on the surface flow rather than on underground supplies.

The case for modern transport facilities, particularly on village routes, remains open to question. Motor transport certainly opens up a much wider market for agricultural products and, by accelerating the commercialisation of agriculture, may sometimes reduce the local output of grains or other subsistence crops, as cash crops are substituted for subsistence crops. As a result, food imports from other regions may become necessary. Where the extension of modern transport facilities leads to the displacement of local carts on village routes and boats on smaller rivers, motor trucks could be restricted to trunk routes, leaving village routes to indigenous means of transport.

On the whole, it is now commonly accepted that 'modern'

agricultural technology, which relies on the intensive use of chemical fertilisers, pesticides and water, requires more labour per unit of land than other types of farming. It is for this reason that the labour requirement in Japanese agriculture is higher than in both India and China for all types of work, particularly interculture and manuring.[16]

Is 'modern' technology socially unjust?

The question of whether 'modern' technology is socially unjust or not is difficult to answer. This question has been raised in the wake of the so-called 'Green Revolution'. The 'Green Revolution' technique with its emphasis on 'hybrids' or dwarf varieties and the intensive use of modern inputs is based on the concept of selective development. Modern inputs, for geographical reasons and/or lack of complementary inputs, cannot be used indiscriminately in all parts of a country and on all farms in a particular region. Since a regular and adequate supply of water is the first precondition for the large-scale use of chemical fertiliser this method of farming, which came to be known in India as 'The Package Plan' can only be used in areas with an assured water supply and which are not regularly flooded. The input requirements are so heavy that they were beyond the means of small farmers in India and so the Government had to rely mainly on the richer farmers.[17] As a result, the main advantages of the new technology accrued to the rich farmers or to regions which already had favourable factor endowments. This aggravated the problems of inequality between persons and regions in India. A selective approach was adopted in China as well, and this led to disparities in income between different communes, brigades and teams.

Undoubtedly, it was the large and medium farmers who were the main beneficiaries of the 'Green Revolution' in India. Some of these farmers bought tractors and other agricultural machinery, which may have had some labour displacing effect. It is not yet certain whether tractors were bought simply as 'status symbols' or as a genuine reaction to shortages of labour during the seasonal peaks and to increased agricultural wages.[18] There is some evidence that agricultural wages were much higher in the 'Green Revolution' areas than in other parts of India.[19]

Certainly there is nothing in the 'package' technique itself which makes it inequitable or even labour displacing. In a recent study it has been indicated that the use of high yielding varieties leads to a 20 to 50 per cent increase in the demand for labour, per hectare, at the farm level.[20] In fact the 'Green Revolution' technique is neutral as to scale of operation and can be used equally efficiently on small and large farms.[21] It is possible that a family farm with surplus labour will devote more care to the new cultivation practices and water management than a large wage-farm. If the small farmer cannot take advantage of the new technology for lack of financial resources or, for that matter, even 'knowledge', the responsibility rests with the planners and policymakers who have been unable so far to devise the right kind of mechanisms and institutions.

In most developing countries the planners and policymakers, the 'elite', are socially and politically nearer to the rich and medium farmers than to the masses. By their training they are basically market orientated and their major concern is with increasing the marketed surplus of food. The small and marginal farmers generally do not contribute significantly to the marketed surplus[22] and so they receive a low priority in agricultural planning. Although some efforts, particularly under the auspices of international organisations such as the World Bank are being made to ameliorate the conditions of the small and marginal farmers, the framework in which these schemes are being formulated continues to be market orientated. Unless there is a fundamental change in planning attitudes the small man will remain underprivileged.

Much the same is true for regions not particularly well endowed with resources. Much modern technology depends critically on water supply, and thus dry zones, with inadequate rainfall and irrigation, are unable to take advantage of the new methods. If regional disparities are to be reduced better methods of sharing wealth and income have to be devised.

The reality of the situation is that in most developing countries, geographical constraints, shortage of money, lack of skills (in the form of researchers and service personnel), will compel large numbers of farmers to continue to rely on 'traditional' methods of farming. This has been clearly recognised by the Chinese leadership which has always emphasised the need for the simultaneous use of 'modern' and 'traditional' technologies. This strategy is symbolised in Chairman Mao's idea of 'walking on two legs'.

Even if it could be established that the 'modern' technology is clearly superior in the three criteria of increasing production, providing increased employment and protecting the interests of future generations, the period of transition from a 'traditional' to a 'modern' agriculture will be a long one. Much greater attention should, therefore, be paid to research and development aimed at improving the 'traditional' technology rather than rejecting it totally.

4 EMPLOYMENT CREATION: THE PLANNERS' ACHILLES HEEL

Since the problem of hunger and malnutrition is closely linked with poverty and lack of jobs, employment creation has always been one of the major objectives of planning in most developing countries. As early as 1951 the First Five Year Plan of India emphasised the need for 'maximum use of idle labour for the purpose of development'.[1] The Second Five Year Plan was an 'employment-oriented plan' which 'implies much more than determining the optimum scale of investment'.[2] It also emphasised that the 'creation of employment opportunities and reduction in underemployment cannot be approached merely in overall terms. The problem needs to be broken up in terms of sectors, regions and classes.'[3] It was aware that 'in spite of concerted efforts for the mobilisation of available resources and their optimum utilization as proposed in the Second Plan, the impact on the two-fold problem of unemployment and under-employment will not be as large as the situation demands'.[4]

Development planners in several other countries have also been aware of the need for creating greater employment opportunities in both the rural and urban areas.[5] International organisations, particularly the International Labour Office (ILO), have also shown a growing concern. One of ILO's earlier reports[6] — by a committee of experts and published in 1961 — remains an important contribution to the analysis of the problem of unemployment in developing countries. In 1969 the ILO launched its World Employment Programme, under the auspices of which employment missions have been sent to Colombia, Sri Lanka, Kenya, Iran, the Dominican Republic and the Philippines. The World Bank, the Organisation of Economic Co-operation and Development (OECD) and other international organisations have also become more employment conscious.

Much of the research sponsored by such organisations has served to underline the important links between poverty, employment and the need for a more equitable distribution of income and wealth. However, it is becoming increasingly clear that any effective solution of the employment problem in many developing countries requires a radical rethinking of development policy, something which may often be unpalatable to the groups in power. As will be argued later, none of the major international organisations, with their present terms of reference and ideological biases, can advocate or finance radical changes. As a result, policies which are only marginally useful will continue to be advocated and adopted and, despite growing national and international concern, the extent of unemployment will continue to grow.

Obviously, one of the main reasons for the growth of unemployment is the rapid rise in the size of the labour force. According to the labour force projections of the ILO, the total world labour force in 1970 was nearly 1,500 million. This is expected to grow by anything between 1.6 and 1.9 per cent per annum reaching a total of 2,588 million by the year 2000. Over three-quarters of this labour force will be in the developing countries. Because of rapid population growth, the labour force in the developing countries is expected to grow by a little over 2 per cent per annum, reaching a figure of 1,946 million by the year 2000, thus adding over 920 million to the existing labour force in a period of 30 years. In almost all developing regions, except for the centrally planned economies, the rate of growth of the labour force in the 1970s is expected to exceed 2 per cent, reaching 2.5 to 2.9 per cent by the end of the century (see Table 7).

It is interesting to compare these figures with the FAO estimates of the total number of economically active people in agriculture for the corresponding period. These figures (see Table 8) are based on the assumption that in the developing countries gross domestic product (GDP) will grow in line with the United Nations income projections for the Second Development Decade and that the growth rate of agricultural GDP postulated in the FAO Indicative World Plan (IWP) for Agricultural Development will be achieved.[7] These projections indicate that while there will be a further decline in the absolute size of the agricultural labour force in the developed countries, the absolute increase in the size of the labour force in the agricultural (not rural) sector in developing countries will continue. But even under the optimistic assumptions of the IWP, the size of the labour force employed in the agricultural sector by the year 2000 will only increase from 671 million to 837 million; thus only 166 million more people will be actively employed in the agricultural sector, as against an increase of over 927 million in the total labour force. Out of this total nearly 124 million is projected to be absorbed in Asian agriculture. With the already high pressure of population on the land this will not be easy to achieve. During the 1960s the availability of land per head of economically active population in Asia fell to 1 hectare. Some further additions to arable land are still possible, but only at a high cost; the

Table 7. Rates of growth of economically active population

	(Per cent per annum)				
	1950-60	1960-70	1970-80	1980-90	1990-2000
Developed market economies	1.0	1.1	1.0	1.0	1.1
North America	1.6	1.5	1.5	1.4	1.6
Western Europe	0.4	0.5	0.6	0.7	0.8
Oceania	2.2	1.9	2.9	1.2	2.0
Eastern Europe & USSR	1.4	1.0	1.2	0.7	0.6
Total Developed Countries	1.2	1.1	1.0	0.9	0.9
Developing market economies	1.6	2.1	2.3	2.5	2.6
Africa	1.6	2.0	2.2	2.4	2.7
Far East	1.4	2.1	2.3	2.5	2.5
Latin America	2.3	2.3	2.6	2.7	2.8
Near East	1.7	2.3	2.5	2.8	2.9
Asian centrally planned economies	3.2	1.6	1.5	1.6	1.5
Total Developing Countries	2.2	1.9	2.1	2.2	2.2
World	1.8	1.6	1.7	1.9	1.9

Source: ILO, *Labour Force Projections*, 1971. See also projections as reproduced in FAO (1973), *The State of Food and Agriculture*, p. 131.

possibilities for adding to arable land lie mainly in Pakistan, the Philippines, Burma and Thailand. Even if the entire stock of potentially arable land in Asia[8] were brought under cultivation by the year 2000 the availability of land per active worker would remain just under 1 hectare. The land-man ratio being more favourable in Africa and Latin America, the absorption of the projected increase in the labour force may not pose as serious a problem in these areas as in Asia. According to these projections agriculture, given present socio-economic relationships, will be able to accommodate less than a fifth of the total increase; the remaining four-fifths will have to be absorbed in non-agricultural employment. Thus in the year 2000 a staggering total of 1,109 million people (761 million of whom will be new additions) more than three times the total in 1970, will be looking for jobs in the non-agricultural sector of the developing countries.

Table 8. Total labour force and economically active population in agriculture (in millions)

	1970			2000		
	Total Labour Force	In agri- culture	Balance	Total Labour Force	In agri- culture	Balance
Developed market economies	305	43	262	414	17	397
North America	90	4	86	141	2	139
Western Europe	149	26	123	182	9	173
Oceania	6	0.6	5.4	11	0.3	10.7
Eastern Europe & USSR	177	57	120	228	19	209
Total developed countries	482	100	382	642	35	607
Developing market economies	645	421	224	1351	573	778
Africa	111	84	27	229	110	119
Far East	389	265	124	800	374	426
Latin America	88	37	51	194	42	152
Near East	55	34	21	124	44	80
Asian centrally planned	374	250	124	595	265	330
Total developing countries	1019	671	348	1946	837	1109
World	1501	771	730	2588	872	1716

Source: FAO (1973), *The State of Food and Agriculture*, pp. 131, 138.

Over 300 million new workers, equivalent to the entire labour force of the developed market economies in 1970, will have to be accommodated outside agriculture in the Asian countries (excluding the centrally planned economies) alone. The absorption of this additional workforce will require a 4 per cent annual rate of growth of non-agricultural employment in the developing countries (Table 9).

Statistics for the actual rate of growth of non-agricultural employ-

ment are only available for a limited number of countries. Because of
differences in the definitions of employment and the coverage of the
data such rates are not strictly comparable between different countries.
Neither are the countries mentioned in Table 10 fully representative
of the regions concerned. However, a comparison of the rates of growth
of employment in all non-agricultural sectors and in manufacturing
in some developing countries in recent years may give some idea of the
seriousness of the problem.

Table 9. Estimated rates of growth of non-agricultural employment
needed to absorb the additional labour force by 2000 AD (per cent
per annum)

Africa	4.0
Far East	4.25
Latin America	3.6
Near East	4.5
Asian Centrally Planned	3.2
Total Developing Countries	4.0

In most African countries for which data were available non-agricultural
employment increased by 4 per cent per annum or more. Similar
growth rates were experienced in some of the smaller countries in
Latin America and Asia. For instance, the rate of growth of non-
agricultural employment was 5.9 per cent in Panama and just over 6
per cent in the Korean Republic, over the period 1964-72. However,
for several relatively large countries such as Egypt, Ghana and India
the rate was much lower. The rates of increase of employment in the
manufacturing sector were similar. In many of the African countries
which recently established new manufacturing industries the rates of
growth of employment were relatively high. The index of employment
in manufacturing rose from 91 in 1968 to 100 in 1970, but by 1972
it had fallen back to 90. In Latin America, employment in manufacturing showed a significant increase in Panama, Peru and Puerto Rico. In
Asia, the Korean Republic and Hong Kong had relatively high rates
of growth. In India and the Philippines, employment in manufacturing
grew at a slower pace than in the entire non-agricultural sector.
Employment in the construction industry had a mixed record; in some
countries, such as Zambia and Tanzania, it was rising at between 10
and 15 per cent per annum, while in Ghana, Sierra Leone, and the
Philippines there was a significant decline.

Table 10. Rates of growth of employment in non-agricultural and manufacturing sectors (per cent per annum)

| | | Compound Annual Rate | | |
		Total Non-Agricultural	Manufacturing	Construction
Africa				
Cameroon	(1964-70)	4.7	2.6	3.2
Egypt	(1968-72)	2.7	—	2.0
Ghana	(1964-72)	0.9	7.3	4.0
Kenya	(1967-72)	3.9	7.0	3.4
Malawi	(1968-73)	9.0	6.0	6.7
Mauritius	(1966-73)	6.4	12.0	—
Sierra Leone	(1964-71)	1.3	1.0	−4.4
Tanzania	(1964-70)	5.5	13.5	10.0
Uganda	(1964-72)	6.5	6.0	14.5
Latin America				
Chile	(1964-73)	—	0.3	—
Dominican Republic	(1964-71)	—	1.7	—
Equador	(1964-72)	—	0.8	—
El Salvador	(1964-73)	2.4	2.9	−1.6
Guatemala	(1964-73)	—	1.0	—
Panama	(1964-72)	5.9	7.6	—
Peru	(1964-72)	—	4.0	—
Puerto Rico	(1964-73)	4.4	4.5	—
Asia				
Hong Kong	(1964-73)	—	6.7	—
India	(1964-71)	2.5	1.6	—
Israel	(1964-73)	4.4	4.0	—
Korean Republic	(1964-72)	6.1	11.7	8.7
Philippines	(1964-73)	4.6	3.7	−6.0
Syrian Republic	(1964-73)	3.3	4.9	—

Based on ILO (1974), *Year Book of Labour Statistics*.

Thus recent increases in employment in the non-agricultural sector, particularly in manufacturing, in developing countries, provide some basis for optimism — especially if the targets for increasing manufacturing output in various developing countries are achieved. According to a recent study, out of the 36 countries for which relevant information was available, 24 were aiming to achieve a 9 per cent average annual growth rate for manufacturing output; 7 were seeking a growth rate of between 7 and 9 per cent and only 5 had targets below 7 per cent.[9] Assuming that direct employment grows at a rate of about one half of the target rates of output, employment in manufacturing in many developing countries will grow at around 4 per cent per annum.[10] If account is taken of the increase in indirect employment as well, the overall rate of growth of employment resulting from an increase in output in the manufacturing sector may come to as much as 6 per cent.[11] Allowance has to be made, of course, for any reduction in employment in the handicraft sector due to increased competition from the organised manufacturing sector.

It is unlikely that the rate of growth of output in the manufacturing sector will continue at the high rates experienced in many developing countries in recent years. In some developing countries these high rates were largely due to their starting from a very low base.[12] With the further expansion of the manufacturing sector the rates of growth will tend to slow down. In fact such a tendency was already apparent in some developing countries even in the 1960s. While employment in manufacturing increased by 4.3 per cent per annum during 1960-5, it was only 2.4 per cent per annum during 1965-70. This decline in the rate of growth of employment was more marked in light industries than in heavy industries.[13] In the industrially more advanced developing countries, the increase in employment in traditional manufactures such as textiles was negligible. The growth industries, particularly in Asia and Latin America, have been metal products, basic metals, chemicals, petroleum products, etc. As a result of the high capital intensity and the new technology embodied in such industries employment per unit of output tends to fall with increasing output. This is reflected in the fact that value added in heavy industries in the 1960s rose much faster than employment.[14]

The pace of future industrialisation in many developing countries will depend not only on the rate of investment but also on their capacity to import capital goods. It has been found that during the 1960s and early 1970s the rate of growth of capital goods imports was similar to the rate of growth of output of the manufacturing sector.[15] In several developing countries in the early 1970s capital goods imports exceeded 40 per cent of gross fixed investment. It is felt that, except for some large developing countries such as Argentina, Brazil, Mexico, India and Pakistan, capital goods imports will continue to be on a significant scale.[16] In view of the limited prospects for increasing their exports, the near stagnation in aid and the increasing burdens of debt servicing, high food and oil prices will almost certainly reduce the capacity of many developing countries to import capital goods and will thereby hold back the pace of industrialisation.

However, some developing countries may gain some advantage in this respect as a result of the increased tendency for multi-national companies to transfer their production of labour intensive components to developing countries. For example, semi-conductors, valves, tuners, and other components are manufactured for a large number of Japanese and American electronics firms in Hong Kong, Singapore, South Korea, Taiwan and Mexico. British, Japanese and American automobile firms subcontract with Taiwan, South Korea, Mexico, India and Thailand for the production of parts and components. The precision drilling for some Swiss watches is now done in Mauritius.[17] There are many other lines of production for which similar possibilities exist.

This kind of subcontracting may become, at least in the immediate future, a significant source of additional employment, particularly in countries such as Hong Kong, Singapore and Taiwan. However, the long-term prospects for such industries being able to continue absorbing an ever-increasing supply of labour are not very bright. Besides, the 'linkage' effect of such industries is rather weak, so that the indirect effects on employment are unlikely to be very great. There is already a significant opposition in the developed countries from trade unions and small businesses to this subcontracting. American trade unions have already launched a crusade against 'runaway' plants.[18] The developing countries themselves will not want to get too closely associated with or dependent upon the developed countries since this will make it more difficult to insulate themselves from the frequent business fluctuations in the richer countries.[19] In any case, as is clearly being recognised, 'even with the best policies, urban industry will continue to be incapable of providing adequate job opportunities or a satisfactory level of living to all those wishing to leave the countryside'.[20]

Most developing countries will have to attempt to retain their surplus population in the rural areas. In rural areas cottage industries and handicrafts have traditionally provided substantial employment, particularly to women. The development of freshwater fisheries and the creation of new rural industries such as the processing of fruit and vegetables, etc., can also absorb some of the fast growing supply of under- or unutilised labour. Such industries can easily be geared to seasonal fluctuations in the demand for labour in farming. Under-employed labour can also be mobilised for the construction of rural public works, such as feeder canals and field channels, small irrigation schemes, terracing, embankments, drainage, afforestation, village roads, houses, schools, etc., most of which need not involve the use of very much capital equipment. The resulting increase in output, some of which may be of capital and intermediate goods, can assist a further expansion of employment. Some economists have been so impressed by this mechanism of capital formation through the more intensive use of surplus labour that they call 'mass mobilisation' the 'first law of development'.[21]

Rural house construction as a means of employing surplus labour should receive special attention, particularly for creating employment opportunities during years of severe droughts which tend to create famine conditions; in contrast with other rural public works, such as feeder roads or irrigation channels, improvements in rural housing do not immediately increase agricultural productivity, although the long-run effects on productivity through health improvements may be substantial. Since improvements in housing can easily be postponed and taken up intermittently this can serve as a good source of employment creation during drought years. Feeder roads and irrigation cannot easily fit this category, because their postponement will affect agricultural production.

It must be remembered that ultimately the expansion of employment in public works or housing is limited by a country's capacity to produce food and other consumer goods.[22] Given the high income elasticities of demand for grains and other basic necessities at low levels of income, the increase in income resulting from increased employment means that the demand for such products rises rapidly, while for lack of resources and because of institutional constraints (such as tenancy and share cropping arrangements, lack of credit and marketing facilities for agricultural products or handicrafts) supply cannot normally rise as fast. As a result there is a serious risk of inflation.[23]

Employment creation by redistribution of income may come up against similar constraints. It is often argued that since poor people on average consume more domestically produced labour intensive goods while richer people consume more capital intensive goods, frequently of foreign origin (partly for status reasons), a more even distribution of income within a country would increase overall employment. However, it is uncertain whether the rich do in fact consume more capital intensive goods on average than the poor, especially when the amount of services (i.e. medical, education, entertainment, domestic service, etc.) consumed by the rich is taken into account. But even if this assertion is accepted it is highly unlikely that there would be any significant increase in employment as a result of a marginal redistribution of income. As soon as any redistribution of income towards the poor is implemented there will be a substantial increase in the demand for grains and other basic necessities. Since the output of these commodities, particularly grains, cannot be increased substantially in the short run, there is likely to be a significant rise in their prices. The ultimate beneficiaries of such a rise in prices are likely to be the landlords, the rich and medium peasants and the traders. The resulting income distribution may be even more unfavourable to the poor than the initial situation. Any major attempt to create additional employment through income redistribution has, therefore, to go hand in hand with efforts to increase the production of basic necessities.

On the basis of the limited information that is available on China it seems that the twin policies of income redistribution and labour mobilisation succeeded in China mainly for two reasons: firstly, by concentrating efforts on traditional labour intensive techniques, and on productive activities with short gestation periods,[24] an attempt was made to increase the supply of food and other consumer goods; secondly, through price controls and the rationing of essential commodities (rice, wheat, sugar, edible oil and cotton textiles), inflation was kept at bay.[25] It is not only for the sake of maintaining ideological purity but also to reduce the 'demonstration effect' on consumption behaviour that contacts between foreigners and the ordinary Chinese citizens are kept to a minimum. The restrictions on foreign travel as well as on movements within the country (i.e. between the villages and towns and between regions) are also, at least partially, motivated by similar considerations.

Chinese experience clearly demonstrates that it is possible to create meaningful additional employment in public works, etc. while simultaneously increasing the production of goods and services to match, to a considerable extent, the increase in effective demand. Most of these public works schemes require only small capital investments and can therefore be financed locally. However, for the successful implementation of such schemes certain preconditions must be met.

Because of differences in factor endowment, topography, climate, the level of skill of local people, transport and communication facilities and other social and psychological factors, many rural schemes are area-specific and the choice of time and place has to be made locally. This clearly requires efficient local organisations which can conceive useful projects, mobilise people in support of them and implement the various stages of the projects. Some projects, such as digging wells, or constructing small embankments can be carried out by mobilising resources solely from within a village, but in the case of large irrigation schemes or embankments the cooperation of several villages or even several districts may be required. Organising labour at this level requires local leadership which can be trusted by the people. Past experience of the community development programmes in India and cooperative movements in several countries indicates that local initiative is not always forthcoming, so that such schemes are usually government initiated or sponsored. However civil servants too often fail to provide effective leadership and, being outsiders, they rarely inspire confidence among local people. In cases where promotion and other job prospects depend on visible records of performance most of their efforts are concentrated on the construction of roads, buildings, irrigation channels and so on, and not on the changes in attitudes and thinking which generate a sense of self-reliance and mutual help. Exaggerated claims of achievements are not uncommon.

In China mass movements to involve people in achieving certain economic objectives (such as during the Great Leap) often led to an enormous waste of scarce resources. On the other hand, in many countries social and institutional barriers stand in the way of peoples' involvement in plans for economic development. For instance, in areas where a large proportion of peasants' gross output goes to landlords, moneylenders and merchants, it would not be surprising to find a definite lack of incentive among the peasants. In such situations the effectiveness of the fuller utilisation of labour depends largely on reorganising the existing agrarian structure. If agrarian reform is a necessary precondition for calling forth the initiative of local people and the 'mobilisation' of surplus labour then, given the vested interests involved, and the political power of the rich and middle farmers in many developing countries, no substantial addition to employment can be hoped for, at least in the foreseeable future. Changes in social attitudes and relationships may become imperative if a society aims at increasing both productivity and labour utilisation in the rural sector.[26]

Undoubtedly, rural industries and public works can greatly supplement employment opportunities in the villages, but in the last resort it is farming (and therefore land) which has to bear the main burden of an increasing population and labour force. In those African and Latin American countries where land is plentiful the redistribution of land, if politically feasible, can absorb a significant proportion of the likely increase in the labour force. But in the densely populated countries of

Asia, a redistribution of land with a view to creating peasant proprietorship, even if politically feasible, will create tiny non-viable holdings.
Any effort to create economically viable units will fail to ameliorate
the condition of vast numbers of landless labour because there is just
not enough land to go round. It can, however, be argued that peasant
families could, as they generally do, absorb the surplus labour of
family members on their own farms since employment on a family
farm can easily extend up to the point where the marginal product of
labour is zero. Generally, the labour intensity and, therefore, output
per unit of land, on a family farm is higher than on a wage-farm, where
the profit maximising economic 'rationality' of the farmer only allows
him to employ labour up to the point where the marginal product of
labour is equal to the real wage.

But even a family farm cannot be expected to carry the surplus
labour of other families. Therefore, in densely populated countries,
the answer to the problem of surplus labour has to be found in some
form of cooperative or collective organisation until such time when
the rate of population growth and the new additions to the labour force
are brought down to manageable proportions capable of being absorbed
in non-agricultural activities. Collective enterprises can be seen as an
extension of the idea of the joint family, tribe, or traditional village
community where the payment for work is not necessarily geared to
the amount of work done by an individual or to the marginal product.
The limited employment opportunities that are available are shared
evenly among individuals. Since unemployment leads not only to a lack
of earnings, but also to frustration and human degradation, more disguised unemployment — spreading limited employment opportunities
evenly among people — is preferable to the complete unemployment
of some. In a country that cannot be made prosperous overnight, the
sharing of limited employment opportunities is a social necessity. By
eliminating the risk of the complete loss of a job during severe
droughts, the sharing of limited employment opportunities can help
prevent famine deaths.

The sharing of employment — in a wider context, the sharing of
poverty — requires a radical rethinking on property relationships,
institutions and economic 'rationality'. Some of these points will be
taken up in greater detail below.

Even if the 'sharing of employment' could be effectively implemented within the rural areas, the differences between rural and urban
incomes and amenities will continue to attract some rural people to
the urban areas. In China in spite of severe restrictions on such

movements and continuing campaigns to send students and other people from the urban to the rural areas, the urban drift has continued.

In the long run the question to be resolved is not only how to provide additional jobs in the rural areas but also how to make life sufficiently attractive so that the incentive to 'drift' to towns is eliminated. Alternatively, there must be a change in attitudes towards material acquisitions and 'modern' living. Until then, if the evils of shanty towns and slums are to be avoided, some authoritarian measures must be employed to restrict movements to the towns and cities.

5 LAND REFORM AND THE POOR

There is now enough evidence to suggest that while technological change in agriculture may succeed in raising output substantially, it does not always ensure adequate employment, income and consequently sufficient food for the very poor. Therefore those who believe in social justice tend to recommend some form of land reform programme involving at least tenancy legislation to curb the excesses of landlords, or, better, the abolition of landlordism, some redistribution of land and the establishment of owner-operated farms (often called peasant proprietorship). At the same time such reforms have to be supplemented by the provision of credit and marketing facilities, not only to increase agricultural output but also to make sure that the new owners do not, for lack of financial resources, lose their land once again to money-lenders and traders. Even those who pin their faith primarily on technological change in agriculture to end food shortages acknowledge that the full benefits of technical improvement cannot be realised until those institutional arrangements which work as disincentives and dampen individual initiative are reformed. Inequitable land tenure systems (such as share cropping or temporary leases), and the lack of credit and marketing facilities, come high up on the list of institutional inadequacies. Thus differences of opinion between the various schools of thought centre not so much on the need for land reform *per se*, as on the extent to which redistribution should go and on the nature of the social and economic reorganisation that should take place after a land reform programme has been implemented.

It can be shown that on the grounds of both technical efficiency and social justice collective solutions to the land problem are more attractive, particularly for the densely populated Asian countries. However, for ideological reasons (or political expediency) 'liberal' thinkers usually advocate a slow and gradual change even though this may not bring about any significant improvement in the conditions of the very poor. It is often stressed, and rightly so, that 'revolutionary' solutions have immense social costs. However, it is debatable whether 'gradualist' solutions, which merely introduce marginal changes and leave the property relations and power structure virtually unaffected, are less costly in social terms in the long run or whether they can, in fact, eliminate or reduce the risks of violent change.

The main aim of a land reform is to eliminate the intermediary interests (often described as feudal and semi-feudal elements),[1] redistribute land and to establish peasant proprietorship. In its traditional and generally accepted sense, land reform refers to the 'redistribution of property or rights in land for the benefit of small farmers and agricultural labourers'.[2] The main argument is a remnant of Ricardian thinking — that intermediaries are not particularly interested in making agricultural improvements and that rent is an 'unearned increment'. As against this, since the 'magic of property turns sand into gold' a peasant proprietor does have the incentive to make improvements. Therefore a change from a landlord-tenant tenure system (or from a communal system) to a system of peasant proprietorship should increase agricultural output.[3]

The anti-feudal streak in land reform programmes comes from diverse and often conflicting sources. The opposition to landlords has come from both liberal thinkers like Ricardo and the leadership of the French, Russian and Chinese Revolutions. In each case the abolition of feudal elements became an important objective of a political programme. For Ricardo, landlords and the Corn Laws represented the *status quo* and stood in the way of industrialisation. For revolutionary leaders in France, Russia and, more recently, in China, the political power of the landlords represented a serious obstacle to the establishment of a revolutionary regime. Thus in both liberal and revolutionary thinking opposition to feudalism represented a fight against the establishment and an emotional hatred of a class which stood against 'progress', as defined by the new ideology. Only the strategy of opposition was different. Because of its mixed heritage, the abolition of intermediaries, the redistribution of land ownership and the establishment of peasant proprietorship have an appeal for people of various convictions.

The ideological overtones — partly a result of the haunting memories of the mass 'liquidation' of rich peasants in Russia, and (to a lesser extent) the elimination of landlords in China on the one hand, and the US Government making land reform an issue in the Cold War[4] on the other — have often inhibited rational discussion of the issues involved in land reform. It is undeniable that in many parts of the world peasants have suffered various deprivations, even indignities at the hands of the landlords, and that landlords in general, and absentee landlords in particular, have not been very interested in agricultural development. On the other hand, eighteenth-century landlords in Britain played a leading role in improving agricultural techniques and practices.

Similarly, some landlords played a vital role in Japanese agricultural development, although instances of parasitic, rack-renting, indifferent, conservative or absentee landlords were not lacking even in Japan. Dore, who is otherwise sympathetic to landlords, summarises the contribution of landlords in the following words:

> Too many factors are involved, however, none of them strictly assessable in quantitative terms, for the verdict on the Japanese case to be other than not proven — with, possibly, the balance of probability on the side of the landlords up to the point at which literacy became common in Japanese villages, and against them thereafter.[5]

Landlords also made some positive contribution to agricultural development in China and India. In both these countries it was customary for the landlords to finance and maintain major and medium irrigation works.[6] Many landlords in Bengal and elsewhere in India cooperated with the British administration in agricultural experiments. Some of the feudal chiefs in India themselves practiced modern farming, advanced loans at low rates of interest for the construction of wells or for the repayment of loans from private moneylenders and made significant contributions to afforestation. One feudal chief took a lead in starting an agricultural college. Nevertheless, it remains true that on balance landlordism (as a system) went against the interests of the tenants and also proved to be an obstacle to agricultural development. However, the converse, that the abolition of landlordism will automatically improve the conditions of the poor farmers and landless labour and provide greater incentives for agricultural development, is not necessarily true. A number of factors have to be considered before such a conclusion can be reached. For instance, in a land reform programme which allows a retention of land only for self-cultivation by former landlords, there is a risk that many small peasants will be evicted. If the new title to land is conditional on proving continued cultivation of a particular piece of land over a period of time, then a poor and illiterate peasant might find it difficult to establish his rights, particularly when many people hold land under customary tenancies and when he possesses no written record of his rights. Often, the tax burden is not reduced; although tenants now come into direct contact with the state, they may continue to pay the same rent as before so that there is no particular financial benefit to the peasants from land redistribution.[7] Sometimes the state takes over the revenue-administration personnel of landlords after the takeover of their estates. In such a situation the same persons who acted as the agents and sub-agents of the landlords now become civil servants. The 'oppression' of the tenants may, in fact, be intensified because it is not often realised that it is not always the absentee landlord who 'exploits' the tenant or the sharecropper; historically many of the difficulties were caused by their agents and subagents who generally lived on the estate.[8] On the one hand, they 'fleeced' the tenant while on the other they 'cheated' their own masters.

Then there is the problem of implementation. Even when reform legislation has been passed the landed interests, through their influence with the political leadership and the Civil Service, can slow down the implementation of the reform. Programmes involving the redistribution of land and ceilings on land holdings have usually been much faster under revolutionary or military regimes than under democratic ones.

Even after the implementation of a land redistribution programme it is not always certain that the new class of peasant proprietors, often with tiny holdings, will be able to retain their holdings. For lack of resources many peasant proprietors are forced to borrow from traders and moneylenders, and often lose effective control over their land, even though the transference of land ownership by sale or mortgage may be illegal. Such transference of land ownership occurred in France after the revolutionary land redistribution and more recently in China after the 1952 land reforms. By the mid-1950s the Chinese leaders were already complaining that the poor peasants were losing control of their land to the rich and middle peasants. This was one of the reasons why the pace of collectivisation was speeded up in China. Another interesting example of this type of development comes from Mexico, where the land expropriated from private estates was redistributed among *ejidos* (peasant communities). Although land ownership rights could not be transferred by sale, many *ejidos*, for lack of credit and sufficient employment opportunities, 'leased their land to business men and worked as employees of their tenants on their own land'.[9] Doreen Warriner emphasises that in Mexico the 'redistribution has not provided a remedy for rural poverty. It has not provided full employment or satisfied hunger for food and land.'[10] Myrdal is as emphatic about Asian countries, where the 'post-war attack in South Asia on agrarian problems by way of land distribution and ceiling legislation' has not accomplished a great deal.[11] Nor have these reforms brought any direct benefit to landless labour.[12]

It is increasingly being felt that land redistribution and the establishment of peasant proprietorship alone will not transform the condition of poor farmers and agricultural labour. Peasant proprietors must be supported by a 'comprehensive programme' including supervised credit, organised marketing, agricultural education and extension services.[13] American scholars use the term 'agrarian reform' to describe such a comprehensive programme. In principle, this type of comprehensive programme is sound enough, but the administration of such a programme is not always easy, particularly in countries where the bureaucracy is both inefficient and corrupt. As Warriner rightly puts it: 'If they have had no system of agricultural credit, no cooperatives, and no agricultural advisers before, governments in underdeveloped countries cannot mount these services at short notice.'[14]

If agricultural administration, including extension services, is one of the main scarce resources, it can be economised on not by maintaining numerous tiny, often uneconomic peasant holdings, but by consolidating them into bigger units. Alternatively, economies of scale in credit, marketing and other services can be exploited by providing multipurpose cooperatives (not necessarily cooperative farms).[15] This is probably what Doreen Warriner has in mind when she says: '. . . grant individual ownership, but provide some form of organization to channel investment and market the produce, thus linking increased inputs with higher output and greater incentives to sell.'[16]

This may be a reasonable approach for peasants who are the beneficiaries of a land redistribution; but in view of the shortages of land in densely populated countries many small peasants would probably only obtain non-viable tiny holdings. Besides, a poor peasant will continue to be at a disadvantage *vis-à-vis* his richer counterparts; for even after land redistribution (unless it is a revolutionary one) some inequality of land ownership will probably persist.

Gunnar Myrdal's brand of peasant proprietorship (capitalist farmer) is hard to justify on his own criteria. A substantial part of *Asian Drama* is devoted to underlining the unfairness of the post-war land reforms in South Asian countries with regard to small peasants and landless labour. Right through the book he is concerned with the under-utilisation of labour. He clearly indicates that the goal for agricultural planners must be *'to increase the utilisation of the at present greatly under-utilised agricultural labor force'*.[17]   But when he comes to propose 'A Potentially More Promising Option'[18] for radical land redistribution and radical land consolidation, he recommends [to India] that 'it may be preferable to make a deliberate policy choice in favour of capitalist farming by allowing and encouraging the progressive cultivator to reap the full rewards of his enterprise and labor, while approaching the fundamental issues of equality and institutional reform from a different angle and by different policy means'.[19] He further suggests that 'Large scale ownership *per se* should not be regarded as an evil if it provides genuine gains in efficiency and productivity'.[20]

It is debatable whether capitalist farming will always increase agricultural output above that of small family farms. There is some evidence to suggest that in terms of per hectare output family farms perform rather better than wage-farms. The impact of large-scale capitalist farming on equality and employment creation will not normally be favourable. It is possible that capitalist farmers, with a view to increasing the scale of their operations, will buy out the small peasant in the neighbourhood. There is no guarantee that they will use intensive farming techniques. If maximisation of profit is the main criterion then farming intensity will certainly fall below what is usual for family farms. It is well known that a family farm, in order to maximise total revenue (or food), works the land more intensively than wage-farms. Myrdal is aware of these difficulties, particularly the risk of the substitution of machinery for labour. He recognises that a government would find it difficult to prevent 'strong vested interests from obtaining equipment, but some degree of control could be exercised'.[21] To the agricultural worker (presumably sharecroppers and landless labour) he offers a 'respectable place in the capitalist agricultural system'.[22] In addition, his scheme would include a programme '*to give a small plot of land – and with it a dignity and a fresh outlook on life as well as a minor independent source of income – to members of the landless lower strata*'.[23] This land would come from currently 'uncultivated waste'. This means, that the land would probably not be very fertile and would provide only meagre incomes which 'would still need to be supplemented from other sources – either through agricultural wage labor or through other types of work in the countryside'.[24]

Since this scheme apparently does nothing to reduce the concentration of land ownership its impact on the existing inequality of land ownership and political power would be minimal. Land given to the landless labour will only be a symbolic gesture; actual land received would be much less than under a land redistribution scheme with a ceiling on land holdings. It would not be easy to find supporting services for such tiny holdings because they would have to compete with the richer farmers, who would continue to be a dominant force in the country. Above all, there would be no job security nor any guarantee that the wage-earners would receive a 'fair' wage on the capitalist farms. In addition, there will always be the risk that an agricultural worker will be thrown out of employment in recurrent droughts. In effect, he will have much less security than a sharecropper. Myrdal's 'promising option' is a recipe for disaster for landless labour.

Admittedly capitalist farming has been successfully operating in the plantation sector of many developing countries but the rights of the farm worker (i.e. the wage labourer) have had to be protected by labour legislation and have not always proved easy to enforce. Two major limitations of plantations have been that the employment provided is often only seasonal and that there is little 'spread effect' of the modern agricultural technology used on such farms.

Myrdal's 'promising option' may be a more appropriate programme for countries with low densities of population, particularly in Latin America, where the size of farm is generally large and land is not the major constraint in creating more employment opportunities, but it is certainly inappropriate for the densely populated countries of Asia to whom his recommendation is directed.

Land nationalisation

Myrdal's support for land nationalisation as a viable alternative to a more radical redistribution of land to the cultivators is a more defensible proposition than his proposal for the establishment of capitalist farms. He rightly stresses that the results of the nationalisation of land would be that the 'problems of fragmentation and the dispersion of small holdings could be overcome; rational land use and planning could be introduced; the technical capabilities of irrigation could be better exploited; and the economies of scale that would accompany a rationalization in power supplies could be achieved.'[25]

Above all, by eliminating private property in land, such a programme would cut at the root of economic and social inequities. Of course, the nationalisation of land, as in the case of industries, creates its own problems; there would not only be a risk of increased red tape and its resulting inefficiencies but also, for lack of incentives, production could suffer. The well-being of an agricultural worker who would be turned into a wage labourer on a state farm, would depend largely on the political commissars of the state which can lead to a sense of alienation.

The experience of the Gezira Scheme[26] in the Sudan indicates that some of these problems can be tackled reasonably effectively if agricultural business after nationalisation is run by an autonomous public corporation. After the expiry of the private foreign concession in 1950 the Gezira Scheme was taken over by the Government and its management was vested in a 'tripartite partnership between the Government, tenants and a managing board'.[27] The rights and duties of the three partners are clearly defined by a partnership agreement: the Government provides the land and water, the tenant is responsible for providing the labour for various agricultural operations, and the Board of Management looks after the provision of finance (partly borrowed from the Government), the marketing of crops and the general running of the enterprise.

The land belonging to the Scheme is divided into standardised small family units which are allocated to the tenants. The Board of Management provides the tenants with agricultural credit against a condition embodied in the tenancy regulations that the cotton crop must be handed over to the management, which is responsible for marketing services such as ginning, grading, baling, transport and storage. The individual tenant is not allowed to dispose of his cotton crop in any other way. It is the management which takes the decisions regarding the rotation of crops and other agricultural practices, and the use of various inputs, including labour. All agricultural operations are strictly supervised by field staff appointed by the management. The field staff are assisted by locally appointed overseers (*samed*) and village councils. These controls and supervision do not apply to food grains (*dura*) and fodder (*lubia*), nor is agricultural credit provided for these crops. However, the tenant is not required to pay for land and water used in the production of food grains and fodder, and he is allowed to retain the whole output of these crops for his personal use.

The net sales proceeds from cotton are divided between the three partners, the state, the Board of Management and the tenants. The tenants' share is 50 per cent of the net proceeds, the Government takes a third and the Board of Management around 10 per cent. The remaining 6 per cent is divided equally between the tenants' reserve fund, local government councils and social service schemes. By building up a leguminous crop in the rotation as a subsistence crop, the system not only guarantees employment and food in the slack season but also assists soil conservation. The provision that a tenant cannot generally have more than one tenancy nor enlarge the size of his holdings has enabled the system to continue as an egalitarian venture. Much still remains to be achieved in terms of increasing tenant participation, but the Gezira Scheme is a successful case of a 'socialised' enterprise with some workers' participation in management. With the degree of compulsion in rotations, seeds, fertiliser use, marketing, etc., and the non-voluntary nature of such services it is hard to see what is left of individual enterprise. It is debatable if the tenants retain any affection they originally had for their own plots when they entered the scheme.[28]

Collectivisation

By now it is widely accepted that if participation in cooperative farming is voluntary, it is unlikely that land will be pooled on any appreciable scale.[29] Also, if the members have the right to withdraw from a co-operative venture, then the stability of the venture is threatened. In the early years of collectivisation in Poland, the voluntary cooperatives frequently had to be reorganised as a result of withdrawals and it became impossible for the cooperatives to set long-term targets for investment or production.[30] Ultimately, the plan for collectivisation had to be given up. In most cooperative farming ventures the membership is limited to those who pool their land and other material resources; landless labour do not qualify for membership. In addition, the right to private property in land is respected, so that initial inequities in economic and political power persist in the management of most cooperative farms. Although in most cooperative farms the system of voting is one-man-one-vote and is not related to the ownership of land, a family with large areas of land at its disposal can split up its landholding so as to have more than one vote on the board of management. Thus, in addition to the difficulties created by the lack of managerial ability and finance and the problem of incentives, two further obstacles to the success of cooperative farms have been the recognition of private property in land and the right of members to withdraw. Similarly, a provision for voluntary compliance has been a serious obstacle to the consolidation of holdings into economically viable units. Various attempts at the consolidation of land in India during the period of British rule achieved only limited success, and the same was true in Japan in the late nineteenth and early twentieth century. This was why in India, after Independence, under the provisions of the joint village management scheme, it was decided that if in any village two-thirds of the peasants decided to establish a cooperative farm, it would be obligatory for the remaining third to join in. Once the need for compulsion is acknowledged it can easily be demonstrated that collectives, particularly along the lines of the Chinese communes, cannot only 'mobilise' labour much more effectively than most other forms of rural organisation but also are more socially just. In terms of productive efficiency there is no reason why communes should be less viable than other types of farm organisation although the problem of material incentives still poses some (not insurmountable) problems.

Even Western liberal thinkers such as Myrdal accept that small
family farms are not particularly suitable for certain output-raising
innovations such as irrigation works and the economic use of animal
and tractor power, while compulsory consolidation

> . . . can insure comprehensive geographical coverage and economies
> of scale unobtainable when private owners refuse to participate.
> Moreover, by wiping out private titles to land, a vigorously ad-
> ministered system of compulsory consolidation could erase the
> traditional cleavages in social and economic status that have rested
> on the ownership of land.[31]

In spite of the considerable advantages of collectives, this form of rural
reconstruction does not receive any support from liberal thinkers,
largely for ideological reasons.[32] The arguments put forward do not
generally stand a close scrutiny. Some of the arguments used by
Myrdal[33] are as follows:

> (1) such an approach is 'ruled out in official discussions because
> democratic consent could not be won';
> (2) 'no enthusiasm for a radical expropriation can be found among
> a peasantry that jealously guards its private title to even small
> plots of land';
> (3) support for such measures is lacking even among the landless
> labour who aspire for 'a plot of their own rather than for participa-
> tion in collective ventures';
> (4) if the state adopts ruthless measures to implement collectivisa-
> tion, there is a risk of creating an 'embittered agrarian population'
> which might sabotage agricultural production rather than assist it;
> (5) there is a lack of the necessary skills 'either in quality or in
> quantity' for the planning and organisation of the use of land and
> to provide technical guidance.

Myrdal's first four objections relate to people's resistance to ideas of
compulsory social change. A risk of some resistance is always there
when state action to bring about a social reform is being contemplated,
the resistance being much greater if the proposed change affects
private property. Any social reform such as the abolition of hanging,
banning racial discrimination or providing maternity benefits to un-
married mothers, put to a mass vote would probably be rejected in

many countries, including the most culturally advanced nations of the West. But such reforms are not dismissed casually; at least some attempt is made to win over public opinion. Similarly, there is a need for reasoned discussion on the issue of collective farming as an alternative to peasant proprietorship.

It can also be argued that the peasantry jealously guard their small pieces of land mainly because they provide their only assured means of livelihood. Besides, in most developing countries they are on of the safest forms of investment as well as being a status symbol. Landless labourers want a small piece of land for much the same reason. If there is a genuine guarantee that the livelihood of a peasant will not be threatened after the abolition of private property in land then he may not have the same kind of attachment to the soil as before. The leadership in Communist countries have always been aware of the desire for land and when organising collective farms have usually provided each peasant with a small 'private plot', at least for a transitional period – an arrangement which should compare favourably with the tiny holding that Myrdal proposes to provide to the landless labour in his 'promising option'. Myrdal is, of course, right about the risk of sabotage, especially by landlords and rich peasants. This happened in Russia and the Eastern European countries and, to some extent, in China too, although in the latter the leadership had learnt from Russian experience and so were prepared to be ruthless with such people, while simultaneously trying to win over other sections of the peasantry. In China the changes were introduced gradually so as to reduce the feeling of 'suddenness and shock among the peasants'.[34] Evidence, though somewhat limited, suggests that the 'enthusiasm for collective farming seemed to have remained high among the majority of poor farmers'.[35] Most farmers joined 'with nothing more than persuasion' and in only a few cases did political and economic leverage have to be used.[36]

Some opposition is inevitable, however mild the particular land reform. Myrdal's fears that this kind of rural reorganisation may not succeed for lack of trained personnel are justifiable but this would apply probably to a greater extent to other forms of rural reconstruction, particularly that of peasant proprietorship supported by a system of service cooperatives, which he seems to prefer to collectives:

> . . . it is difficult to see what advantages could be obtained from this [collective] approach that could not be obtained with far less social strain through a program combining a radical redistribution of land with service cooperation and intensified agricultural

extension programs.[37]

It is difficult to see how the requirements of trained administrative personnel and planners could be lower in the above scheme than in a collective. The larger number of units to be serviced would make the problem of coordination, if anything, more serious than in the collective approach. Moreover, the greatest social tension (and resistance) arises in the course of a radical redistribution and not so much after it. But Myrdal's alternative does not rule out a radical redistribution.

Since it is being argued here that a collective form of rural reorganisation is a more viable alternative for developing countries, particularly the densely populated ones, it is instructive to look in detail at the organisation of the Chinese communes. The Chinese experience is more valid than the Russian one for densely populated countries. Moreover, Russia's collectivisation programme was the first attempt in that direction — other countries have learnt to avoid some of the major pitfalls.

The Chinese communes

The basic philosophy behind the Chinese communes is that agricultural policy must aim at improving all aspects of rural life and, as far as possible, on the basis of self-reliance and self-government. This is similar to the philosophy behind the Community Development Projects in India, which did not make much progress, one of the main reasons being the lack of real mass involvement. From the very inception of the idea of the communes in China, the Communist Party stressed that

> ... the people's commune is the organiser of the production and life of the people, and the fundamental purpose of the development of production is to satisfy to the maximum extent the constantly growing material and cultural needs of all members of society. In leading the work of the commune, the Party must give all-round attention to the ideological development, production and livelihood of commune members.

It was stressed that:

> ... in order to do their work well, the communes must practise a high level of democracy, consult the masses on all matters, faithfully represent their interests and reflect their will.[38]

A commune is subdivided into production brigades which, in turn, are subdivided into production teams. An average production team consists of 30 to 40 households and roughly coincides with a traditional village; for all practical purposes the village continues to be the basic social unit. A large village with over 200 households, on the other hand, is analogous to a production brigade. Under the present set-up the production team is an accounting unit and is responsible for its own profits and losses and for organising its production and distribution of income. Ownership of land is vested in the production brigade but is given permanently to the production team for use. Draught animals and farm tools are owned and maintained by production teams. Expensive tools such as tractors, water pumps, and threshing machines are more commonly owned by production brigades which also own forests and trees (with the exception of fruit trees near peasants' homes) which they lease out to production teams on contract or on a sharecropping basis. Industrial enterprises are generally owned and managed by the communes. Peasants own their homes which are heritable by their children; the construction of homes can be privately undertaken. For all practical purposes permission to build new houses is rarely refused. Families, are allocated a 'private' plot of land, and, although the ownership is not vested in the family, the right to use it is heritable. They may also own a small number of pigs, poultry and ducks and can take part in private side-line occupations (e.g. basket-making, knitting, sewing, etc.) to add to the income earned by collective work. In many communes private sources of income constitute up to a quarter of household income.

Participation in collective activities is compulsory for commune members and payment for labour is made mainly according to work done. Although there are several methods of work assessment, the work-point system is the most common. With this method members are classified according to the level of their skills and capacities; the more difficult (or skilled) the job, the more work-points are assigned to it. For instance, carrying heavy loads on shoulder poles receives more work-points than weeding of fields or picking vegetables. Women earn the same number of work-points as men for similar jobs. Invariably, however, more arduous jobs are given to able-bodied men: while an able-bodied man can earn as many as 10 work-points a day, able-bodied females can earn only around 8.5. Some work-points are assigned for innovational activities and, until recently, for 'political consciousness' which was largely assessed on the basis of attendance at political meetings. During the slack season when peasants are drafted for creating infrastructure such as roads, irrigation works, etc., they continue to earn work-points from their own commune and only a small cash payment is made by the employing agency. However, the workers employed by the commune industries, and jobs relating to livestock, earn a fixed salary and other fringe benefits as do their counterparts in urban industries.

It is obligatory for the production team to meet the agricultural tax (effectively around 6 per cent of output) levied by the state and to deliver the quota of grains and cash crops to the state at a pre-determined price. This quota is fixed by the state, in consultation with the County and the Commune Revolutionary Committees (management committees) which consist of representatives from the three groups of people (i.e. peasants, cadres and soldiers), and is communicated to the production teams. In fixing quotas, the production capacity, past performance and food needs of the team are taken into consideration. After meeting the tax and the state delivery quota, allowance is made for seed, feed and other production expenses; of what remains 8 to 10 per cent of total output is allocated to the public accumulation fund (capital formation) for the purchase of machinery and other investments; and another 3 to 5 per cent goes to the welfare fund, which is divided equally between education and public health.[39] The remaining 50 to 55 per cent of output is distributed among members according to the total number of work-points credited to each member. Payments are made both in cash and in kind, with a cash component of around 70 per cent. Members are free to sell their receipts in kind, if they so desire, either to the state procurement agencies or to the 'private' rural markets, where the prices are regulated by the state and are kept almost 10 per cent higher than the procurement price.

Production teams can borrow money from the Peoples' Bank, which charges differential interest rates. Rates on loans for major developmental purposes like buying tractors, or for the construction of irrigation works are lower than those for running expenses. Peasants receive interest of up to 1½ per cent on their bank deposits and can borrow money for their individual requirements; loans for consumption and ceremonial purposes are charged at punitive rates.

Various organisational levels within the commune are responsible for their own welfare activities; generally there is a hospital or a dispensary at the commune level, a health clinic in each production brigade and a health worker, called the 'bare-foot doctor', in each production team. The 'bare-foot doctor' is a para-medical worker who receives short-term training for nearly six months in public health, sanitation, rudimentary medicine and acupuncture. He is also responsible for family planning advice and the distribution of free contraceptives and pills; some 'bare-foot doctors' are also trained to undertake abortions by the vacuum aspiration method. Minor ailments are handled by the Brigade Clinics and minor operations are carried out in the Commune Hospital, which has three to four qualified doctors. Commune members are required to pay 1.5 to 2.5 yuan per annum and the production team pays 2 yuan per head per annum out of the welfare fund into a cooperative medical insurance fund, which finances medical treatment for everyone living on the commune. In cases where a patient has to be moved to an urban hospital either for detailed medical examination or for treatment, the extra expenses are met out of this medical insurance fund. Since the Cultural Revolution the production teams have been given more freedom with regard to the disposal of the welfare fund.

The management of the three levels of the commune is vested in the corresponding representative assemblies elected[40] by the members. The actual day-to-day management is the responsibility of a permanent body called a revolutionary committee at the commune and the brigade levels and 'a leading group' at the production team level. The committee and the group have a tripartite representation: the peasants, the cadres (i.e. the management personnel) and the army and/or peoples' militia. Some representatives on these committees and groups are members of the Communist Party but they are not always in the majority. Leading groups at each level are responsible for drawing up production plans based on the targets set by the state, the potential of each unit and local needs. A draft plan is circulated among the people for discussion and is revised in the light of suggestions for modification. It cannot be denied that the Party has the overwhelming power to push its decisions through, but whilst it prescribes the broad outline, in much the same way as an indicative plan, the details are left to be decided by the communes at their various levels. Apart from the fact that the commune has to meet a compulsory delivery quota, it has a fair degree of freedom to make its own decisions. Whether the peasants do, in effect, have any influence on decision-making will remain a debatable issue, but they are at least made to feel that they have such an influence.

A high degree of managerial inefficiency was experienced all over China during the early years of the communisation movement. Many of the difficulties arose from a lack of coordination and guidance which

resulted from the enormous geographical coverage of individual
communes, which were arbitrarily carved out, neglecting the natural
configuration of traditional marketing communities.[41] According to
Skinner:

> ... the many and grave difficulties encountered by the communes
> during 1958-61 stemmed in significant part from the grotesquely
> large mould into which they had in most cases been forced, and in
> particular from the failure to align the new unit with the natural
> socio-economic systems shaped by rural trade.

After the initial setbacks, the Chinese leadership realised its mistake
and the size of the communes was drastically reduced by splitting the
initial 24,000 communes into more than 70,000; at the same time,
attempts were made to align them with the traditional marketing
system.[42]

The leadership has been conscious of the other major limitation of a
collective enterprise, i.e. the lack of personal incentives. In addition to
work-points, private plots, privately owned pigs and poultry, and the
freedom to engage in side-line activities, rural free markets were
organised to provide further material incentives. In the early stages of
communisation, it was intended that a large part (almost half) of the
distributable income should be given out in the form of 'free supply',
such as free meals at the mess halls; in some cases free clothing and
other benefits were provided according to need and not work. When it
was realised that this diminished the incentive to work and encouraged
wasteful consumption, the Chinese leaders themselves acknowledged
that there was a 'universal lack of incentives in rural China'.[43] By 1961
'free supply' came to an end and the mess halls were closed down.
Private plots, private livestock and the rural markets, which were
abolished during the establishment of the communes, were revived.
Collective incentives are provided through reductions in taxation, or
by manipulating the prices of products or agricultural inputs. In recent
years taxation on agriculture has been reduced from around 12 per cent
to 6 per cent of total output. The actual amount of tax remains fixed
for a number of years, so the commune gains materially with every
increase in output. The prices at which grain quotas are bought by the
state are also fixed in advance. Any sales in excess of the quota receive
a higher price, usually 30 per cent more than the guaranteed price.
Relative prices are manipulated to bring about a reallocation of resources in the desired direction. Often the supply of scarce inputs such

as chemical fertiliser is linked with the fulfilment of the delivery quota. Differential interest rates are charged on loans, depending on the use to which they are put. Long-term loans for development purposes are charged at lower rates of interest than short-term loans for recurring expenses. On the whole it is reasonable to suggest that even though the Chinese leaders have not yet devised a satisfactory way of providing individual incentives, they have made good use of the manipulation of prices, taxation and subsidies to provide collective incentives. The use of such non-Communist weapons of economic management is clear evidence of the pragmatism of the Chinese leadership. It is quite wrong to say that: 'The Communist conception is wrong in ignoring incentive and indeed every economic aspect except that of getting the peasants under control.'[44]

The role of the communes in mobilising labour and the creation of employment opportunities, in the creation of infrastructure such as irrigation and transport networks, or in bringing industries to the rural areas is widely acknowledged.[45] Another aspect of this employment creation, which has not yet received serious attention, is the approach to the problem itself. Even a casual visit to the countryside in China will suggest that there is overmanning on farms, in rural transport and in the retail trade. This virtually amounts to relieving the problem of unemployment by creating more disguised unemployment. Traditional social institutions, such as the family, or tribal and communal villages have always done this whenever the need has arisen. This lesson from China should be taken seriously by other developing countries. The conventional wisdom that tolerates inequality of wealth and power on the grounds of increasing savings and investment loses its force in countries where the state is the major investor.

A collective rural organisation seen as an extension of traditional social organisation[46] and not necessarily as an instrument of class struggle, as a communist theorist might argue, may make it more palatable to liberal thinkers and governments in both developed and developing countries.[47] Some western social scientists are already acknowledging that 'group agriculture is a realistic possibility for rendering agriculture more meaningful in many under-developed countries'.[48]

Obviously, collective farming has some serious limitations and is not a panacea for all rural evils; nor can it be recommended for all countries alike. But if it is rejected, it must be on rational grounds and not merely on ideological preconceptions.

In conclusion it must be remembered that whatever form a land reform takes, if successfully implemented, it will inevitably undermine the economic and political power of the landed interests, and the rich and medium peasants. It is natural for them to resist a change which undermines their authority or threatens their very existence. The opposition to such a change will certainly be milder if the reforms do not radically alter the existing distribution of power and wealth. This is one of the main reasons why 'liberal' thinkers advocate slow or marginal changes. What they fail to admit, however, is that just tinkering with the problem commits millions to life-long starvation, misery and degradation. On the other hand, a radical land reform may involve considerable violence and the loss of numerous lives. Thus the brutal truth is that the choice between a slow and gradual change on the one hand and a swift and radical one on the other is not a choice between peaceful transition and violent change, as is widely believed. It is essentially a choice between the possible instantaneous death of many and the slow and painful end of many more. 'Morally it makes no difference whether a man is killed in war or is condemned to starve to death by the indifference of others.'[49] A society which is — rightly — appalled by the former should show an even greater distaste for the latter.

6 CREDIT, MARKETING AND PRICE POLICY

Any kind of land reform scheme, whether it aims to establish peasant proprietorships, cooperatives or collectives, must be supported by appropriate credit and marketing organisations and by policies which encourage the peasants to increase output and introduce innovations. The kind of supporting services provided are of considerable importance to very small producers and landless labourers. It is argued in this chapter that market-orientated policies for credit and marketing do not have much to offer the very poor. Even cooperatives and state-owned institutions such as marketing boards fail to safeguard the interests of these groups. Ultimately, their interests can only be protected through their direct involvement and participation in decision-making. The extent of this involvement will depend largely upon the levels of education and the degree of politicising of the masses of poorer peasants and landless labour.

Credit

As in any other business, an agricultural enterprise requires finance for investments: long-term finance for land improvements, housing, irrigation or agricultural machinery; medium-term for livestock, and short-term for seeds and fertilisers, and for wage payments. In the case of family farms, where most labour is provided by the family, short-term credit may also be needed for consumption. The practice of labelling borrowing for consumption purposes as 'unproductive' is justified only for conspicuous consumption. Any loans obtained for food consumption generally add to the productive efficiency of poor families. Money borrowed for medical treatment should also qualify as 'productive' expenditure.

It is widely accepted that a lack of sufficient credit at 'reasonable' rates of interest is one of the main bottlenecks in agricultural development. Credit cooperatives were established in several developing countries early this century but even now only a very small percentage of farmers receive institutional credit. In Africa no more than 5 per cent of farming families receive any institutional credit; in Asia and Latin America this proportion is about 15 to 20 per cent. Much of this institutional credit is 'cornered' by the richer and politically more influential sections of the farming population. Poor farming families, for lack of finance or a significant supply of saleable products, cannot take a direct share in the ownership and administration of credit and marketing cooperatives. The small farmer has to look for other sources of credit and he invariably ends up borrowing from village traders and moneylenders and is forced to pay high rates of interest; sometimes he has to mortgage his crop to the moneylender and/or trader.[1]

Besides, there are technical issues involved. If the granting of a loan is conditional on the borrower being able to provide a collateral as security a tenant or landless labourer will, almost by definition, not be eligible. Much the same would apply to a small owner-occupier once he mortgages his piece of land. Moreover, some of the purposes for which the poor require credit (such as expenses for illness and funerals) are fairly urgent. A system which involves considerable red tape and scrutiny leading to delays will not be able to meet these needs. It is in this respect that the village moneylender scores over any credit institution. He is usually resident in the village and is aware of the financial conditions of his clients; he usually operates on his own and does not need to get the approval of any higher authority outside the village.

One of the most crucial issues relates to the financial viability of credit institutions. Since the object is to bring about the self-sustaining growth of such institutions they must operate at a profit and not be dependent upon regular government subsidies. Interest rates charged on rural credit must cover administrative and supervisory costs, losses resulting from defaults and delinquencies and the opportunity cost of (foregone earnings on) capital. It has been estimated[2] that the administrative and supervisory costs of existing agricultural credit programmes are around 20 per cent, the cost of defaults around 30 per cent and the opportunity cost of funds nearly 10 per cent. Thus the total cost averages around 60 per cent. These costs relate to average farmers, so the cost of special programmes for poor farmers will probably be even greater. Supervising a large number of small loans costs more than a small number of large ones because subsistence farmers are more likely to default; a subsistence farmer borrows largely for consumption purposes and does not generate a significant marketable surplus, so he may have greater difficulties in paying off his debts. However, contrary to what might be expected, the incidence of default is greater among rich farmers than among poor farmers. Among rich farmers there is a high incidence of deliberate 'delinquency' as a direct consequence of the misuse of political influence.

A rate of interest which covered the various costs indicated above would probably be nearly as high as those charged by private moneylenders. Therefore, if the aim is to provide cheap institutional credit to small and marginal farmers, interest rates will have to be heavily subsidised. There may, in fact, be a case for charging differential rates; rich farmers could be charged a rate of interest which reflects the realities of the market and is consistent with the rates of interest charged by commercial banks and other credit institutions whilst subsidised low rates could be charged on small loans to poorer farmers. The principle of a two-part tariff is a well-established practice in charging for public utilities. Since the supply of credit is a service the principle of marginal cost pricing should also be applicable to institutional credit. Once a credit institution has been established for supplying credit to rich and middle farmers, its fixed costs are already met; the marginal cost of providing services to poorer farmers will only be a little higher than the opportunity cost of capital. Since low rates of interest will only be applicable to small loans there will not be much risk of the misuse of the system through inter-group transfers. Credit institutions using a two-part tariff can be run as profit-making (though not profit maximising) enterprises; if they charge a reasonably high rate of interest on loans to their richer borrowers they should be able to afford to pay commercially competitive rates of interest to their depositors and thereby attract capital. This is assuming, of course, that delinquency rates on large loans are kept low. If losses are incurred on loans to poor farmers they could be underwritten by the state. However, an unconditional guarantee by the state to this effect would be an open invitation to inefficiency.

The success of a credit institution which aims at helping the poor will depend upon a new breed of administrators who can rise above red tape, graft and corruption, whilst having a great deal of patience. The granting and supervising of large numbers of small loans and dealing with largely illiterate masses of poor peasants may often be frustrating. A business-school trained 'elitist' manager may prefer to deal with a limited number of large customers where transactions can be more easily conducted and where the profitability of the enterprise is more assured.

It is interesting to note that these problems have emerged even in the Communist countries where profitability may not be the main criteria of credit institutions. For example, during the Cultural Revolution in China the credit cooperatives were criticised for being 'too business-minded' and 'divorced from the poor and lower middle peasants'. It was suggested that they paid too much attention to the financial background of commune members asking for loans. It was alleged that their staff had little contact with the conditions of the poor and lower-middle peasants; these peasants had to walk long distances to make deposits, draw money and seek loans — yet they sometimes failed to obtain the assistance of the credit personnel. Subsequently, on the basis of Mao's directives, credit stations were set up in the production brigades, and poor and lower-middle peasants' management committees were set up at the team level to cater to the needs of these peasants.

In recent years, even in non-Communist countries, increasing thought has been given to group responsibility in the administration of credit. As much as a fifth of the World Bank's resources in the field of agricultural credit are channelled through cooperatives. Other social groups, such as village societies in Turkey and tribal groups in Mexico have also been used. It is increasingly being felt that group responsibility for credit provided to individual members of a group might facilitate improved loan recovery. It has rightly been argued that:

> . . . joint production systems, in which even very small farmers may acquire an interest, offer an excellent base for group credit. This type of model, however, requires a shift from individual to joint property or, at least, management rights in rural enterprises. Credit could be used for such group facilities as machinery pools, irrigation installations or collectively operated livestock enterprises. The resulting larger operations (in which individual members hold shared interests) have a better chance of economic survival than their component units.[3]

A credit programme must be linked with a programme of debt redemption. New devices to grant prompt loans with some flexibility concerning security and the purpose of the loans have to be devised. The integration (or at least coordination) of credit and marketing agencies may facilitate improved loan recovery. A contractual document between the marketing agency and the peasant may be accepted as collateral by the credit agency. However, any attempt to eliminate the moneylender will fail unless credit institutions have substantial resources and the procedures for obtaining loans are made easier and more prompt. In this respect it may be desirable to concentrate limited resources on small areas rather than spread them thinly over large areas. If the agencies for institutional credit can provide *effective* competition with the moneylender, it will have a sobering effect on him. The need for eliminating the moneylender altogether will no longer arise.

Marketing

There is a similar need for caution in formulating policy prescriptions for agricultural marketing. While it is true that middlemen and traders have often 'cheated' small peasants with regard to the proceeds from the sale of agricultural commodities, it is also a fact that these middlemen and traders have often provided virtually the only link between the small producers and the distant markets. In the absence of reasonable transport and storage facilities traders do undertake definite risks in collecting, storing and distributing agricultural produce. What is a 'fair' price for these services is not easy to assess. It is also not proven that the elimination of middlemen and the creation of cooperatives and marketing boards will necessarily improve the lot of the small producers. If the administrative and political machinery is inefficient and corrupt, extending the domain of public enterprise may simply be a recipe for increasing the misery of both producers and consumers. Marketing experts have always recognised that:

> . . . however well adapted to local conditions and requirements, a marketing board scheme may still prove completely ineffective when, for instance, the required reliable higher caliber staff or financial reserves are lacking, or when the board is hampered in the elaboration and implementation of its price and marketing policy by political and/or sectional pressures.[4]

As well as improving the efficiency of domestic food distribution, marketing boards can be used to stabilise producer prices, particularly for export crops, and also as a source of government revenue. In many African countries where the system of taxation is still not fully developed, and where export crops are the main source of public revenue, marketing boards are major revenue-earners for the state. Their monopoly profits are a useful means of financing economic development. The ultimate impact of their pricing policies on economic development depends upon how they affect the levels of savings and investments, their ability to control the output of export crops, and how the money so procured is used. If the funds raised by marketing boards are merely used to build monuments to the memories of the rulers, or for military expenditure, then the sacrifices of the peasants are futile. On the other hand, if the surpluses are used for agricultural development, the dissemination of technical knowledge, the creation of infrastructure, or for improving the supply of farm inputs such as irrigation, fertilisers and pesticides, then the contribution of marketing boards to state revenue may provide further incentives for increasing the production of export crops.

It must be remembered that fixing the prices to be paid to producers does not guarantee that small producers will not continue to be exploited by local buyers, subagents and quality inspectors from the marketing boards.[5] Some of the present malpractices can be substantially reduced by employing cooperative societies as agents for the marketing boards to handle the local purchase and collection of crops. Marketing experts often recommend the creation of parallel channels of marketing; if private traders are operating in competition with cooperatives then this competition alone will probably ensure that small producers actually receive the fixed prices. To minimise the likelihood of unfair practices they also recommend the compulsory public display of the minimum prices for each grade of each commodity.[6]

These measures would certainly improve the bargaining position of small producers but whether they can safeguard their interests *vis-à-vis* the traders on the one hand and the cooperatives and marketing boards on the other will depend on whether the producers have easy access to institutional credit. If the cooperatives or other credit agencies do not have sufficient funds to assist the small producers, then they will continue to be dependent upon village traders and moneylenders.

The risk of bureaucratic and unfair practices by the staff of cooperatives and state-owned enterprises cannot often be reduced by creating 'watchdog' bodies such as anti-corruption departments. Such departments themselves tend to degenerate in due course. In such a situation the rights of the small producers can best be safeguarded by creating organisations in which they have a reasonable degree of participation. It is mainly through mass involvement, active participation in and criticism of the running of these enterprises that some of the evils of corruption, nepotism, etc., can gradually be eliminated. The involvement of the small producers in credit and marketing organisations requires a long process of education and politicising of the people. In the last analysis, credit, marketing and technical improvements in agriculture, and land tenure reforms cannot be viewed simply as isolated issues concerning economic efficiency and technological choice; they must form part of the process of creating new attitudes towards socio-economic development in rural areas. The answer to various agricultural problems lies ultimately in some kind of integrated rural development based on relatively self-reliant, self-governing rural democracies.

Price incentives

The commonly observed market phenomenon that the output and supply of grains (or any other product) are positively correlated with price support underlies the conventional wisdom among economists that high prices motivate producers to invest in agricultural improvements and that the state must therefore ensure that:

> . . . farm prices are remunerative to efficient producers in relation to the prices of the inputs required for increased production and to their living expenses at the levels they are used to with hope of some improvements.[7]

This has become an article of faith not only for economists and the policymakers associated with farmers' lobbies but also for those who believe in social justice. In the developed countries farm incomes have usually lagged behind non-farm incomes, so that price (or income) subsidies work in the direction of greater equity in income distribution between the rural and urban areas. The situation is quite different in most developing countries since inequality is largely due to the concentration of land, wealth and income in the hands of landlords and rich peasants. The really poor are, as seen earlier, the small, largely subsistence farmers and the landless labourers whose output is not usually marketed. Even the somewhat richer farmers are dependent on the traders and moneylenders to such an extent that any price incentive rarely reaches them. It is necessary, therefore, particularly for those who believe in greater equity and social justice, to reconsider the argument for high grain prices. Academic support for high prices comes from a large number of econometric exercises published in the last twenty years. Many of these exercises were single-equation models limited to one or two crops, one of them often being an export crop. Sometimes the determining variable used was the relative price rather than the price of the crop itself. It is doubtful whether so-called empirical testing, on the basis of single-equation models, is really worthwhile. If the intention was to prove that peasants react positively to changes in relative prices, or the opening up of markets, then there is a wealth of historical evidence from all parts of the world to substantiate this. After all, as a result of the contact with Europeans, and the introduction of new means of transport and communication, peasants all over the world started producing cash crops such as cotton, jute, indigo, sugar cane, tea and coffee. Many of these crops were developed by the peasants on their own farms and not just by planters.

More recently, the opening up of the countryside in most developing countries has resulted in the increased commercialisation of agriculture.

However, the effect of high prices on food grain production and investment in agriculture as well as on the economy as a whole is far too complex to be satisfactorily explained by a single-equation model. The FAO Study referred to above was partly aware of this problem and stressed that:

> Most of the published data, however, relate to the behaviour of a single crop, and there is always the possibility that the increase in production may have occurred at the expense of another crop for which price relations were less favourable. It would be valuable to evaluate the effect of price supports over a wide range of crops on aggregate farm output in a developing country, although such a study would be difficult to carry out.[8]

However, the FAO Study did not adequately underline the fact that the effects of high food prices may reach far beyond the agricultural sector. Through their impact on the cost of living and wage levels they may, in fact, slow down the pace of industrialisation and the creation of infrastructure such as roads and irrigation facilities, and thereby not only slow down the overall rate of economic development of the economy but also adversely affect the prospects of agriculture itself. It does not require much ingenuity to prove that in many developing countries high food prices might be socially unjust not only to the urban population, but also to the rural poor and the landless who have to live wholly or partly on purchased food. If, however, the increase in profit from high grain prices is spent on manufactures, then the increasing demand for industrial products will increase their profitability and will lead to the situation visualised by Adam Smith where the town and country will support each other's development. If, on the other hand, the increasing profits of the landed interests are devoted to conspicuous consumption, land speculation or hoarding and speculation in grains, the increasing prices will not have favourable effects on capital formation, industrialisation or overall economic development. Increasing agricultural prices and profitability do not inevitably lead to increased investment in agriculture, nor do they automatically increase the marketed surplus. Furthermore, increased savings and investment by the rich landowners may be more than compensated by a decline in profits, and therefore savings and investment in the non-agricultural sector; such a redistribution may not always be desirable, even for social equity.

Historical evidence is not conclusive on this point even within a given country. As Habakkuk points out:

> The low or stationary agricultural prices of the earlier decades of the [eighteenth] century had a depressing effect on agricultural investment and indirectly on the demand for industrial goods. The rising prices over most of the second half of the century stimulated agricultural investment and led to increased demand for industrial goods; they led not so much to a shift of income between the industrial and the agricultural sectors as to an increase in the income of both.[9]

As against this, it was during the Great Depression in agriculture, resulting from the increasing imports of American grain, that British agriculture underwent its major restructuring and implemented some major innovations. It is in years of falling prices that farmers are forced to take recourse to cost-saving devices. It was in the last quarter of the nineteenth century that the reaper and the binder came into general use in Great Britain. Improvements were made in the methods of seeding and threshing wheat, and chemical fertilisers came to be more commonly used.[10]

The adverse effects of high food prices on a country's economy was a much discussed issue during the Corn Law controversy in Britain in the first half of the nineteenth century. It was clearly argued by the advocates of free trade that the:

> . . . high food prices, fostered by the Corn Laws, not only injured the working classes but also had adverse effects on trade and industry. Dear food reduced the purchasing power of the population for manufactured goods, while our failure to buy the food exports of our foreign customers prevented them from buying as much of our manufactures as they might.[11]

Ricardo unequivocally stressed that: 'If landlords could be sure of the prices of corn remaining steadily high, which happily they cannot be, they would have an interest opposed to every other class in the community.'[12] The repeal of the Corn Laws did not prove disastrous to British agriculture. Wheat prices fell but the prices of barley and oats, meat and dairy products rose substantially.[13] There is a general consensus among British historians that: 'Once it had recovered from the short-lived depression immediately after the Repeal, agriculture was generally and increasingly prosperous.'[14] As Chambers and Mingay stress, it was only wheat and wool which were seriously prejudiced; arable farmers benefited from the rising prices of barley, oats, hay and straw since they were already switching over to producing feed for stall-fed cattle. The landed interests were not very seriously affected in any economic sense.[15]

The post-Corn Law phase of British history is very instructive to those policymakers in developing countries who feel that lower grain prices will always be disastrous to agriculture. Among those who advocate high grain prices there is a tendency to regard grain production as synonymous with agriculture and to treat agricultural interests as if they constituted a homogeneous group. A decline in the price of a particular grain (say wheat) changes the relative price of wheat *vis-à-vis* other grains and other agricultural products. Since the price response of farmers is normally positive there would be an increase in the output of these other products, while the output and supply of wheat would probably decline. So far as the peasants are concerned there will be little effect on the income and level of living of the subsistence farmer, even if wheat is his only crop, although he may have to sell a little more wheat than before in order to meet his rent and interest payments and to purchase those essential consumer goods which he cannot produce himself. If he has the possibility of changing over to some other crop he will probably do so. The effect on landless labour is difficult to analyse. A decline in the income of wheat farmers as a result of a fall in price may lead to reduced employment on wheat-farms; this may or may not be compensated for by increases in employment on other farms. For example, the fall in wheat prices may induce a decline in the price of coarse grains. This may result in an expansion of the livestock sector since this sector is generally more labour intensive than arable farming; a decline in grain prices may lead to an increase in total agricultural employment. Landless workers are likely to gain in real terms with falling grain prices, because they have to buy at least a part of their food requirements on the market.

On the other hand, large and medium wheat farmers will probably lose (at least in the short run) as a result of low wheat prices. They may, however, be forced to introduce cost saving devices. High prices tend to keep inefficient firms in business so that if the aim of agricultural policy is to increase production through technological change, it is always preferable to subsidise modern inputs such as chemical fertilisers, pesticides, etc. Even when subsidising agricultural inputs there is a need for careful selection of the items to be supported. In densely populated countries a subsidy on tractors may sometimes lead to the displacement of labour.

If employment and equity are among the main objectives of agricultural policy, high prices for grains may often be undesirable on both counts; they tend to hurt the poor both in the rural and urban areas and, as suggested earlier, by changing the net barter terms of trade against industry they may slow down industrial development. High grain prices in many developing countries simply enhance the economic power of the richer peasants, traders and grain speculators. With their increased resources the latter group are able to extend their activities. This adds to inflationary pressures and consequently to the hardship and misery of the poor. If governments were able to siphon off inflationary profits from the rich farmers, traders and speculators and use these funds for capital formation, the sacrifices of the poor would not be in vain. In the absence of any meaningful taxation of the rural rich, guaranteeing high prices for grains is morally indefensible and economically wasteful. Much of the inflationary profits of the rich farmers and traders go into property speculation, luxury housing construction and conspicuous consumption. These activities divert scarce resources into non-productive uses (e.g. steel and cement in luxury housing rather than in dams and reservoirs). It is surprising, therefore, to find present day 'liberal' economists and the international agencies which are 'committed' to a more equitable sharing of benefits between the rich and the poor continuing to advocate high prices for grain. For example, a recent World Bank policy document suggests that:

> ... such [input] subsidies lead to undesirable distortions in the economy, are costly to implement, and are available only to those in contact with and enjoying the confidence of the organisations through which they are provided. *The small farmer, typically, is excluded from the advantages. In general, therefore, it is more beneficial and less costly to provide* incentives by guaranteeing minimum prices.[16]

If, as is often the case, the small farmer does not have a large surplus to sell, how is he going to benefit to any significant degree from guaranteed minimum prices? Besides, if he is vulnerable to exploitation by rich farmers and traders how would he actually receive the guaranteed prices?

Admittedly, the provision of credit and marketing facilities and price
incentives are indispensible elements in any agricultural development
policy in any form of rural organisation. What is questionable is
whether, given the economic and political power relationships in most
developing countries, these measures in themselves are adequate to
ameliorate the conditions of the very poor. There is growing evidence
that the richer sections of the community are able, through their
political control of credit and marketing institutions and the administrative machinery, to reserve for themselves the lion's share of the
facilities. It is increasingly being felt that: 'for many really marginal
farmers, the ability to use credit facilities for investment is limited by
fragmentation and other institutional and technological problems.'[17]
The tragedy of schemes designed to help small and marginal farmers[18]
is essentially that credit and marketing institutions are grafted on to an
agrarian socio-political base which is inherently biased against the poor.
Unless this imbalance of economic and political power is redressed,
leading to the effective participation of the poor, none of these ameliorative measures will reduce the misery of the poor to any meaningful
extent. Those who abhor violent social change must urgently devise
ways and means of sharing equitably not only resources and opportunities, however limited they may be, but also the political power
which determines social priorities.

7 NEED FOR NEW IDEOLOGY

By now it is clear that none of the measures being seriously discussed
by market-orientated 'liberal' social scientists, or implemented by
planners in non-communist countries (with or without the support of
the international organisations) are anything more than mere palliatives,
barely doing more than touching the fringe of the problem of the poor.
If the main answer to the problem of the poor lies in an equitable
sharing of limited opportunities and resources then purely 'materialistic' ideologies have little relevance for the poorer countries, at least
for the foreseeable future, and there is a need for having a closer look
at alternative ideologies.[1] The main ideologies discussed here are:
(a) 'modified' materialism (the Club of Rome type ideology); (b) the
Gandhian view of the poor man's *swaraj*[2]; and (c) Mao's mass-line.[3]

Modified materialism (the Club of Rome ideology)

Essentially the Club of Rome thesis is a sophisticated extension of
the Malthusian view of population pressure on the world resources.
It suggests that: 'If the present growth trends in world population,
industrialization, pollution, food production, and resource depletion
continue unchanged, the limits to growth on this planet will be reached
sometime within the next one hundred years. The most probable result
will be a rather sudden and uncontrollable decline in both population
and industrial capacity.'[4]

Such a catastrophic situation can be averted only by establishing
'a global equilibrium' in which 'the basic material needs of each person
on earth are satisfied and each person has an equal opportunity to
realise his individual human potential'.[5] In such an 'equilibrium state'
advances in material production or technology would simply
increase leisure time which could be devoted to education, art, music,
religion, basic scientific research, athletics, and social interaction.[6]

The broad policy recommendations of the Club lay great emphasis
on population control, but, unlike Malthus,[7] the Club recommends a
more equitable distribution of resources between people and nations.
It recognises that the 'world equilibrium can become a reality only
if the lot of the so-called developing countries is substantially improved, both in absolute terms and relative to the economically developed nations',[8] and calls for a 'joint venture based on joint conviction,

78

with benefits for all'.[9] This would involve the richer countries in encouraging 'a deceleration in the growth of their own material output while, at the same time, assisting the developing nations in their efforts to advance their economies more rapidly'.[10]

So far the Club has not said anything about the actual implementation of a strategy for reaching the 'equilibrium' state except that: 'Entirely new approaches are required to redirect society toward goals of equilibrium rather than growth. Such a reorganisation will involve a supreme effort of understanding, imagination, and political and moral resolve.'[11] The dangers of 'population explosion', serious inequities in the distribution of wealth and political power and the growing problems of ecological imbalance are well known. A mathematical model can, at best, dramatise the problems but certainly cannot 'mobilise forces' to bring about a 'radical reform of institutions and political processes at all levels, including the highest, that of world polity'.[12] Social and political realities are such that just wishing them away is not much help; the Club has to look more into social and political phenomena, which it has completely ignored and come out with a plan of action. The second Report[13] of the Club is an improvement over the first Report in so far as it emphasises the role of individual values and attitudes and the role of education in changing such attitudes. It emphasises the need for developing a world consciousness which makes every individual realise his role as a member of the world community; a new ethic in the use of material resources compatible with the 'oncoming age of scarcity'; the development of an attitude of harmony rather than conquest towards nature; and identification with future generations.[14] Much of the programme of action recommended by the second Report is relevant as a 'Code of Conduct' mainly for the richer countries. Its relevance for the developing countries is mainly as a warning against the risks of uninhibited pursuit of 'growth' and urbanisation in terms of ecological imbalance. While the Report rightly underlines the horrors of unrestricted urbanisation it does not provide any 'alternative' strategy by which the poorer countries can effectively solve the problems of poverty and unemployment in rural areas which lie at the root of large-scale migration to urban areas.

Even with regard to the development of a 'world consciousness' which may ultimately lead to a more equitable distribution of world resources between the richer and the poorer countries, the Report is rather ambivalent. In fact, there is an inherent contradiction in the second Report between the desire for the emergence of 'world consciousness' and the conclusion that:

'The most preferable solutions' always involve 'harmony' or 'compromise' among 'balanced' participants. But there is no balance between participants like the United States or the Soviet Union on the one hand and Dahomey or Singapore on the other. In order to achieve *balance between regions in global development a more coherent regional outlook must be developed in various parts of the world* so that the 'preferable solutions' will be arrived at of necessity rather than good will . . .[15]

Thus, what the second Report is recommending is the creation of economic and political power blocs [16] – to act as counterveiling forces against each other. The cooperation between nations or blocs does not come about as a result of a change in attitudes in favour of the international ownership and control of world resources and their equitable distribution, but out of a fear of retaliation by other equally powerful nations. In the Club of Rome's vision of the world there is no room for smaller nations; nor is there any scope for a world government.[17]

If economic and political power continue to be the main determinants of the bargaining strength of the regional blocs it is difficult to visualise an end to the arms race and the reckless exploitation of natural resources. Under present conditions, it is not easy to visualise a harmonious relationship between man and nature. For example, there is considerable emphasis in the Japanese culture and tradition on man's harmony with nature. Yet this did not stop Japan, in search of economic power, from pursuing a policy of indiscriminate industrialisation which created some of the worst problems of environmental pollution anywhere in the world. With the growing awareness of these problems in Japan, there has been an increasing effort to improve the domestic environment while, at the same time, the industries and processes which created the worst pollution problems are being transferred to developing countries.

Gandhi's poor man's *swaraj*

Two of the most comprehensive politico-economic programmes for providing social justice are Mao's mass-line and the Gandhian concept of 'sarvodaya'. Although in basic philosophy and strategy the two approaches are fundamentally opposed to each other – one believing in class conflict and advocating violent revolution, the other strongly believing in non-violence and 'sarvodaya' – welfare of all – yet they share a fundamental concern for the poor and their economic and political programmes of social justice are quite similar. Gandhi resented a situation of gross economic inequality in which 'a few roll in riches and the masses do not get even enough to eat'.[18] He clearly saw the link between unemployment and hunger. As early as 1921 he stressed that: 'To a people famishing and idle, the only acceptable form in which God can dare appear is work and promise of food as wages.'[19] To him unemployment was degrading:

> What a calamity it must be to have 300 millions unemployed, several millions becoming degraded every day for want of employment, devoid of self-respect, devoid of faith in God. I may as well place before the dog over there the message of God as before those hungry millions who have no lustre in their eyes and whose only God is their bread. I can take before them a message of God only by taking the message of sacred work before them. It is good enough to talk of God whilst we are sitting here after a nice breakfast, and looking forward to a nicer luncheon, but how am I to talk of God to the millions who have to go without two meals a day?[20]

In Gandhi's scheme of things no one should suffer from want. Everybody should get sufficient work to enable him to procure the basic necessities of life. This ideal could be realised:

> . . . only if the means of production of the elementary necessaries of life remain in the control of the masses. These should be freely available to all as God's air and water are or ought to be; they should not be made a vehicle of traffic for the exploitation of others. Their monopolization by any country, nation or group of persons would be unjust. The neglect of this simple principle is the cause of the destitution that we witness today not only in this unhappy land but in other parts of the world too.[21]

According to Gandhi, civilisation, in the real sense of the term, consisted not in the multiplication but in the deliberate and voluntary reduction of wants.[22] This ideal could be translated into action not by state power or force but by non-violence and necessary changes in personal life so as to reduce one's wants to a minimum. To him the possession of private property beyond this minimum[23] was immoral:

> This denial of the very concept of private property stemmed from his belief that all riches, not only material but also physical and intellectual, belonged to God, and could be held by the

individual, only as a trust.[24]

Therefore those who have superior intellect or superfluous wealth will not use it merely for self-advancement at the expense of others, but 'for the service of those who are less favoured in that respect than they'.[25] This idea of trusteeship has often been misunderstood not only in the West but also in India. Nehru was one of its critics. Myrdal calls it 'a concept that fits into a paternalistic, feudal, pre-democratic society. It is so flexible that it can serve as a justification for inequality.'[26] Such criticisms represent a misinterpretation of the Gandhian view. Gandhi did not leave the matter entirely in the hands of the charitable instincts of the rich. Indeed he was very emphatic in suggesting remedies.

> If, however, in spite of the utmost effort, the rich do not become guardians of the poor in the true sense of the term and the latter are more and more crushed and die of hunger, what is to be done? In trying to find out the solution of this riddle I have lighted on non-violent, non-cooperation and civil disobedience as the right and infallible means. The rich cannot accumulate wealth without the co-operation of the poor in society. If this knowledge were to penetrate to and spread amongst the poor, they would become strong and would learn how to free themselves by means of non-violence from the crushing inequalities which have brought them to the verge of starvation.[27]

According to Gandhi the exploitation of the poor can be ended not by the sheer physical destruction of a few rich people, 'but by removing the ignorance of the poor and teaching them to be non-cooperative with their exploiters'.[28] He had strong reservations about machinery and large-scale production because of their undesirable effects on employment and social justice. He explains:

> What I object to, is the 'craze' for machinery, not machinery as such. The craze is for what they call labour-saving machinery. Men go on 'saving labour' till thousands are without work and thrown on the open streets to die of starvation . . . Today machinery merely helps a few to ride on the back of millions. The impetus behind it all is not the philanthropy to save labour, but greed. It is against this constitution of things that I am fighting with all my might.[29]

Thus his oppositon to machinery was due to the fact that it concentrated production and distribution in the hands of a few. He hated privilege and monopoly, and anything that could not be shared with the masses was taboo to him. He accepted the need for factories for the production of key capital goods, but these factories should be nationalised or state controlled and should be operated 'not for profit, but for the benefit of humanity, love taking the place of greed as the motive'.[30]

He was convinced that India's salvation lay in the villages. Relatively self-reliant and self-governing (but not completely closed) mini-economies were, to him, the key to the poor man's *swaraj*:

> . . . every village's first concern will be to grow its own food crops and cotton for its cloth. It should have a reserve for its cattle, recreation and playgrounds for adults and children. Then if there is more land available it will grow *useful* money crops, thus excluding *ganja*,[31] tobacco, opium and the like. The village will maintain a village theatre, school and public hall. It will have its own waterworks ensuring clean supply. This can be done through controlled wells and tanks. Education will be compulsory up to the final basic course. As far as possible every activity will be conducted on the cooperative basis. There will be no castes such as we have today, with their graded untouchability. Non-violence with its technique of *Satyagraha* and non-cooperation will be the sanction of the village community. There will be a compulsory service of village guards who will be selected by rotation from the register maintained by the village. The government of the village will be conducted by the *Panchayat* of five persons, annually elected by the adult villagers, male and female, possessing minimum prescribed qualifications. These will have all the authority and jurisdiction required. Since there will be no system of punishments in the accepted sense, this *Panchayat* will be the legislature, judiciary and executive combined to operate for its years of office.[32]

There was a need for the leadership to identify themselves with the villagers:

> We must identify ourselves with the villagers who toil under the hot sun beating on their bent backs and see how we would like to drink water from the pool in which the villagers bathe, wash their clothes and pots, in which their cattle drink and roll. Then and not till then shall we truly represent the masses and they will, as surely as I am writing this, respond to every call.[33]

Gandhi, like Mao, wanted to eliminate the growing gulf between the rich and the poor, the intellectuals and the workers, the rulers and the ruled, and the town and the village. He asked the youths to settle down in villages, where they would find unlimited scope for service, research and true knowledge. He considered manual labour[34] a blessing. If everyone engaged in manual labour, sufficient to provide for his own food, then invidious distinctions of rank would be obliterated.

Gandhi's reliance on the power of the masses was complete. To him democracy was 'the art and science of mobilizing the entire physical, economic and spiritual resources of all the various sections of the people in the service of the common good of all'.[35] True democracy could not be worked through a handful of men sitting in capitals, it had to be worked from below by the people of every village. There was a need for educating the masses: 'We must train these masses of men who have a heart of gold, who feel for the country, who want to be taught and led.'[36] Since such a programme of training would be dependent upon the ability and sincerity of political workers, the role of 'cadres' was central to the achievement of his programme. He was keenly aware of the interrelationship between social and moral progress and political work. He stressed that no part of life in a democracy can be seen in abstraction from politics.[37] He did, however, underestimate the likelihood of cadres being 'corrupted' by their own success. In actual fact, many of his own followers failed to keep the high Gandhian moral standards once they got accustomed to high offices.

Mao's mass-line

It was Mao's concern for the poor peasants[38] and his faith in their power that led him to base his revolutionary strategy on the peasantry. Contrary to orthodox Marxism he kept the poor peasantry in the vanguard of the revolution.

As with Gandhi, the subordination of self-interest to the greater good of society is an important facet of Mao's strategy:

> At no time and in no circumstances should a Communist place his personal interests first; he should subordinate them to the interests of the nation and of the masses of the people. Hence selfishness, slacking, corruption, striving for the limelight, etc. are most contemptible, while selflessness, working with all one's energy, wholehearted devotion to public duty, and quiet hard work are the qualities that command respect.[39]

However, since Mao believed in class conflict he had no hesitation in recommending the confiscation of land from the landlords and its distribution among the poor and lower middle peasants. This programme was implemented soon after the liberation in 1949. Subsequently, under Mao's leadership, land was cooperativised and ultimately collectivised by 1958. Thus private property in land in China came to an end. As seen earlier, Gandhi did not believe in private property in land in excess of what was needed for minimum subsistence. However, he did not believe in violence as a means of eliminating private property in land. In his scheme, this would have come about through landlords voluntarily relinquishing their titles to land. Later this programme found expression in Vinoba Bhave's *Bhoodan Movement*.[40] The overall experience of this movement cast doubt on the possibilities of radical changes in landowning relationships by voluntary means.

Unlike Gandhi, Mao supported heavy industrialisation but, at the same time, he was conscious of the difficulties created by a lack of balance between heavy industries, consumer goods industries and agriculture. As seen earlier, agricultural activities in China are organised by various organs of the commune. Each level of the commune is organised as a self-governing, self-reliant village or group of villages. Although the system of payment continues to be related to the quality and the amount of work done, which often results in income disparities, the basic minimum of food, clothing, shelter, education and medical facilities is provided to everybody. Thus the various levels of the commune come very close to the Gandhian dream of the 'poor man's *swaraj*'. Both Gandhi and Mao stress the need for the decentralisation of economic and political activity.

Like Gandhi, Mao detests privilege and the growing gulf between the intellectuals and manual workers, the town and the countryside, the rulers and the ruled. Mao stresses the need for the intellectuals, the white collar workers and the students to go and work with the masses on their farms and in factories. Since the Cultural Revolution manual work has become obligatory for white collar workers and millions of students have been sent to the villages. Mao questions Stalin's contention that the abolition of private property in the means of production automatically creates a classless society.[41] According to Mao, the party which leads the revolution creates its own vested interests. Political power and the privileges attached to it creates a new elite and the gulf between this elite and the masses progressively widens. Thus even after the physical disappearance of classes, the state of mind, i.e. class attitudes (capitalist tendencies) persists. Therefore, there is a

need for continuous revolution. It is the 'rectification' of the individual
which is the key to Mao's thinking. This 'rectification' involves the
changing of a capitalistic into a proletarian attitude. Here Mao's thinking comes very close to that of Gandhi who argued that the destruction
of material possessions does not necessarily destroy possessiveness. It
is the latter, the attitude of mind, that has to change.[42]

In both Gandhi and Mao the 'rectification' is attained through the
vigilant masses. Mao encourages the masses to come out in revolt
against the establishment whereas Gandhi calls on them to stop co-
operating with the elite if the latter default in their duty. It is not
inconceivable that if Gandhi were alive today he, like Mao, would have
come out in rebellion against the establishment.

Mao probably would not go as far as Gandhi in supporting the
negation' of wants or the willingness to sacrifice material progress; in
fact Mao advocates the use of consumer goods as a means of providing
incentives. However, as Gray suggests, Mao follows Gandhi in believing
that 'no society which is unjust can be efficient, that only when society
operates and is seen to operate in the interests of the majority can the
energies and talents of that majority be harnessed to progress'.[43]

In both Gandhi and Mao, social justice can be brought about by
'rectification', or a change in the attitudes of the 'elite' and the 'education' of the masses to assert their rights. Therefore, politicising the masses
is one of the key elements in ensuring that they get their 'fair' share.
Such changes in attitudes can only come about slowly and that too by
a process of education. However, if social justice is one of the major
objectives of development policy, then the nature and purpose of
education will have to be fundamentally different to the 'formal'
education currently being provided in most developing countries.

Education 'the best leveller'

Much of the discussion about education in the development literature
is centred around the contribution education makes to economic
development in relation to its cost, i.e. its cost-effectiveness. Educa-
tionalists assert that: 'In the Third World education and economics
are closely interdependent, for it is necessary to ensure that there are
enough persons with all the skills needed for economic growth, and
also enough jobs to take advantage of their skills — a balancing act that
requires continuous adjustment.'[44] Given the poor resource base of
most developing countries, and the pyramid-like nature of the job
market, a case can be made out for some kind of general education at a
fairly low level for the vast mass of the population with a more

advanced level of education and training for a select group. For economic and political reasons the advantages of such a scheme would accrue mainly to the richer sections of the community. What Tawney said about British elementary education in the nineteenth century is equally true for primary (and to some extent secondary) education in most developing countries today:

> In origin a discipline, half-redemptive, half-repressive, for the lower orders, elementary education has been, throughout its history, not an educational, but a social, category. It had been designed for those for whom it was expedient to provide the rudiments of instruction, since, if wholly untaught, they were a danger to society, but inexpedient to provide more, since they were equally a danger, if taught too much.[45]

The poor frequently find it difficult to take advantage of even the very rudimentary type of education provided for them. As Bhagwati[46] points out, for the poor there is a high opportunity cost in sending children to school since they could otherwise work for the family and add to the family income, however small the increment may be. Since employment opportunities for the poor in rural teaching jobs requiring education (e.g. postmaster, school teacher) are rather limited the private rate of return of primary education is usually low while, for institutional reasons, the cost of capital to the poor against which this rate of return is to be compared is high. Similarly, if primary education assists in increasing the agricultural productivity of labour, little advantage will accrue to landless labour in the absence of the opportunity to translate training into action. Bhagwati suggests that some of these deficiencies could be overcome by suitable policy measures, such as broadening the employment opportunities for the lower income groups, asking the higher income groups to pay the full economic price for their children's education, while subsidising the poorer groups and increasing the number of jobs reserved for them.[47] In addition, legal prohibition on the 'back door' appointments of the sons of businessmen to lucrative jobs in public limited companies could be imposed. However, even if such policies were actually introduced, Bhagwati argues[48] that genuine equality of educational opportunities would still not be available to all classes for at least three reasons: since nutritional deficiencies in childhood can cause lasting damage to intellectual ability, children from poor families cannot compete on equal terms with children from richer families;

similarly, to the extent that family background and other 'environmental' factors affect the motivation to intellectual attainment, the poorer families will always be at a disadvantage; thirdly, if richer parents can 'buy' a better education for their children through expensive private schools then their children will usually have the edge over the children of poorer families in any competitive selection process.

Bhagwati concludes that the:

> ... problem of ensuring to the children of the lower-income groups genuine equality of access (in its fullest sense) to education must thus remain one at the solution to which the capitalist LDCs would thus appear to remain inept and inferior, in principle, to LDCs following the Chinese model. In all these regards, therefore, the success of genuine egalitarianism in China would seem to be impressive, and not merely in the matter of reducing *income* differentials (whether rural *v.* urban, region *v.* region, educated *v.* uneducated) to which Sinologists have drawn our attention.[49]

In general terms Bhagwati's conclusions are correct although it must be remembered that privileges in education, 'back-door' appointments of the children of the leading cadres, etc., were very common in China prior to the Cultural Revolution. The Cultural Revolution was essentially directed against the misuse of power and privileges by the elite.

Systems of higher education and the widening gulf between the 'elite' and the masses

It is widely acknowledged that the educational systems, particularly at the higher levels, of most developing countries continue to be run along predominantly European lines and tend to reflect the legal, and literary and cultural traditions of the former 'mother country', with an extreme exaltation for 'liberal' education and an utter disdain for manual work.[50] In recent years some developing countries have gone over to American business-school-type institutions. These institutions are a definite departure from the traditions of 'liberal' education and have insisted on a high level of technical competence. An obsession with technical excellence to the neglect of social and political norms generates a sense of intolerance of mediocrity. This insistence on 'quality' in western educational systems has resulted in what Balogh calls the 'closely restricted circles of culture'. Access to such an education is limited to the very privileged few in most developing countries. In fact, 'foreign qualifications' are the means through which the elite perpetuates its vested interests within a country. The richer countries, through various programmes of educational support, scholarships, fellowships, etc., have tried to maintain their cultural domination of the poorer countries. In this context Macaulay's dream of creating 'a class of persons, Indian in blood and colour, but English in taste, in opinions, in morals, and in intellect' continues to be all-pervading. In fact, it is through identifying themselves with their ex-colonial masters that the elite find the fulfilment of their own dreams; this can be seen in the way the emerging elites in developing countries copy the life style of the expatriate colonial officials. This identification with an 'alien' culture and mode of life is a reflection of the continuing inferiority complex of the elite in many developing countries. In their 'assumed' role the elite not only find it difficult to identify themselves with the masses, but deliberately create barriers of life style and of language between themselves and the masses.[51]

As has already been mentioned, in both the Gandhian and the Maoist strategies, any meaningful 'fair deal' for the poor presupposes the involvement and identification of the elite with the masses; any system of education and training that keeps the groups apart is self-defeating. An identification with the masses can only come about through the elite's self-confidence and respect for their own culture and people. Without cultural emancipation it is difficult to develop mutual understanding and respect among nations.

If growing out of an inferiority complex is to be one of the main objectives of education, then many developing countries must take a serious look at their educational systems, particularly at higher levels, as well as at their programmes for sending students abroad. Foreign educational institutions, by commission rather than omission, attempt to reinforce rather than reduce the inferiority complex. For instance, in most development schools the courses stress *ad nauseam* the *mistakes* the developing countries have committed in the past. There are few references to the mistakes committed by the present-day developed countries in their earlier stages of development.[52] Frequently (though not necessarily deliberately), when comparisons are made between developed and developing countries an 'ideal' description of life in the developed countries is compared with the commonplace situation in developing countries.[53] When a young student returns to his home country he is often convinced of the 'superiority' of the country in which he was trained.

There is certainly a need for foreign training in science and technology if the developing countries are to raise their levels of living.

Since they have to operate in an international community and fight for their 'fair share' in the world's income and resources they need to study the psychology and motivations of the people, particularly the ruling elite, in the richer countries. Above all, people from developing countries must study the past history of the developed countries so as to familiarise themselves with some of the pitfalls that have to be confronted in the process of development.[54] They must learn from their mistakes. One important lesson that can be learnt from the experience of the 'West' is that without 'confrontation' the underprivileged will rarely get their fair share of national wealth in a capitalist society. It is a strange irony that the USA, one of the great 'democracies', has failed to secure basic human dignity for a substantial number of its citizens.

It may, however, be in the interests of the poor countries not to send their students abroad until they are mature enough to discriminate between myths and realities. In fact, it may be preferable to arrange on-the-job training rather than academic work for people who need to be trained. This may give trainees from the developing countries an opportunity to match their wits and abilities with their counterparts in the richer countries. However, such an arrangement does not always work satisfactorily. For example, doctors from the developing countries working in the UK rarely get jobs in the institutions where they could receive adequate training. Most often they have to work in peripheral hospitals. Even in the field of joint research between institutions or scholars from the rich and poor countries, the scholars from the richer countries usually have the upper hand not necessarily, as Streeten suggests, because of the *fact of superiority*[55] but simply because they control the purse. As a generalisation it may be true that the average social scientist from a developed country is better equipped than his counterpart from a developing country, but in joint research arrangements, where the financing is under technical assistance, the donors do not always send the most appropriate or best qualified persons. In many instances the people sent are fresh from universities with little experience and certainly no familiarity with the problems of developing countries. The 'experts' sent to developing countries are usually placed in fairly high-level appointments, often higher than better-qualified indigenous personnel.

Certainly, personal contact, cooperation in research and on-the-job training can help trainees from developing countries to shake off their inferiority complex, but there is always the risk that in search of international 'respectability' they may take up research topics which are irrelevant, esoteric, and grossly abstract.[56] Or perhaps they may decide to migrate to a developed country. It is often argued that the 'brain drain' is detrimental to the interests of poorer countries. Strange though it may sound, the loss of these people may not, in the long run, be such a bad thing for a country. They are obviously more involved with personal attainment than with the welfare of the country, or are attracted by 'materialistic' considerations. Invariably, such people have always been part of the elite which is psychologically incapable of identifying with the masses. Even if they remain in the country their life style makes them alien to their own people. Their attitude to equality and social justice is often one of 'paternalistic', 'armchair' concern for the poor. Their presence or absence in a country does not make any significant difference.[57] A society which aims at 'changing the man' can do without such people. 'Excellence' with no social purpose is of no real value. While 'social purpose' can be 'defined and tailored' by the ruling elite to serve their own interests, probably the best safeguard against this is the increasing involvement and participation of well-informed masses in the political process. If, for reasons of scarcity of resources, a choice has to be made between pushing the 'average' levels of education for all a little higher, on the one hand, and 'excellence' for a few on the other, a developing country should opt, at least for a time, for mediocrity rather than excellence.

8 WORLD TRADE AND THE DEVELOPING COUNTRIES

It is undeniable that much of the effort to eradicate poverty and reduce inequities of wealth and opportunities in the developing countries have to come from indigenous sources. Scarcity, both of human and material resources, makes the process of development a slow and painful one. The resource constraint is further aggravated by the present structure and organisation of world trade and foreign investments in developing countries. This structure is largely the product of the colonial economic relationships of the past two centuries. This system has continued to operate to the advantage of the developed countries and has led to a significant transfer of resources from the poorer to the richer countries. The need for reorganisation of the world economic system towards a more equitable distribution of resources is being increasingly recognised, at least in principle, even by the richer countries. This is reflected in a recent speech by Harold Wilson, the British Prime Minister:

> I want to make it clear in what I propose today that my government fully accept that the relationship, the balance, between the rich and poor countries of the world is wrong and must be remedied ... that the wealth of the world must be redistributed in favour of the poverty stricken and the starving. This means a new deal in world economies, in trade between nations and the terms of that trade.[1]

In practice, however, the developing countries have failed so far to obtain any significant trade concessions even though exports are by far their most important source of foreign exchange.[2] Both processed agricultural products and manufactures from developing countries continue to face enormous tariff and non-tariff barriers in the developed countries. The recently negotiated Generalised System of Preferences (GSP) which provides for a non-reciprocal abolition or reduction of tariffs on imports from developing countries is 'studded with exceptions, limitations and safeguards'.[3]

This has meant that, in spite of the recent trends towards the diversification of exports, most developing countries remain heavily dependent for their foreign exchange earnings — badly needed for financing the increasing import requirements of capital goods, technical know-how, fertiliser, food and fuel — upon exports of agricultural products and minerals, which have been increasing much more slowly than world trade as a whole.

At the same time, the terms of trade for primary products have also, except for a very short period in 1972 and 1973, declined. This has meant that just to maintain the same level of export earnings the developing countries have had to export more and more. Besides, export earnings have experienced considerable short-term fluctuations which introduce a considerable degree of uncertainty into development planning. Some of the difficulties experienced by the developing countries are due to the nature of the commodities traded. Most primary commodities, particularly beverages and agricultural raw materials have a low income elasticity of demand and so their demand rises rather slowly in response to increases in incomes. But it is undeniable that many of the difficulties facing the developing countries are a direct outcome of the existing world trading system. In this section some of the problems of trade facing the developing countries will be discussed.

World trade in the 1960s

Total world trade increased by nearly 10 per cent per annum between 1961 and 1971. As against this, the total export earnings of the developing countries increased by roughly 7 per cent per annum; as a result, the share of the developing countries in world exports fell from around 30 per cent at the beginning of the 1950s to only 17.8 per cent in 1970. World trade in primary products grew at a much slower pace than total world trade or trade in manufactures. The annual rates of growth for the various product groups for the developing countries are given in Table 11.

The rate of growth of the agricultural exports of the developing countries was much slower than for the exports of minerals and manufactures. This meant that the share of agricultural exports (in value terms) in the total exports of the developing countries declined from 57 per cent in 1955 to only 32 per cent in 1971, while the share of fuels and manufactures showed a significant increase. The slow growth of exports of agricultural raw materials was mainly the result of increasing competition from synthetic fibres and research and development efforts in the developed countries aimed at reducing the raw material content of finished products. This took various forms, including the development of blends of materials and synthetics as well

Table 11. Foreign trade of developing countries by product groups

| | Annual rates of change (1958-60 to 1969-71) | Shares in the total | |
		1955	1971
		(per cent)	
Total exports (f.o.b.)	7.2	100*	100*
Agricultural products	3.0	57*	31.6
Non-fuel minerals	9.0	9.9	9.1
Fuels	9.0	25.2	38.4
Manufactures	15.0	7.7	18.3

Source: GATT (1974), *International Trade 1973/74*, Table 35, p. 104.
* Totals may not add up because of the inclusion of non-classified traded goods.

as efforts to reduce losses in transport, storage, and handling. In the case of tropical beverages, a low income elasticity of demand was probably the main reason for the slow growth in export earnings. To what extent malpractices in auctions, such as price-rigging by the major buyers in the developed countries have had an effect is still uncertain. The export of basic food grains and vegetable oils by the developing countries was adversely affected by increasing domestic demand, resulting from population growth, the rise in incomes and consequent changes in food consumption habits. In any case, much of the trade in grains and feed stuffs is largely in the hands of richer countries.

Competing agricultural exports from the developing countries face enormous tariff and non-tariff barriers in the developed countries. Tariff protection is very high on those imported agricultural products which compete with domestic production. Naturally, the temperate zone agricultural products face the highest tariffs, often supplemented by non-tariff measures such as import restrictions, variable levies, taxes, reference prices, etc.[4] For example, in the USA in 1968 the nominal rate of tariff protection on peanuts was only 69 per cent but the effective protection[5] worked out at 204 per cent. In the case of cotton, nominal protection was only 0.3 per cent while the effective protection was 101 per cent.[6] Similarly, in the EEC many of the nominal *ad valorem* equivalents of the variable levies affecting the agricultural imports of the Community exceeded 50 per cent in 1967, and in the case of butter approached as much as 300 per cent.[7] The tariff schedules of the developed countries are so constituted that raw materials not available in these countries are generally admitted duty free or at very low rates. The tariff rates tend to increase with the level of processing, with moderate tariffs on semi-manufactures and higher tariffs for finished products.

As a result of the various impediments to their growth, the agricultural exports of the developing countries in the sixties grew at only half the rate of growth of agricultural exports of the developed countries;[8] as a result the developing countries' share in world exports of agricultural products declined steadily from 42 per cent in 1955 to 28 per cent in 1971.[9]

However, during the sixties the developing countries, in their efforts to diversify their economies as well as their export trade, have achieved significant progress (Table 12) in spite of the continuing restriction on imports of some of their major manufactures. The share of manufactures in the exports of developing countries more than doubled between 1955 and 1971. But it still constitutes only one-fifth of the total exports of the developing countries and the share of the developing countries in the total world export of manufactures is still only 6 per cent.

There is no doubt that exports of manufactures from the developing countries suffer from various limitations of market information, design, quality control, advertising, packaging and marketing; the initial acquisition of expertise is generally expensive in these fields. But on the other hand there is no denying that tariff and non-tariff barriers in developed countries remain *the* major obstacle to the expansion of developing countries' exports of manufactures. The tariffs facing manufactures from the developing countries in the markets of the developed countries are on average higher than those levied on imports from other developed countries. The tariff cuts negotiated during the Kennedy Round in 1967 mainly included items such as chemicals, machinery, and transport equipment which are traded largely between the developed countries. In the case of items such as textiles, leather and leather goods, which are of special interest to the developing countries, only small tariff cuts were made.[10]

An attempt to ameliorate the situation was made in 1968 when the Generalised System of Preferences (GSP) was negotiated during the UNCTAD II in Delhi. The GSP provides for a non-reciprocal abolition or reduction of tariffs on imports from developing countries. Individual schemes vary in scope with regard to commodity coverage, the extent of tariff cuts, safeguard mechanisms, etc. Although the schemes cover manufactures and semi-manufactures, textiles, leather goods and petroleum products have been excluded. As mentioned earlier, agricultural products are covered only marginally. The schemes have so far

Table 12. Rates of growth of exports of manufactures* from selected developing countries

Countries	Manufacturing as a percentage of total exports (1969)	Growth rate of exports in manufactures (1962-69)	Total export growth rates (1960-70)
		(per cent per annum)	
Hong Kong	67.4	20.1	13.8
Taiwan	57.0	36.5	24.2
India	30.0	6.1	3.9
Mexico	27.0	19.8	6.2
South Korea	60.8	77.1	38.2
Brazil	10.6	16.2	8.0
Argentina	13.0	11.7	5.0
Pakistan	28.1	23.7	6.3
Philippines	15.3	10.2	6.6
Iran	6.3	8.7	10.9
Malaysia	8.1	18.0	3.6
Nigeria	4.2	18.1	10.1
UAR	4.7	4.8	3.0
Colombia	4.3	19.6	4.8
Chile	2.0	8.4	9.2
Indonesia	2.8	21.3	3.9

* Manufactured exports excluding petroleum products and unworked non-ferrous metals.

Source: Helleiner, G. K. (1973), 'Manufactured Exports from Less-Developed Countries and Multinational Firms', *The Economic Journal*, Vol. 83, No. 329, March.

been implemented by Australia, Austria, Bulgaria, Canada, Czechoslovakia, the EEC, Finland, German Democratic Republic, Hungary, Japan, New Zealand, Poland, Norway, Sweden, Switzerland, and the USSR. The US Trade Act, passed in December 1974, which authorised the Government to provide GSP to developing countries, was to be put into effect from January 1976.[11]

The EEC scheme provides for the duty-free entry of manufactures and semi-manufactures of phosphates, aluminium, iron ore, copper, lead, zinc, tin, rubber, wool, cotton and jute, but excludes pig iron and unwrought non-ferrous metals up to the stage of ingots. Preferential treatment for cotton textiles is limited only to the signatories of the long-term arrangement on trade in cotton textiles (LTA) and the arrangement on international trade in textiles. The signatories of these arrangements have 'voluntarily agreed' to limit the growth in their exports to the EEC. The preferential treatment with regard to cotton textiles is extended also to those countries which have entered into bilateral agreements with the Community. The total number of developing countries receiving preferential treatment from the EEC in 1974 was limited to only sixteen. For jute the preferential treatment is limited only to India and Bangladesh.[12] The Japanese scheme provides for duty-free entry for all the products listed above except that unwrought aluminium, some woven woollen fabrics, some cotton yarn and other woven fabrics, jute yarn and woven jute fabrics have been granted only 50 per cent tariff cuts. In the US scheme textiles, footwear and petroleum will be excluded. In addition, countries whose imports into the United States of a particular product exceed $25 million or 50 per cent of total US imports of that product from all sources, will be excluded from the preferential treatment. The US Trade Act (1974) excludes the Organisation of the Petroleum Exporting Countries (OPEC) and other cartel countries from the benefits of the GSP. It also excludes those countries that fail to observe the US view of what is the proper procedure for the nationalisation of foreign industries and those that do not cooperate with the US Government in drug control.[13]

Both the EEC and Japanese schemes provide for ceiling limitations. Normal duties are payable on imports in excess of these ceilings. The ceilings are calculated on the basis of 1968 imports with a small provision for growth. By 1970, imports into the EEC under the GSP already exceeded these ceilings.[14] The Japanese scheme allowed for a 3 per cent annual rate of growth for the GSP group of products against an actual increase of about 20 per cent per annum.[15] Of course, the freer entry of manufactures from developing countries may sometimes create social problems within the developed countries. This has been particularly the case with textiles in various developed countries. Cheaper textiles, though they benefit the consumer, have adverse effects on employment, particularly in areas which have a high concentration of textile mills. These problems can only be avoided by a planned phasing out of such industries, supported by a retraining programme for the people who are made redundant as a result of increasing foreign competition. Unlike the developing countries, the developed countries possess the resources to be able to undertake such programmes effectively. If, however, it is felt that some developed countries such as the UK, Italy or Spain cannot finance such a programme of restructuring their industries the UN system ought to provide 'adjustment' grants to countries which plan to phase out their industries so as to accommodate the increasing volume of imported manufactures from developing countries.

The biggest limitation of the GSP is that it does not deal with non-tariff barriers. These barriers include quantitative restrictions such as quotas, licensing, prohibitions and embargoes, variable levies, health and sanitary controls, as well as packaging and labelling regulations. Government procurement policies, by providing preferential treatment to domestic goods, also have a restrictive effect on imports.

The product groups most frequently affected by non-tariff barriers include meat and meat preparations, cocoa and cocoa products, wheat, barley, corn and rice products, oranges and tangerine products, sugar and sugar preparations, tobacco products, oleaginous products, banana and banana products. Among the manufactures and semi-manufactures, jute, wool and cotton products face the most severe quantitative restrictions, mainly in the form of 'voluntary' restraints. Phosphates, pig iron and zinc products also face some restrictions.

Among the kinds of non-tariff barriers, variable levies and discretionary licensing are the most common. Variable levies[16] are applied by the EEC, Austria, Finland, Sweden and Switzerland, mainly with a view to protecting the real incomes of their farming populations. Prohibitions and embargoes have generally been applied on sugar (raw and refined) and zinc. Health and sanitary regulations have frequently been used in developed countries to restrict imports of processed and semi-processed agricultural products. The governments of many developed countries assist the domestic producer *vis-à-vis* the importers by means of discriminatory state trading[17] both in primary commodities and in manufactures and semi-manufactures.

Similar criticisms can be levelled against the Communist countries in their trade with the developing countries, which has been expanding rapidly in recent years. The developing countries' total exports to the Eastern trading areas[18] amounted to roughly $1.2 billion in 1960; by 1973 it had gone up to $5.4 billion — but it still constitutes only 5 per cent of total exports of the developing countries. On the whole, the nature of the trading pattern between the Soviet Bloc and the developing countries is similar to that between the 'West' and the developing countries. The Bloc countries mainly export manufactures, particularly armaments, while raw materials, food and beverages still account for 85 per cent of the Bloc's imports from developing countries.[19] Opinions differ as to whether the prices charged for exports of machinery from the Soviet Bloc are more or less favourable than from the developed countries. Kidron, in the case of Pakistan, found that machinery export prices were lower than world prices, while Datar[20] felt that machinery and equipment obtained by India from the Bloc countries was costlier than those offered by other countries. There is, however, agreement on one point. The performance of the Bloc countries in providing back-up facilities was poor. Spares were expensive and often superseded by new incompatible models.[21] The suppliers have often been unwilling to deal in small quantities or to adapt to local conditions. However, the socialist countries seem to have given a slightly higher price than the other importers for the raw material imports from the developing countries.[22]

Recent developments

The opening years of the 1970s coincided with a cyclical low in business investment in most rich countries. In 1970 and 1971 total world material production increased by less than 4 per cent per annum against a long-term trend rate of growth of 5.5 per cent between 1961-71;[23] the combined GNP of the OECD countries increased by only 3 per cent per annum. In the USA there was actually a decline in GNP in 1970. The revival which started in mid-1972 brought about an exceptionally strong investment and production boom. With a sharp increase in investment there was a substantial rise in the demand for capital goods, raw materials and semi-manufactures, particularly metals. World output (excluding services) rose by 8 per cent in 1973 and the combined GNP of the major industrial countries rose by 6.5 per cent.[24] The dollar value of world exports increased by 20 per cent in 1972 and by 37 per cent in 1973, against a trend rate of growth of slightly under 10 per cent between 1961 and 1971. Although a substantial part of this increase was due to the devaluation of the US dollar, and world-wide inflation, the volume of world exports still increased by 8 per cent in 1972 and 13 per cent in 1973.[25] Agricultural exports registered a 50 per cent increase in value terms in 1973, but their volume remained at the 1972 level; however, exports of minerals and manufactures increased in volume by 8 and 16 per cent respectively. The increases (in value terms) were 40 per cent for minerals and 33 per cent for manufactures.

The volume of exports of the developed countries increased in 1973 by 14 per cent (imports by 12 per cent). For developing countries as a whole the value of exports rose by 18 per cent in 1972 and 37 per cent in 1973 against a trend rate of growth of 7 per cent over the period 1958-60 to 1969-71. The value of exports of the developing countries continued to rise in the first half of 1974 mainly due to the increased value of oil exports and other raw materials. The volume of agricultural exports from the developing countries, however, increased only slightly in 1972. There was hardly any change in the following year but exports of minerals increased by nearly 12 per cent.[26] Fragmentary data suggest that exports of manufactures from the developing countries, particularly to Japan, increased considerably in 1973 making Japan the second largest single market for manufactures after the USA. The diversification of exports of the developing countries continued so that by 1973 engineering products accounted for nearly one-fifth of the developing countries exports of manufactures to the developed countries.[27]

Not all the developing countries shared equally in this export expansion. The most rapid rate of growth of exports was experienced largely by those countries which had a heavy concentration of exports in either manufactures (e.g. South Korea and Singapore) or petroleum (e.g. Ecuador, Saudi Arabia, Nigeria and Indonesia).[28] The countries which continued to concentrate largely on agricultural exports (23 countries) had relatively slower rates of growth. Many of these were in the Sahelian Zone, East Africa and Asia where crop failures had reduced the quantity of output available for export. Countries such as Malawi, Sri Lanka, Bangladesh and India, which concentrate mainly on tea, jute and bananas, gained only marginally.[29]

Export earnings in these countries did not rise fast enough to match their import bills, particularly in those developing countries which are net food importers. Food imports of the developing countries increased by nearly 12 per cent in 1972 as against a long-term trend of 5 per cent per annum over the period 1955-71. In 1973 they increased by 60 per cent. Some of this increase resulted from widespread crop failures in many of these countries. At the same time there was a considerable reduction in the quantities delivered under various food aid programmes.

For the first time since the Korean War the trade balance (c.i.f.-f.o.b.) of the developing countries showed a surplus of $3 billion in 1972, increasing to $11 billion in 1973. Most of this surplus accrued to the petroleum exporting countries, whose combined surplus increased from $12.5 billion in 1972 to over $21 billion in 1973.[30] The balance of payments situation of the non-petroleum-exporting developing countries deteriorated during this period, their deficit amounting to nearly $10 billion in 1973. Within this group individual countries had varying experiences. For instance, because of the exceptionally high rates of growth of exports of soya beans, iron ore and manufactures the volume of Brazilian exports rose by nearly 15 per cent in 1973, while the value increased by about 55 per cent. Between 1972 and 1973 the volume of imports increased by 20 per cent, and the value by 43 per cent. As a result Brazil's trade balance moved into surplus in 1973. This, coupled with a large net capital inflow, led to an increase in reserves. Largely as a result of higher prices for grain, oilseeds and vegetable oils, and wool, there was a 57 per cent rise in the dollar export receipts of Argentina in 1973; the dollar value of imports increased by only 10 per cent. Both trade surplus and reserves increased sharply. As against this Mexico's exports, in value terms, increased by about a third, while imports rose by 41 per cent, almost half of this increase in imports being caused by rises in the prices of petroleum, cereals and steel. A sharp deterioration in Mexico's merchandise account led to a considerable deficit on current account in 1973. Nevertheless, there was some increase in reserves as a result of large-scale borrowing abroad. In India, on the other hand, exports increased (in value terms) by only 22 per cent, during 1973. This rate was less than half the combined average increase for all developing countries, one of the main reasons being that the prices of some of her main exports such as tea, cashew nuts, tobacco and iron ore rose much more slowly than the prices of other primary commodities. However, the value of imports increased by nearly 30 per cent, particularly because of the sharp rise in the prices of grains, petroleum and fertilisers. The consequent trade deficit in 1973 led to a decline in reserves.

Trends of commodity prices

Much of the gains in export earnings in 1972 and 1973 were the outcome of increases in commodity prices. The UN commodity price index (which includes petroleum but excludes non-ferrous metals) rose by an unprecedented rate, since the Korean War, of 61 per cent between the fourth quarter of 1972 and the fourth quarter of 1973. Since the peak of the Korean boom in 1951 and 1972 there have been two distinct phases of the trend in commodity prices. During the first phase (1951-62), commodity prices declined by nearly 3 per cent per annum, and by as much as 7 per cent per annum for cotton and wool, while the export prices of manufactures, after an initial decline between 1951 and 1954, showed a consistent increase of nearly 1 per cent per annum. Consequently, the terms of trade of the developing countries declined to 92 in 1958-61 (100 = base 1950-3) and this decline continued throughout the first half of the 1960s,[31] even though commodity prices started showing some improvement from 1962. In the second phase, from 1962 to 1971, commodity prices increased at an annual rate of 2 per cent, though towards the end of the period (1968-71) this rate accelerated to 5 per cent. Some commodities such as tea, wheat, wool, jute and rubber experienced a sharp decline in prices during the 1960s while prices of copper, bauxite, fish, beef, cocoa, lead, tin and zinc showed a significant increase.

The phenomenal rise in commodity prices in 1973 was influenced by various short- and long-term forces. As indicated earlier, mid-1972 was a period of cyclical recovery in the richer countries; total manufacturing production in the industrial countries as a group increased by 10 per cent in 1973. The output of the base metal and engineering industries rose by 12.5 per cent, engineering by 13 per cent, chemicals 10.4 per cent, and textiles 4.7 per cent.[32] This led to a substantial increase in the demand for non-ferrous ores and metals, and fibres such as cotton and wool. The consequent increase in income in both developed and developing countries created additional demands for cereals, vegetable oils and beef.

While the world demand for agricultural products was soaring, widespread crop failures created shortages even in countries such as the USSR, which in normal years had food surpluses. Droughts in Asia and Africa reduced the supply of oilseeds. This coincided with an increased demand for animal feed such as oilcakes and soya bean as a result of the disappearance of anchoveta (a small fish used for animal feed and fish-meal) from the Peruvian Coast. The combined effect was an escalation in the prices of feed grains, soya beans and oilseeds. This, in turn, reduced the profitability of livestock production, particularly pig meat, poultry and eggs.

The widening margin between the demand and supply of primary products led to a serious reduction in stocks of various commodities. Huge Soviet purchases of grain from the USA in 1973 reduced US grain reserves to an all time low, which meant that the gap in demand and supply could not be met from reserves and this, in turn, led to an emergency psychosis in the market.

Speculative tendencies in world commodity markets were reinforced by speculation in exchange rates, monetary uncertainties and rapid inflation. Commodities came to be accepted as a hedge against inflation. Another important factor in the rise in commodity prices was the growing confidence of the developing countries (in the wake of the success of the OPEC countries in raising the price of petroleum) and their efforts to maximise their own market power by forming cartels. This was followed by the seven leading bauxite exporters forming the International Bauxite Association (IBA).[33] Four leading copper producers formed the International Council of Copper Exporting

Countries (CIPEC). After the expiry of the International Coffee Agreement the major coffee producers, through a series of interlocking marketing companies and stockpile financing arrangements, sought to obtain greater control over world coffee prices. Similarly, the tin producers attempted to increase the guaranteed floor price through the International Tin Agreement. Five leading banana producers started levying sizeable duties on banana exports. The four major tea producers began to coordinate their marketing arrangements and to establish a floor price in a more meaningful way.

The boom in 1973 was followed in 1974 by a serious recession in several developed countries. The combined GNP of seven industrial countries (USA, Canada, Japan, West Germany, France, Italy and the UK) declined at an annual rate of 1.5 per cent during the first half of 1974. During the same period inflation averaged 14.8 per cent. The exports of these countries increased at 10 per cent per annum between January and June 1974, only half the rate attained during the first half of 1973. Their imports during this period grew at a rate of only 3.5 per cent. Except for West Germany and the USA all these countries had considerable balance of payments deficits.

Although the value of exports from the developing countries continued to grow rapidly in the first half of 1974 much of this was due to oil exports. There was a marked difference in the behaviour of the prices of primary products. The prices of agricultural raw materials, such as cotton, wool and rubber reached a peak in the early part of the year and then experienced a significant decline. In the case of wool the decline was so drastic that in both Australia and New Zealand the wool boards had to intervene in the market. However, jute and sisal prices continued to increase. Coffee, tea and cocoa prices also showed some decline in the second half of 1974. Most vegetable oil prices retained their gains, with soya beans and soya bean oil registering a significant increase, while copra suffered a serious decline. As against this, grain prices in general, which had shown some decline in the second quarter of the year, picked up once again around September and October, though the price of rice continued to decline. The rise in cereal prices was the result of disappointing harvests in 1974: in North America the total output of cereals was lower[34] than expected because of drought in the Midwest and an early frost; similarly, there was a decline in output in both the USSR and Oceania as compared to 1973. In the Far East the late and rather erratic monsoon cereal production was considerably below 1973 levels.

As a result the UN index for food continued rising throughout 1974.

This price rise, coupled with the reduced availability of food aid, exacerbated the balance of payment difficulties of several food-deficit developing countries and this continued into 1975. At the same time, the prices of non-food agricultural commodities had been declining since the beginning of 1974. Between the first quarter of 1974 and the first quarter of 1975 the index fell from 228 to 202, i.e. by nearly 13 per cent. However, during the same period the prices of non-food commodities originating from developing countries declined by 21 per cent as against only 1 per cent for the developed countries. Most non-oil-producing developing countries are in a situation of continuing uncertainty and efforts are being made to organise schemes for cutting back production or stockpiling. Past experience with such arrangements does not provide much cause for optimism. In the discussion that follows an attempt will be made to explain why in the past commodity arrangements have failed to achieve their objectives and to assess whether any of the ideas and schemes currently being advocated have a better chance of success.

Instability of export earnings

Recurrent short-term fluctuations in the prices of primary products have been a major cause of concern for planners in most developing countries. One of the main reasons for these fluctuations is the inherently inflexible nature of supply and demand. Particularly in agriculture production is not only vulnerable to the vicissitudes of the weather, but also relatively rigid production cycles make it difficult to bring about adjustments in supply in response to short-term fluctuations in demand. The product cycle is as long as a generation or more for forestry, 5 to 10 years for crops such as coffee, cocoa, tea and rubber; and for livestock it is 2 to 3 years. Even in the case of grains, planting has to be done several months in advance of the time when output is placed on the market. Agricultural production is also vulnerable to drought, floods, and diseases and pests. The incidence of such natural calamities can only be reduced gradually and that only through huge capital investments for which many developing countries do not possess the necessary resources. On the demand side the price and income elasticities of demand for most agricultural products are relatively low and decline with increasing income. Consequently, the demand for most agricultural products has not risen significantly in the markets of the richer countries. As indicated earlier, the demand for raw materials has tended to be sluggish because of competition from synthetics. Thus the low elasticities of demand, coupled with the inherent inflexibility of supply can result in sharp fluctuations in the prices of primary products.

In recent years commodity speculation has exacerbated the instability of primary commodity prices. Although future trading in commodities started in the second half of the nineteenth century in the USA, its recent growth has been phenomenal. Between 1960 and 1973 trading on the US commodity markets increased from $5 billion to more than $135 billion and on the London Exchange from $4 billion to $70 billion.[35]

The growth in turnover for individual commodities between 1960-2 and 1973 has also been phenomenal (see Table 13). Much of the increase in the volume of trading since 1970 has been due to speculation. Trading in commodity futures became very active in 1973 and the first half of 1974. This tendency was strengthened by the economic and monetary uncertainties created by continuing inflation, the collapse of the gold-dollar system and the declining value of the two major reserve currencies, the dollar and pound sterling. Sharp falls in equity markets during 1970-4 further strengthened the movement towards commodity speculation. The availability of cheap short-term credit on the Euro-dollar market also made it easier to speculate in commodities.

Under normal conditions, future trading helps to reduce price instability because speculators buy when prices are low and sell when prices are high. But in the recent bout of speculative activity, speculators expected a further rise in prices, and so were reluctant to sell. The resulting instability in prices has alarmed both national governments and the international organisations.[36]

The price instability of primary products, through its impact on export earnings, may have an adverse effect on the process of economic development in many developing countries. Primary producing developed countries are as vulnerable to price instability as the developing countries, but generally it can be seen that their economies are better able to cope with the adverse effects of fluctuations. Not only do the richer countries have more efficient and experienced administrative machinery which can normally take fairly effective counter-cyclical monetary and fiscal measures, but also trade in primary products forms a relatively small proportion of their total exports. Moreover, the composition of their primary product exports is usually more diversified than in the developing countries so that losses on some items can often be compensated for by gains on others. Most developing countries, on the other hand depend on only a few commodities for their export earnings. Macbean,[37] on the basis of a

Table 13. Annual volume of turnover on commodity futures markets in London and New York

| | Volume of futures turnover | | Futures/import ratio | |
| | 1960-2 | 1973 | 1960-72 | 1973 |
	(Thousand long tons)			
Cocoa				
London	379	11,363	0.37	7.39
New York	1,402	5,769	1.38	3.75
Coffee				
London	60	761	0.02	0.23
New York	210	3,057	0.08	0.92
Sugar				
London	2,458	42,282	0.11	1.94
New York	2,231	51,515	0.10	1.69
Rubber				
London	179	599	0.09	0.19

Source: Labys, W. C. (1974), 'Speculation and Price Instability on International Commodity Futures Markets' (mimeo.), p. 4.

cross-country regression, argued that there was only a very weak, if any, correlation between commodity concentration and instability of export earnings. But, on the basis of country case studies, he was prepared to admit that for some countries such as Malaya and Indonesia rubber prices in the period under study 'have been highly unstable and undoubtedly are the major proximate cause of their export instability'.[38] The instability of export proceeds in Pakistan and the Sudan is mainly explained by their heavy concentration on natural fibres. Macbean included Ghana, Bolivia and Haiti among the countries where instability of export earnings stemmed largely from specialisation in the production of one or two commodities.

It is debatable whether short-term instability in export earnings is an important obstacle to economic development. Much depends on the nature of the development strategy and the role that foreign capital goods and technical personnel play in the development process. If foreign aid and investment can be made available to meet the foreign exchange requirement, a fall in export earnings may not hurt. However, to the extent that foreign exchange is a real bottleneck, short-term export instability may seriously impair the ability of some developing countries to achieve high rates of economic growth. Even Macbean does not rule out this possibility.[39]

Furthermore, the instability of export earnings would certainly have an adverse effect on the incomes of the producers themselves. Whilst, in the case of plantation crops, some of the loss from a drop in price can be borne by the companies themselves, part of the loss will probably be passed on to the workers in the form of reduced wages or employment or both. Uncertainty about price and/or demand will certainly have unfavourable effects on investment and hence on future output. The governments of most developing countries have attempted to reduce price instability by various devices. However, it has increasingly been felt that, without international cooperation, it is not always possible to satisfactorily safeguard the interests of the producers.

International Commodity Agreements were originally intended as a major international instrument to bring more rationality into the world markets in agricultural and mineral products. The main objective of these agreements is to moderate fluctuations in commodity prices, although this often involves some stabilisation of quantities of internationally marketed products as well — through production or sales quotas for producing countries and forward contracts for buying countries. In some cases there is a provision for international buffer stocks, to hold prices within a certain range; if prices rise beyond the ceiling, part of the stock is released on to the market to bring the price back down; when the price drops below the floor a part of the surplus is siphoned off from the market. Since World War II only six formal international commodity agreements have been worked out in a systematic way, under the auspices of the United Nations, and their overall achievements have been rather scanty.

Most of the agreements require a fair amount of discipline among both producers and consumers. It is essential that all major producers and consumers join such arrangements and do not opt out when prices outside a scheme are more favourable to them. In the past, the consuming countries have generally remained inside a scheme when prices are high but have opted out when world prices are lower. The United Kingdom has been one of the main offenders, particularly with regard to the International Wheat Agreement.

It is also imperative that national policies are consistent with the aims of these schemes and are adjusted according to changes in the international situation. For instance, when the market price falls to the 'reference' price the governments of member countries should intervene by adding to their stocks of that particular commodity.

One of the major obstacles to the success of many International Commodity Agreements has been the uncompromising attitude of the US Government. Because of the dominance of the USA in world agricultural trade,[40] no international arrangement can succeed without US cooperation. It is surprising that, even though US agriculture is so highly protected by tariffs, quantitative restrictions, and price discrimination, the US Government representative at international negotiations continues to argue against commodity arrangements on the grounds that they distort 'free market forces'. Much of the opposition to commodity agreements in the US Congress comes from various lobbies; for example, the US Government, under pressure from instant coffee producers, has frustrated all Brazilian efforts to enter the US instant coffee market.[41]

Recently there seems to have been some shift in the US position. In a speech in mid-1974, President Nixon's special trade representative responsible for multilateral trade negotiations suggested that, although the US Government will continue to oppose the traditional type of commodity agreements which carve up markets among existing producers at prices fixed in perpetuity, they will have an open mind on new kinds of international arrangements which provide:

> . . . for both suppliers and customers to shoulder their responsibilities of being good sellers and good buyers, an arrangement under which the natural forces of supply and demand would be permitted their fullest and most efficient interaction in normal conditions, but which would provide sovereign nations with guidelines for an acceptable range of actions to help level off peaks of surplus and valleys of shortage. An arrangement which would permit the entry of new producers and new production into world markets, and perhaps most important an arrangement which would provide for any government intervention to phase out automatically as conditions no longer warranted it. Such arrangements could apply not only to agriculture but also to petroleum, bauxite, copper, tin, and other materials . . .[42]

More recently, during the Seventh Special Session of the UN General Assembly the USA announced that she would sign the International Tin Agreement, subject to Congressional consultation and ratification. She is already taking part in the negotiations on coffee and has indicated her willingness to join cocoa and sugar negotiations. But the US Government still continues to favour the idea of a loose type of consumer-producer forum rather than a commodity agreement.[43] Any concessions from the richer countries, particularly the US Government, on these issues will depend largely on the producing countries remaining united even in the face of declining world primary product prices. If such price declines are serious and last for a long time the chances are that this unity might disintegrate.

Compensatory financing of export fluctuations

In view of the shortcomings of international commodity agreements and the continuing opposition of the richer countries — particularly the USA — to them, the search for alternative means of reducing extreme fluctuations in the export earnings of developing countries has continued. Efforts in this direction have come from the IMF, UNCTAD and a number of academics. The earliest attempt in this direction was outlined by F. G. Olano,[44] a member of a UN expert group, as early as 1953, but with the increasing militancy of the developing countries alternative schemes have attracted more attention in recent years. Olano suggested a 'Mutual Insurance Scheme' which would compensate member countries, both developed and developing, in the case of losses arising from their terms of trade declining below a 'reference' level. This 'reference terms of trade' could be calculated using the prices of 60 to 70 primary products and about 500 manufactures. Thus when a country's terms of trade rose above the 'reference' level it would be required to make payments into the insurance fund. Another UN expert group proposed a similar scheme[45] in which the payment from the insurance fund was to be based on the short-fall in total export earnings and not on the terms of trade. Although this proposal did not exclude developed countries, it was biased in favour of the developing countries. The compensatory payments were to be made partly in unconditional cash grants and partly in loans to be repaid when export earnings once again exceeded the 'reference' level. Outstanding loans were to be written off after a certain specified period. In 1965 the World Bank[46] produced a new proposal of a rather longer term nature than the two UN schemes above which were intended to operate over a period of 2 to 5 years. The World Bank scheme aimed at supporting development programmes which were unduly affected by adverse export movements. A major innovation was introduced in calculating the standard of reference; it was to be estimated on the basis not only of past performance but also of future expectations regarding export earnings. The scheme was not visualised as a self-financing one. Payments of compensation were to be made in the form of contingency loans to be repaid initially by the excess of realised exports over projected export earnings. If, however, these initial payments could not be made during the specified period (usually the Plan period) then outstanding balances were to be converted into long-term loans. The rate of interest and the period of maturity were to be determined according to the overall financial and economic situation of a country. A part of the payment could also be made by drawing on a country's own reserves or its IMF drawing rights.[47]

At present only the IMF runs a modest compensatory financing scheme[48] which began in 1963 and was revised in 1966. Compensation is paid when total export earnings fall below a predetermined 'norm', calculated as a 5 year moving average centred on the short-fall year. The payment is made only if the country concerned is facing overall balance of payments difficulties. It is further stipulated that outstanding loans should not normally exceed 25 per cent of the members' contribution to the IMF within a twelve month period, nor amount to more than 50 per cent of its quota at any time. If, however, a member country takes advantage of the IMF facility for the financing of buffer stocks then its aggregate borrowing rights are reduced to only 25 per cent of its quota. Repayments have to be made within 3 to 5 years and standard IMF rates of interest are charged. The IMF scheme, though helpful, has proved somewhat rigid so that borrowings under the scheme have remained low. Borrowings so far have been about SDR 90 million per annum between 1963-74. Outstanding loans have never exceeded SDR 600 million as compared to the theoretical provision for borrowings of over SDR 3 billion.[49]

According to the UNCTAD, the usefulness of the IMF scheme would be greatly increased if the following modifications were made:[50]

(1)   the criteria for assistance should be more flexible and take account not only of a country's overall balance of payments situation but also of the problems of individual commodity sectors and their impact on the economic situation as a whole and on the longer term balance of payments prospects;
(2)   the limits of compensation ought to be based not so much on the IMF quotas, which are invariably small for the smaller and poorer countries but on the extent of short-falls in export earnings;
(3)   since many poorer countries still do not possess adequate export statistics, IMF insistence that the short-fall should be calculated with respect to the latest twelve-month period for which

the IMF has data means that some countries may find it difficult
to use the IMF facility. UNCTAD would recommend, at least for
the immediate future, easier requirements with regard to the
provision of the statistical data on which a request for assistance is
to be based;

(4)   the repayment of loans should be more clearly linked to the
recovery in the level of exports and the insistence on complete
repayment within 3 to 5 years should be relaxed;

(5)   finally, compensation should be linked to the changes in the
import purchasing power of a country's exports, not to their money
value.

Compensatory financing schemes as outlined above have certain basic
advantages over International Commodity Agreements. Unlike the
latter, compensatory financing schemes do not interfere with the
market; therefore, they should not be so strongly opposed by market-
orientated economists and politicians in the richer countries nor by
international organisations dominated by such western economists.

Since a member country cannot improve its prospects by opting
out of the system, as can happen with Commodity Agreements, compensatory financing schemes have better chances of survival. In principle, such schemes should not involve too much political interference
in the domestic policies of developing countries, particularly when
they are operated by international organisations. In practice, however,
the IMF and the World Bank have often pressurised developing countries into changing their development strategies and even, sometimes,
their ideological standpoint. In particular, this has been due to the
influence of the US Government.

However, the schemes for compensatory financing and International
Commodity Agreements are essentially complementary and an integrated
scheme of this kind has recently been advocated by the Secretary-
General of the UNCTAD. The recent Lomé Agreement between the
EEC and forty-six developing countries in Africa, the Caribbean and
the Pacific is also based on the idea of an integrated scheme.

The UNCTAD integrated program for commodities[51]

The proposal currently being discussed in UNCTAD aims at negotiating
multilateral arrangements for a comprehensive range of commodities
in the form of a package deal (instead of a traditional commodity-by-
commodity approach) consisting of five basic elements: buffer stocks,
a common fund, agreements on multilateral commitments to buy and

sell commodities, compensatory financing arrangements and mechanisms to promote exports of processed products. Under the proposed scheme international commodity arrangements will include the improvement of marketing systems, diversification (both horizontal and vertical) of the domestic industrial structure, expanded access to markets, measures to counter inflation and the maintenance of stable and remunerative prices. The principles and objectives on which the proposed programme should be based are as follows:

(a) 'There is a need to seek solutions simultaneously and urgently to the problems of a number of commodities of major interest to developing countries, both as exporters and importers, in view of the considerable threat to the interest of these countries posed by prospective developments in the world economic situation in both the short-term and the longer term';

(b) 'International action on commodities should take due account of the interests of both exporting and importing countries';

(c) 'Cooperative action by producing countries has a legitimate and important role to play in solving the problems of individual commodities';

(d) 'Arrangements for the stabilization of prices, in the sense of the smoothing out of irregular or cyclical fluctuations, are required for many commodities in order to allow correct responses to price incentives in production, to help stabilize export income and import bills, and to improve the competitive position of natural raw materials facing competition from synthetics;'

(e) 'Commodity prices should be at levels which provide incentives for the maintenance of adequate levels of production, which are just and remunerative, which take due account of world inflation, and which are consistent with development objectives';

(f) 'Diversification and the expansion of processing of commodities in developing countries should be encouraged';

(g) 'The improvement of marketing and distribution systems, more advanced technology, and research should be actively promoted in the interests of both importers and exporters';

(h) 'International commodity arrangements should seek to ensure liberal access to protected markets for exporting countries and security of supplies for importing countries'.

With a view to the increasing risk of a sharp decline in commodity prices the proposal suggests that international stocks should be established for a wide range of commodities. Provisionally eighteen

commodities are considered suitable for stock-piling.[52] The cost of
acquiring the necessary stocks of the eighteen commodities is provisionally estimated at US $10.7 billion, $4.7 billion of which is for
grains and $3.2 billion for sugar, coffee and copper. The estimate for
grain stocks is based on the World Food Conference estimates of world
requirements. According to the UNCTAD this scheme should be
financed by means of a common fund supported by both exporting
and importing countries. Some assistance could be provided by the
international financial institutions. The Fund should also attempt to
attract investment from other sources if sufficient security for the
investment and reasonable returns could be assured. The Fund could
also be allowed to raise funds from the market on terms and conditions
similar to those for other international agencies.

Besides the establishment of stocks of essential commodities the
UNCTAD proposal stresses the need for multilateral supply and purchase
commitments by governments regarding the approximate amounts of
a commodity that each government expects its economy to supply or
demand in any period. Such reciprocal trading commitments would
assist forward planning, particularly of foreign exchange resources.
The system of forward commitment is envisaged as a three stage process:[53]

(1)   'a projection of global potential for trade between exporters
and importers over a specified period, at least annually and prefer-
ably over the medium term';
(2)   'consultations between producers (or consumers) as a means of
resolving significant coverages in annual export availability or in
import demand, the range of prices applicable, or other terms of
arrangement';
(3)   'agreement in form of purchase and supply commitments
concluded multilaterally, but without specification as to the
direction of trade'.

It is acknowledged that the international stockpiling-policy and forward
commitments may still leave some countries vulnerable to export
instability. Countries which produce or export perishable commodities
not easily amenable to stockpiling or multilateral commitments will come
in this category. For such countries the UNCTAD proposals recommend the liberalising of the IMF compensatory financing or some
additional compensatory measures.

The proposal rightly stresses that the:

. . . contribution of commodity production and trade to the economic development of the developing world will only be realised rapidly and efficiently if shifts in resources within the primary sector of the developing countries and within their economies in general can occur. The measures above would create more favourable conditions for appropriate diversification and for freeing resources in a more broadly based economic structure. But in addition, separate and more constructive attention will be required in the international community to develop means of expanding the processing of primary products, removing trade discrimination in this respect and to encourage the transfer of technology and research with this objective.[54]

The UNCTAD scheme, with its multi-commodity approach and its buffer-stock provisions is certainly conceptually sound. However, the very comprehensiveness of the scheme can be both a liability and an asset. A multi-commodity approach, under normal conditions, will help to keep the cost of operations low because purchases of some commodities can be offset by sales of others during a particular period. Similarly, losses on one account can be compensated by gains on another. However, if a serious slump were to occur simultaneously in a number of commodity markets there would be a genuine risk of the scheme collapsing. A scheme of such a wide ranging nature may also have managerial difficulties to overcome. Incorrect decisions as to buying or selling stocks will not only lead to serious losses and waste of resources but will also have a destabilising effect on the market. Inefficiencies and delays in the management of food reserves may add to hardships and human miseries.

The greatest weakness of the UNCTAD scheme is its likely political unacceptability to the developed countries, particularly the USA.[55] If the Lomé Agreement between the EEC and ACP (African, Caribbean and the Pacific countries) is any indication, the EEC countries may be moving in favour of such agreements. However, it is natural for the USA, as oligopolistic leader in the market for agricultural products, to resist any development which might undermine its power. By the same token, it is important for the consumers (and producers of commodities in which the USA is a major buyer) to have a countervailing power in the market. The EEC countries as a group have some such power; Japan also has some, though not much, political and economic leverage; but the developing countries, except through oil and raw materials, have none. Even the UNCTAD scheme will not go far enough in providing the necessary safeguards for the developing countries, unless the present inequities in the distribution of political power in the UN system are redressed in favour of the developing countries and the UN agencies acquire sufficient powers to enforce internationally agreed decisions.

The Lomé Convention

The Convention[56] signed (on 28 February 1975) between the EEC and forty-six developing countries in Africa, the Caribbean and the Pacific (ACP) is symbolic of the recent changes in attitude of the developed countries, particularly the Europeans, towards the commodity problems of the developing countries. The Convention aims at an integrated scheme incorporating trade, aid, the stabilisation of export earnings, cooperation in agricultural and industrial development, the transfer of technology, improving economic and social infrastructure, capital movements, etc.

In the field of trade, manufactures and agricultural products not covered by the Common Agricultural Policy (CAP) will be admitted into the EEC free of customs duties, levies or quantitative import restrictions. For most items, except molasses and some temperate fruit and vegetables covered by the CAP, the EEC will provide more favourable terms of entry to goods from the ACP. Under this arrangement 96 per cent of the exports of the ACP will enter the EEC duty free. Special arrangements have been made for beef, rum, bananas and sugar. The Convention does not require the ACP countries to provide reciprocal treatment for commodities originating in the EEC as was the case with the African associate states prior to the Convention. However, the ACP will grant EEC countries the same terms as would be applicable to any other developed country. The ACP can not discriminate between individual members of the Community; countries which were already providing preferential treatment to a member country can continue to do so provided similar preferences are given to the other members of the Community.

The ACP will receive aid in terms of loans and grants from the European Development Fund and loans from the European Investment Bank. The total resources available have been raised to 3,390 million units of account (equivalent to SDRs), out of which nearly 375 million will be earmarked for stabilising export earnings.

The stabilisation scheme includes twelve basic export products: bananas, cocoa, coffee, coconuts, cotton, palm products, hides and skins, sisal, tea, timber and iron ore. A 'reference' level will be calculated on the basis of actual earnings from each product over the previous four years. If in any one year there is a fall in earnings below the 'reference' level compensation will be paid directly to the governments in five equal annual instalments. The better-off ACP countries will be required to pay back the 'transfer' when their export earnings rise above the 'reference' level.

The Convention includes a comprehensive programme for assisting the industrialisation of the ACP countries through training programmes, the transfer of technology, advisory services and assistance to small and medium firms in priority areas decided by the ACP countries. The Convention provides for a Joint Committee on Industrial Co-operation to supervise and coordinate industrial cooperation.

It is too early to pronounce judgement on the working of the scheme but if it works it may, as the Minister of Overseas Development (UK) said in Parliament recently, be a precursor of a wider scheme encompassing other developed and developing countries as envisaged by the UNCTAD. Much would depend on whether the European countries succeed in persuading the US Government to give up their ideological inhibitions on such issues.

In conclusion it can legitimately be argued that, in spite of continued efforts at international level the developing countries, almost until the Lomé Convention, were unable to obtain any major concessions from the richer countries on trade issues. Nor did the richer countries agree to any comprehensive international scheme which could protect the poorer countries from the harmful effects of fluctuations in commodity prices. The recent change in the attitudes of the richer countries is largely due to the increasing militancy of the Third World countries. It is almost certain that the magnitude of future 'concessions' in the course of GATT and UNCTAD IV negotiations will depend mainly on the continued solidarity of the developing countries.

9 DEVELOPMENT ASSISTANCE AND THE POOR

If the recent record of trade liberalisation does not provide much hope for the developing countries, then the prospects for the transfer of financial resources particularly in the form of official development assistance from the richer countries are still more depressing. In spite of the protestations of the Pearson Commission and the declarations of the development strategy for the Second United Nations Development Decade, the frustration and disillusionment with 'aid' continues in developed and developing countries alike. In nominal terms the total annual transfer of resources from the developed to the developing countries showed a significant increase from $8.57 billion in 1963 to $24.43 billion in 1973. However, if allowance is made for inflation and currency realignments and the flows are expressed in terms of 1970 prices, the total transfer of resources rose from $10 billion to only $17 billion (Table 14) over the period 1963-73. A significant part of this increase resulted from the greatly increased inflow of private capital. Official development assistance (ODA) during this period increased, in nominal terms, from $5.77 billion to $9.41 billion but in constant value terms the real volume of these resources actually declined by 7 per cent.[1] The contribution of the six major donors (Canada, France, Germany, Japan, UK and USA) was reduced from $6.26 billion in 1963 to $4.98 billion in 1973. This was caused mainly by the reduction in the US contribution from $4 billion in 1963 to $1.84 billion in 1973 (Table 15). As a result the US share of total official development assistance fell steadily from 58 per cent in 1962 to 32 per cent in 1973.

During the period 1963-73 the total net flows from the Development Assistance Committee (DAC) members to the developing countries as a group never approached the 1 per cent of GNP target urged by the Pearson Commission. The nearest they came was 0.81 per cent of GNP in 1971. Among the individual countries only Belgium, France, Japan, the Netherlands and Portugal exceeded the 1 per cent target. There was a substantial decline over this period in the flows from Germany, Italy, Switzerland, the UK and the USA.

This decline was even more marked in the case of official development assistance as opposed to total flows for the DAC group as a whole. ODA as a proportion of GNP declined steadily from 0.51 per cent in

Table 14. Total net flow of resources from selected DAC countries 1963-73 (in billion US $)

Countries	1963	1968	1973
	(in real terms, 1970 prices)		
Canada	0.15	0.32	0.74
France	1.45	1.81	1.94
Germany	0.75	1.89	1.19
Japan	0.30	1.12	4.04
UK	0.83	0.92	0.82
USA	5.48	6.48	5.70
Other DAC members	1.91	2.94	4.05
Total	10.17	14.48	17.18

Based on OECD *Development Cooperation Review, 1974*. Adjusted for prices and currency realignments on the basis of OECD deflators.

1963 to only 0.30 per cent in 1973. In the case of the USA it declined from 0.59 per cent to only 0.23 per cent. This was against a background of a UN target for ODA of 0.7 per cent of GNP, incorporated in the International Development Strategy.

On the whole, the concessional flows (ODA) as a proportion of total flows have declined appreciably from 67 per cent to 39 per cent over the period (Table 16). In the bilateral (ODA) flow, grants declined from about 30 per cent of the total in 1970 to 27 per cent in 1973. During the same period concessional loans declined from 17 to 12 per cent.[2]

Obviously, part of the disappointing 'aid' performance of the DAC countries is due to their financial difficulties. But the major factor is the change in the US attitude to 'aid'; the USA remains the largest donor, accounting for almost one third of total ODA. The 'aid' performance of the communist countries has been no better. In quantitative terms the entire communist bloc has provided only a small fraction of the 'aid' provided by the 'western' countries. On average between 1970-3 the total aid provided by the communist countries was roughly equal to one-sixth of the official development assistance provided by the DAC countries. The contribution of the USSR in 1973 was $750 million representing only 0.16 per cent of its estimated GNP. The other Eastern European countries together contributed only around $300 million. The terms of the Soviet Bloc 'aid' are often tougher than for DAC aid. Soviet 'aid' consists largely of loans; grants

Table 15. Net flow of official development assistance (ODA) from selected DAC countries 1963-73 (in billion US $)

Countries	1963	1968	1973
	(in real terms, 1970 prices)		
Canada	0.07	0.18	0.32
France	0.98	0.89	1.01
Germany	0.49	0.63	0.71
Japan	0.15	0.37	0.65
UK	0.48	0.46	0.45
USA	4.09	3.40	1.84
Other DAC members	0.47	0.78	1.31
Total	6.73	6.71	6.29

Based on OECD *Development Cooperation Review, 1974*. Adjusted for prices and currency realignments on the basis of OECD deflators.

Table 16. Composition of the total net flow of resources from DAC countries (per cent)

	1963	1973
Official Development Assistance	67.3	38.5
Other official flows	2.9	10.6
Private flows	29.8	50.9
Total	100.0	100.0

Source: OECD, *Development Cooperation Review, 1974*, Table VII-3, p. 117.

are made only in exceptional cases. All Soviet aid, including the contribution to the UNDP, is fully tied.[3] The People's Republic of China (PRC), though itself still a developing country, has emerged as one of the major communist donors. Its gross aid disbursements in 1973 are estimated to have exceeded $500 million, representing roughly 0.3 per cent of GNP. PRC 'aid' is highly concessional; the major part of its 'aid' is in the form of interest-free loans repayable over 10 to 30 years with a grace period of 5 to 15 years.[4]

'Aid' from the communist countries, particularly the Soviet Bloc, has never been very significant in quantitative terms. In its earlier stages its major contribution was in its impact on the overall aid climate. The USSR was the first donor to accept the principle of giving development loans on concessional terms, by offering lower rates of interest. In accepting repayment in kind the Soviet Bloc countries were far ahead of other developed countries in recognising the need for linking trade and aid policies.[5] The USSR was the first to underline the principle of 'non-interference' in the internal affairs of developing countries, in any shape or form, whether with regard to development strategy, priorities or policies. Soviet aid has been mainly directed towards public sector industries. This form of 'aid' is better suited to the aspirations of industrialisation and economic freedom of the newly emerging countries.[6] The Soviet Bloc countries were the first to adopt the practice of announcing credit arrangements well in advance so as to enable the recipient countries to incorporate foreign assistance into their own development plans.[7] However, in recent years there has been an increasing tendency towards 'hardened commercialism' among the Soviet Bloc countries. With increasing political understanding and cooperation between East and West, such commercial tendencies may well be further strengthened, and the Bloc countries may try to drive harder bargains with the developing countries; the latter may find it difficult to resist without some kind of collective bargaining on their side. On the whole, the prospects for any significant increase in aid from the Soviet Bloc are rather bleak.

Contrary to popular belief in the West, the aid commitments of the OPEC countries have increased significantly since 1973; the official economic assistance of the OPEC countries increased from around $500 million per annum over the period 1970-3, to $16 billion in 1974.[8] Of this, at least $10 billion was on soft loan terms containing a grant element of 25 per cent or more. This was 50 per cent more than the entire official development assistance of the DAC countries in 1973. Several OPEC countries contributed 5 to 10 per cent of their GNP in development assistance. Their loan terms compare favourably with those of the DAC countries. They have made significant contributions to multilateral agencies, including $3.1 billion to the IMF in connection with its oil facility and $1 billion to the World Bank.[9]

In view of the increased foreign exchange requirements for importing oil, grains and fertiliser as well as the increasing burden of debt servicing, and at a time when the traditional donors are reluctant to increase their own contributions, this substantial increase in economic assistance by the OPEC has not only provided some relief to the developing countries but has also given them a new confidence. They are becoming increasingly conscious of the need for greater solidarity. The interests of individual developing countries are often divergent and any meaningful degree of solidarity among them will take some time to develop; however, the increasing militancy of the Third World has often surprised the delegates of the richer countries at international conferences.

Food aid

Being essentially a surplus disposal programme conceived by the US Government to get rid of its embarrassingly large grain surpluses, the fortunes of 'food aid' have been closely linked with US grain harvests. In its initial years the major part of food aid was given in the form of cereals, particularly wheat and wheat flour. Whenever surpluses of other commodities appeared, they were also included in the food aid baskets. Dairy products, butter, oil, and sugar produced in the EEC and Japanese rice are other examples of surplus commodities included in food aid programmes.

In its early stages US food aid was given in the form of concessional sales payable in local currencies. This provision went a long way towards relieving the foreign exchange difficulties of food deficit recipient countries. However, the terms of these sales stipulated that at least 50 per cent of food aid commodities had to be shipped in US vessels. Often US freight rates were higher than the ruling international freight rates. The US embassy and other expenses incurred in the recipient country were also met out of the income received from these sales. Therefore the actual saving of foreign exchange was much less than the face value of food aid. Furthermore, a recipient country could not ease its foreign exchange problems by substituting 'food aid' for commercial imports. It was expected that a recipient country would continue to import through commercial channels the quantity of food that it normally imported. As a result of demands from the other grain exporting countries, elaborate international arrangements[10] were made to supervise the disbursement of food aid so that it did not interfere with the normal pattern of production and international trade.

With the reduction in the size of grain surpluses in the USA, the grant element (through sales for local currency) was gradually phased out and by 1971 had been replaced by dollar loans at concessional rates. At the same time there was a progressive decline in the total volume of food aid. In 1964 food aid constituted nearly a quarter of

world official development assistance; in 1973, as a result of the changed
world food situation, it was only 12 per cent (Table 17). The poorer
countries were thus deprived of food aid when they most needed
it. The actual quantity supplied in 1973 was only 6 million tons as
against 16 million tons in 1963. This was largely the result of a drastic
cut in the food aid bill of the US Government from $1.2 billion in
1963 to only $0.6 billion in 1973.[11]

Table 17. Value of total bilateral and multilateral food aid and cereal
volume received under food aid

	1964	1969	1973
Nominal value (US$ million)	1,529	1,174	1,130
Food aid as a percent of total ODA*	26	18	12
Real value (US$ million) at 1968 prices	1,390	1,236	553
Cereal volume (in million metric tons)	16	13	6

Source: OECD, *Development Cooperation Review, 1974*, Table V-1, p. 87.
* Calculated on the basis of the total ODA given in the above report.

There is no doubt that the massive US food aid programme not only
played a major role in alleviating misery during emergencies but also
assisted economic development in some countries by relieving
inflationary pressures and the foreign exchange constraint; but because
of its close association with US foreign policy its full potentialities
were never realised. The US Government was not prepared to give a
reasonably long-term assurance about the continuation of food aid, so
no developing country could make it a part of its long-term development strategy. On various occasions food aid to individual countries
was discontinued on political grounds. This further discouraged the
recipients from relying too much on food aid. Some of these limitations
could easily be remedied by 'internationalising' the food surplus but
the US Government has vehemently opposed any such proposals.
Under the pressure of world opinion it agreed to the establishment of
the World Food Programme (WFP) in 1963 — under the joint aegis of
the United Nations and the FAO. Initially the WFP was started on an
experimental basis for three years (1963-5) to provide emergency
relief, as well as aid for economic and social development, particularly

with regard to the nutrition of the most vulnerable groups. Resources
at the disposal of the WFP averaged around $100 million a year
between 1963 and 1972. This would be roughly equivalent to 10 per
cent of the food aid or just over 1 per cent of the official development
assistance of the DAC countries. Thus the creation of the WFP is, at
best, a symbolic gesture to the 'multilateralisation' of food aid.

In view of the assurances given by the richer countries during the
World Food Conference (Rome) in 1974 there is a distinct possibility
that food aid will increase in the future. It is not yet clear whether it
will reach the target of 10 million tons. According to the FAO, the
total availability of food aid was nearly 9 million tons in 1974-5.[12]
However, much of this food aid will continue to be administered
through bilateral channels. As a result, the sense of insecurity
among the developing countries will continue, the more so because the US Government representatives have made it clear that
their Government may, in future, use food as a political weapon
much more than in the past. The multilateralisation of food aid
in itself does not provide a watertight guarantee that food aid will
not be used as a political weapon. Because of its dominant position in
the UN agencies, the US Government has often been able to use these
agencies for its own political ends. The refusal to provide WFP grain
to Turkey, or the blocked World Bank loan to Chile are examples of
the international agencies giving way under US pressure.

Bilateral aid and the poor

In recent years increasing attention has been paid to the special problems of the least developed countries. They received relatively more
aid during 1969-72 than previously, on rather softer terms *vis-à-vis*
those developing countries with higher *per capita* GNPs. During this
period the developing countries with *per capita* incomes below $200 per
annum received an average of $2.6 billion annually representing 43 per
cent of bilateral development assistance.[13] However, in *per capita* terms,
the poorest countries still received less official development assistance
than many of their more developed counterparts. In fact their share of
bilateral disbursements (1969-72 annual average) worked out at $3.2
per capita as against $6.3 for countries with *per capita* incomes of
$200 to $375 and $5.2 for countries with *per capita* incomes of
$700 to $1,000.[14]

Even among the very poorest developing countries, the countries
of South Asia, where the number of very poor peasants, landless
labour and urban poor — the World Bank's 'target' groups — is highest,

received much less in *per capita* terms than the average for the least developed countries. For instance, *per capita* gross ODA disbursements (annual average of 1969-72) to Bhutan were only $0.2, Bangladesh $0.7, India $1.4, and Nepal $1.7, as against Botswana $26.7, Laos $22.7, Central African Republic $9.0 and the Gambia $7.6.[15] It does not appear, therefore, that bilateral assistance is particularly directed towards the 'target' groups. 'Aid' continues to be heavily concentrated on areas where the richer countries have special trade or political interests.

This is also clear from the sectoral allocation of 'aid'. Since the majority of people still depend upon agriculture for their livelihood in most developing countries, particularly the least developed countries, the proportion of aid going to agriculture should be one of the main indicators of the donors' desire to assist the 'target' groups. The share of agriculture in total aid commitments in 1973 works out at 8 per cent for the DAC member countries and 25 per cent for the multilateral agencies.[16] Among all the DAC members[17] except for New Zealand, Norway, Sweden and Switzerland, less than 10 per cent of aid commitments in 1973 were directed towards the agricultural sector.[18] A much larger proportion of the bilateral aid commitments of the major donors (Canada, France, Germany, Japan and the UK) was directed towards public utilities, some of which might indirectly benefit agriculture. With Japanese aid, industry, mining and construction received nearly six times as much as agriculture. All the major donors, apart from Japan, provided several times more aid for education than for agriculture. A significant part of this 'aid' to education was probably directed towards technical and engineering subjects, only a small percentage going to agricultural education. In addition, much of the 'aid' to education has been spent on 'elitist' education, bringing scholars from developing countries to universities in the developed countries or sending scholars from the rich countries to the poorer countries. If one considers that one of the effects of this kind of 'education' is the perpetuation of the 'western' market-orientated, capitalist ideology in the developing countries it is debatable who gains most from such 'aid' — the donors or the recipients; but it is indisputable that the direct benefit to the very poor from these educational expenditures is negligible. Except for France, all the major donors directed less than 10 per cent of their 'aid' to health, social infrastructure and welfare in 1973. On the whole it seems reasonable to conclude that so far bilateral assistance from the richer countries has not been particularly directed towards eliminating the poverty of the very poorest groups.

Multilateral aid

In recent years one welcome feature of the aid business has been the significant growth in the activities of the multilateral agencies.

In 1963 multilateral aid constituted only 12 per cent of the net official development assistance of the DAC countries. By 1973 it had risen to nearly 27 per cent. The disbursements of the World Bank and its associates were only about $317 million in 1963; by 1973 they had reached $867 million. Thus the share of the World Bank and its associates in the net transfer of resources from the DAC countries and multilateral agencies to the developing countries increased from about 5 per cent in 1963 to nearly 10 per cent in 1973.

Table 18. Net disbursements by multilateral agencies 1963-73 (in million US $)

	1963	1968	1973
IBRD	263	221	613
IDA	38	202	608
IFC	8	19	98
Total loans	383	453	1470
Total grants	270	424	861
Total loans and grants	653	877	2331

Source: OECD, *Development Cooperation Review, 1974*, Table 67, p. 261.

There have also been some welcome changes in the attitude of the World Bank towards rural development and the problems of the poor. The share of agriculture has increased from 6 per cent of total Bank lending between 1948-60 to around 24 per cent in 1973-4.[19] Traditionally the Bank financed mainly irrigation and infrastructure projects; now it also finances storage, marketing, processing, fisheries and forestry projects and health as well as the construction of rural roads and water supply facilities. A much larger proportion of the Bank's resources for agricultural development is directed towards the least developed countries. The share of disbursements going to those countries with *per capita* incomes of under $150 has increased from 22.5 per cent in 1968 to around 38.2 per cent between 1969 and 1974.[20]

These changes are certainly in the right direction but the magnitude of the problem is immense; the Bank clearly appreciates that, despite its own activities, millions will continue to suffer. Robert McNamara, the President of the World Bank, in his Nairobi address in 1974 set a target of raising production on the 100 million farms with areas of less than 5 hectares, so that by 1985 their output would be growing at 5 per cent per annum.[21] According to the World Bank estimates this could cost anything between $70,000 million and $100,000 million per annum. The Bank is expected to invest about $7,200 million over a five-year period (1975-9) on agriculture and rural development, roughly half of which would be on rural development, or an average of $700 million per annum. Thus World Bank resources will provide only about 7 to 10 per cent of the resources needed to meet the objectives set by its President. Even after allowing for recipient governments' contributions only about 15 to 20 per cent of the total estimated expenditure has been provided for.

The Bank's experts themselves accept[22] that:

> the Bank's program — ambitious as it is — will scarcely keep pace over the five year period with the increase in the numbers of the rural poor resulting from population growth. The increase could amount to 70 million, while the number of the rural poor benefiting from these programs will probably not exceed 60 million. The total number of beneficiaries, including those outside the target groups, can be estimated at 100 million.[23]

The situation will continue to be particularly serious in the South Asian countries which have a much higher proportion of the very poor in their populations.

The Bank is certainly aware of its losing battle against poverty. It is also conscious of the fact that at least

> in some developing countries, present policies and institutional structures are so far from favorable to rural development that a policy shift could only follow a major political change. This is a key problem in situations demanding extensive land reform; it applies even more where the government itself is dominated by special interests unsympathetic to the objectives of rural development.[24]

It is doubtful whether the Bank authorities really believe in radical institutional and political change; if they did they could use whatever leverage they have over their borrowers to that end. They have done so in the past on several occasions but always in an attempt to 'rectify' departures from private enterprise and the 'market'. Radical land redistribution or changes in property relationships which undermine private property are almost an anathema to the World Bank. Seen in this ideological context it is not difficult to understand why the World Bank President, within a couple of years of his widely publicised slogan for the redistribution of income and wealth,[25] has categorically stated that future World Bank programmes 'will put primary emphasis *not on the redistribution of income and wealth* — as justified as that may be in many of our member countries — but rather on increasing the productivity of the poor, thereby providing for a more equitable sharing of the benefits of growth'.[26]

In a more recent speech he explained why the Bank will not advocate the redistribution of income and wealth: '. . . we do not believe we can correct the "skewness" by redistribution of the existing income. It is too small. If you redistribute it evenly it would still be unsatisfactory.'[27]

Whilst his arithmetic may be right, the *qualitative* difference in life resulting from a more equitable distribution could be immense. It has already been forcefully demonstrated in the Chinese case that the kind of redistribution that he rules out has virtually eliminated the misery and deprivation of the very poor. One can rule out such a programme on the grounds of political feasibility but not because of any inherent weakness in the idea itself.

Private foreign investment

This is not the place to go into a detailed analysis of the merits and demerits of private foreign investment; many divergent views[28] have been expressed on its desirability. On the credit side, it is claimed that foreign investment constitutes a net addition to a country's investible resources, that it is instrumental in the introduction of new technology and skills, better management and marketing techniques and that it opens up new markets for the products of developing countries. Foreign investment also provides contacts with overseas banks, capital markets, sales organisations and other institutions. It may create new employment opportunities and thereby raise total wages.[29]

On the debit side, it has been suggested that foreign investment leads to:

the importation of unsuitable technology and unsuitable products, the extension of oligopolistic practices such as unnecessary product differentiations, heavy advertising, or excessive profit making, and the worsening of income distribution by a self-perpetuating process which simultaneously reinforces high income *elites* and provides them with expensive consumers goods.[30]

Many of the critics of private foreign investment feel that, with the elimination of some of the above limitations, it could assist the economic development of poor countries. Their policy recommendations include stringent control over foreign investments, hard bargaining, shopping around for better deals and the exchange of information and coordinated action by the developing countries.[31] At the other extreme there are some who believe that foreign investment is inevitably an instrument of neo-imperialist exploitation.

These opinions mainly reflect the economic and political ideology of the analyst; Lall rightly emphasises that there cannot be a 'value free' or 'truly objective' assessment of foreign investment. Furthermore, the experience of the developing countries has been varied and generalisations can be misleading.

A few basic premises may, however, be in order. Paul Chambers, a prominent British industrialist, has clearly indicated that the economic development of the 'recipient' country can, at best, only be a secondary consideration in an investment decision:

It is no part of the duty of the Directors of any private enterprise company to use the funds of the stockholders to help the development of any underdeveloped country in such a way that the profits accruing to the shareholders are less than if the funds were used in some other way.[32]

It is for this reason that foreign private investment largely flows to the richer countries, only about a third of the total private foreign investments of the richer countries going to the poorer countries.[33] Of the investment that does go to the developing countries the bulk of it goes to the relatively more developed countries or to those which possess exploitable raw materials rather than to the least developed countries.[34] There has been a significant increase in total foreign private investment in recent years (Table 19).

The considerable increase in direct private investment from about $3.5 billion in 1970 to over $6.6 billion in 1973 reflects the growing

Table 19. Total net private capital flows from DAC countries to developing countries (in million US $)

	1963	1970	1973
1. Direct investment		3,529	6,655
2. Portfolio investment and other long-term lending		1,200	3,219
3. Net changes in guaranteed private export credits outstanding		2,142	1,199
Total	2,557	6,871	11,072

Source: OECD, *Development Cooperation Review, 1974*, Table IX-1, and Appendix Table 7, pp. 142, 205.

fears in the richer countries of shortages of raw materials. A substantial part of this increased investment went into securing oil supplies. Another important factor was the transfer of industries, particularly components, to the developing countries; this was largely due to the increasing cost of labour in the developed countries. While such a transfer of industries might create some new employment opportunities in the developing countries, much of the fruits of this cheap labour accrue to foreign shareholders in the form of monopoly rents and profits for the package of capital, enterprise management and technical know-how.[35]

In recent years the developing countries have increasingly asserted their sovereignty over their natural resources, have demanded more local participation, and have been increasingly reserving particular sectors of the economy, such as banking, insurance, transport, public utilities and natural resources for domestic operators.[36] Most oil producing countries have either nationalised or greatly increased state participation in the production and distribution of oil; Iraq and Libya have nationalised their oil industries whilst state participation has greatly increased in Saudi Arabia, Kuwait, Abu Dhabi and Nigeria. Some other countries have nationalised mining industries and public utilities. Some examples are copper and public utilities in Peru, phosphates in Togo, diamonds in Zaire and transport in Bolivia.[37] When foreign investment is allowed, there is greater insistence by local governments that foreign companies enter into joint enterprises, often as minority partners. There has been a tightening of restrictions on remittance of profits and attempts are being made to control and regulate the manipulation of transfer prices for transactions between the parent company and its subsidiaries. For example, in a recent attempt to check the over-invoicing of imports the Bank of Tanzania employed the Swiss General Superintendence Company to inspect shipments of goods to Tanzania in order to check that qualities, quantities and prices were correct.[38]

Although some firms do operate successfully in partnership with governments or local private capital, on the whole they consider minority holdings to be a nuisance.[39] Western firms have a strong 'faith' in private enterprise and the 'price mechanism'. Strong left wing governments, given the increasing trend towards nationalisation of foreign enterprises, mean that foreign firms are becoming more and more reluctant to invest in developing countries. Stamp is right in suggesting that 'in real, and perhaps even in money terms, foreign private investment may tend to decline in the future'.[40] To what extent this tendency will be offset by the OPEC countries and some of the industrially more advanced developing countries establishing joint ventures in other developing countries remains uncertain. In addition to providing official aid the OPEC countries are also contributing to joint investments in developing countries. Some non-OPEC developing countries are doing the same. For example, in 1974 alone Indian industry entered over eighty joint ventures in several developing countries.[41] Whether private investors from these countries will behave differently to the western firms is extremely doubtful. The optimistic should take this warning from a western industrialist seriously:

> Those who worry about the poverty of the world and feel that it is the duty of those who are relatively well-off to help those who are relatively badly-off, have to recognise that the problem cannot be solved by leaving it to private investment. Private investment leaves out the poorest and most needy countries, just as in a national framework it finds no employment for those who are stupid or otherwise economically unproductive.[42]

While the pace of resource transfer from the rich to the poorer countries, particularly in terms of 'aid', has slowed down, in recent years as a result of the increasing cost of domestic labour in the developed countries and the need for securing future supplies of scarce raw materials, foreign private capital has continued to move into certain developing countries. However, unless the developing countries assert their rights and act in concert to regulate and control the activities of the multinationals it is likely that colonial-type relationships between the poor and the rich countries will continue to prevail.

10 INEVITABILITY OF CONFRONTATION

Despite the somewhat more hopeful outcome of the Seventh Special Session of the UN General Assembly, recent international conferences and preparatory meetings and inter-government consultations under the auspices of international agencies have tended to suggest that the 'era of cooperation' between the rich and poor countries is coming to an end and the battle-lines are being sharply drawn. In the face of the oligarchic structure of international decision-making, both within and outside the UN framework, the developing countries often have been unable to safeguard their economic and trading interests. The international agencies which really matter have, because of their voting structure and the composition of staff at decision-making levels, either ignored the major issues facing the poorer countries or have put forward vague generalised schemes containing numerous safeguard clauses; this has often meant that such schemes either cannot be made operational or, if put into operation, cannot make any appreciable difference to the existing state of affairs. As a result, the developing countries have become increasingly frustrated and have now been forced to take a more militant line in international negotiations. Even in the Seventh Special Session of the UN General Assembly (September 1975), which in the end was a victory for the 'moderates' on both sides, the 'compromises' were not easy to reach. In spite of the more conciliatory line adopted by the developed countries, it seems that the risk of confrontation has only been averted and not completely eliminated. It is argued in this chapter that there is a need for a radical rethinking on both sides in relation to a 'fairer' sharing of world resources and political power at the international level if 'confrontation' is to be avoided. This would require not only major concessions from the richer countries on trade and aid issues but also a major restructuring of the international organisations and negotiating machinery in order to provide a much greater say for the poorer countries in international trade, investment and monetary arrangements.

So far, organisations such as the General Agreements on Tariffs and Trade (GATT), the World Bank and the International Monetary Fund (IMF) have been a preserve of the rich. The dominant members of the GATT have never, in practice, believed in free trade and some

of them have established restrictive tariff groupings (e.g. the EEC).
Yet the GATT still conducts its business as if the 'free play' of international forces by itself led to the optimum expansion of world trade
and the most efficient utilisation of the world's productive resources.[1]
Initially the GATT had only selected countries as members and trade
negotiations were dominated by the developed countries. Now that
most developing countries belong to the GATT, some of the developed
countries are becoming disenchanted with it and favour making greater
use of the OECD as a forum for discussing trade policies.[2]

The presidency of the World Bank is reserved for a US Government
nominee. The voting structure is based on the financial contribution
to such an extent that the richer countries control nearly two-thirds
of the votes. The US alone, with more than one-fifth of votes, exercises
effective veto power. The OPEC countries as a group control only 5
per cent of the votes. The developing countries control only 31 per
cent; however, in the World Bank nomenclature, 'other developing
countries' include Greece, Spain, Turkey and Portugal. So the
effective share of votes of the developing countries is much less.
Similarly, the developing countries are poorly represented in the
World Bank staff, particularly at senior levels. In recent years some
attempt has been made to recruit young university graduates from
developing countries. Even in this case preference is given to people
trained in foreign universities. There is a definite bias towards recruitment of technique-orientated professionals with little or no field
experience or training. Such professionals, particularly those at senior
levels who are responsible for policy decisions, have hardly any experience of living, working or policymaking in a developing country; as a
result they fail to appreciate the importance of non-quantifiable,
economic and socio-political variables.[3]

Both with regard to the voting rights and staffing much the same is
true of the IMF. In practice, the developing countries have little control
over the workings of the IMF as well. Voting rights at the IMF are
allocated in such a way that the rich countries have two-thirds of the
votes. The USA and the EEC together have 38 per cent of the votes.[4]
Since a binding vote requires a majority of 85 per cent, they can veto
any proposal. Therefore, whilst the developing countries as a group
can be effective in blocking a proposal they cannot successfully initiate
a proposal unless it has the backing of the richer countries. Most major
decisions regarding world monetary problems have been taken without
consulting the developing countries even though their vital interests
have been involved; as a result, they have suffered considerable losses

due to currency realignments. One of the most significant decisions of late was the Smithsonian Agreement of December 1971, which was signed by the finance ministers and Central Bank governors of the world's ten richest countries, forming the 'Group of Ten'. The Group 'agreed on an interrelated set of measures designed to restore stability to international monetary arrangements and to provide for expanding international trade',[5] and decided that the 'measures will be communicated promptly to other governments'. The hope was expressed 'that all governments will cooperate through the International Monetary Fund to permit implementation of these measures in an orderly fashion', i.e. including those governments that were not a party to the agreement. The decisions were taken exclusively within the framework of the Group of Ten under the Chairmanship of J. B. Connally, the then Secretary of the US Treasury, even though the Group's meeting was attended by the Managing Director of the IMF.

It was only after increasing pressures, as reflected in the Lima Action Programme and the negotiations within the UNCTAD framework, that the Group of Ten was enlarged to form a new Group of Twenty so as to accommodate some developing countries. To date it appears to have been an empty gesture. On the question of Special Drawing Rights (SDRs) and the 'link' the developing countries have yet to obtain any concessions. Under the present system SDRs are distributed to countries according to their quotas in the IMF. On 'sound' banking principles overdraft facilities depend on the 'creditworthiness' of the individual client. Any deviation from this principle would not be acceptable to the dominant rich countries. The 'link' scheme aims at allocating the bulk of the SDRs to the developing countries to be later used by them for purchases from the industrialised countries. Thus the 'link' would serve two purposes simultaneously: provide additional resources for the development of the poor countries while simultaneously meeting the need for reserves of the richer countries. The most significant opposition to the idea has come from the US Government.[6]

From its very inception, UNCTAD's advocacy of the Third World's cause has been disapproved of, if not resented, by the richer countries. While they see an important role for the OECD (which is exclusively a rich man's club) in the international monetary and trade negotiations, they have discouraged a similar role for UNCTAD.

Similarly, the UN General Assembly has now earned the disfavour of the richer countries,[7] particularly the US, who are increasingly concerned about the 'tyranny of the majority'. They are finding

that the institutions which in the past they successfully manipulated to their own ends are now slipping out of their control.

In this debate it must be remembered that it was through the manipulation of the UN General Assembly that many of the rich countries
succeeded until recently in depriving the Peoples' Republic of China
of its legitimate seat in the UN and the Security Council. If the in-
transigence of the Chinese over Korea and Taiwan was sufficient
justification for their being barred from UN membership then similar
sanctions should have been applied against the USSR over Czechoslovakia and Hungary as well as the USA over Vietnam and the Bay of
Pigs.[8] Such double standards have always created a sense of disenchantment with international organisations among the developing countries.[9]
With the recent trend towards increasing solidarity and militancy, this
disenchantment has been reflected in the passing of resolutions which
are clearly aimed at annoying the Western Alliance, and particularly
the USA. The suspension of the South African delegation from the UN,
and the red-carpet treatment afforded to Yasser Arafat, the leader of
the Palestine Liberation Organisation (PLO), in the UN General Assembly have to be seen in the overall context of the past high-handedness
of the richer countries in their handling of the world institutions.[10]

The hardening of attitudes has been clearly demonstrated in various
recent meetings. The UN General Assembly, in its Sixth Special
Session in May 1974, adopted a Declaration and Programme of Action
on the Establishment of a New International Economic Order. This
Programme of Action highlights the continuing anxiety of the poor
countries with regard to 'the continuing severe economic imbalance in
the relations between developed and developing countries'. The
measures called for in the Programme of Action were as follows:

'An end to all forms of foreign occupation and alien domination
and exploitation';

'A "just and equitable relationship" between prices that developing
countries receive for their raw products and the prices they must
pay for imported goods';

'Net transfer of real resources from developed to developing countries, including increases in the real price of commodities exported
by developing countries';

'Improved access to markets in developed countries through a
system of preferences for exports of developing countries and

through the elimination of tariffs and non-tariff barriers and restrictive business practices';

'Reimbursement to developing countries of customs duties and taxes imposed by importing developed countries';

'Arrangements to mitigate the effects of inflation on developing countries and to eliminate the instability of the world monetary system';

'Promotion of foreign investment in developing countries in accordance with their needs and requirements';

'Formulation of an international code of conduct regulating the activities of transnational corporations';

'Measures to promote processing of raw materials in the producer developing countries';

'An increase in essential inputs for food production, including fertilisers, from developed countries on favourable terms';

'Urgent measures to alleviate the burden of external debt'.

Many of these proposed measures are simply a reiteration of previous demands, but the resolve for joint action among the developing countries is gaining ground.

During the World Population Conference the majority of the Third World delegates, while acknowledging the importance of domestic social and institutional changes, argued that since population policies can only succeed as part of an overall economic transformation, the fundamental solution to the population problem lies in the establishment of a new economic order; a fairer distribution of world resources would assist the developing countries in accelerating the necessary changes in institutions and attitudes which favour population planning. As usual, the developed countries argued that the current high rates of population growth put enormous strains on the world's resources.[11] The immediate retort from the developing countries was 'the depletion of resources by the prosperous populations was vastly more dangerous'.[12] The draft Plan of Action which originally represented the views of the developed countries was drastically revised. The US proposals for including specific targets for future rates of population growth, life expectation, and birth rates for the whole world, as well as for specific groups of countries, were defeated.

The Food Conference gave further evidence of hardening of attitudes.
The Conference Secretariat had prepared a National and International
Program for Action which called on governments to make specific
commitments. The proposals included:

(a)   'Measures for increasing food production in developing countries within the wider framework of development';
(b)   'Policies and programmes for improving consumption patterns
in all countries, and aiming at ensuring adequate availability of food
in developing countries, particularly to vulnerable groups';
(c)   'The strengthening of world food security through measures
including inter alia a better early warning and food information
system, more effective national and international stock-holding
policies and improved arrangements for emergency relief and food-
aid';
(d)   'Specific objectives and measures in the area of international
trade and adjustment which are relevant to food problems, including measures towards stabilisation, and expansion of markets for
exports from developing countries'.

Henry Kissinger had at the very outset made it clear that the developing countries cannot have it both ways. If OPEC and other groups
want to exploit their own potential, in the spirit of UNCTAD 3, they
cannot at the same time expect the West to go on doling out free
subsistence on the Victorian workhouse principle which has governed
aid until now. [13] As a result of the deliberations in Committee I, a
resolution was put forward calling for an International Fund for
Agricultural Development. Among the final list of thirty-three co-
sponsors only three — the Netherlands, Australia and New Zealand —
were developed countries. Traditional donors, whilst agreeing to increase their contributions, stated that they were quite happy with the
existing bilateral and multilateral arrangements.[14] In Committee II,
which was handling World Food Security, the USA and the EEC
together saw to it that the proposal for an international reserve of
500,000 tons earmarked for emergencies was dropped. They were convinced that such a stock was unnecessary, and that the present system
was adequate. According to the UK delegate, this was in the interests
of the developing countries themselves.[15] After all, 'if a country
knows that it will receive food supplies come what may, then it may
well be tempted to divert some of its immediate effort away from
agriculture'.[16] As a consolation prize the developing countries were

assured that food aid would be increased to 10 million tons per annum, although most of it will continue to be administered on a bilateral basis. On the proposal for an early warning system the Socialist camp and some developing countries felt that revealing likely future short-ages might aggravate speculative tendencies. Ultimately, a compromise resolution was passed calling for the establishment of a 'voluntary' system.

An attempt to discuss the stabilisation of commodity prices in Committee III was strongly opposed by the richer countries. As usual the US delegate reiterated the virtues of free markets, although the US Government had been busy organising a rich man's consumers cartel to face up to the OPEC. Japan and the EEC supported the US hard line. The Scandinavian, Canadian and Australian delegates made some conciliatory noises but in the rich man's fraternity they are only half-brothers. The Mexican draft resolution containing demands for the control of commodity prices, rationing of foodstuffs between nations, indexing Third World import costs to their export prices, and also indexing its agricultural import costs to the price of harvested products was totally unacceptable to the US delegate. With a view to killing the draft the US delegation claimed that they had no mandate to negotiate on such issues and they they had to seek new instructions from Washington which, as expected, never arrived.[17] Few meaningful concessions on trade and stabilisation issues emerged out of the deliberations in Committee III.

The Rome Conference was not a total failure. The main positive achievements can be summarised as follows:

1. *The creation of the World Food Council.* The Council has the function of looking in an integrated manner at problems connected with food production, food aid and food security. It is also expected to see that the policies of the Conference relating to food aid and food security are implemented. It is too early to say what the future shape and status of this new body will be. From its inception it has some serious handicaps to overcome; for example, its recommendations are not mandatory; it has no control over the International Fund for Agricultural Development; and it has little say on trade and aid issues (except for food aid).

2. *The establishment of an International Fund.* The operational details as to its size, the nature of its governing board, its links with the UN, the World Food Council, and other international agencies are not yet clear. A Committee of 27 nations, 18 developing (including 9

OPEC countries) and 9 developed nations has been constituted to draw
up its charter. Since it will depend mainly on voluntary contributions
its success will largely depend on the continued interest of the richer
countries.

3. *An international undertaking for world food security.* In the
words of the outgoing Director-General of the FAO, 'The Undertaking'
is a 'modified form of at least part of the original strategy of Lord
Boyd Orr'.[18] In fact the idea of an internationally coordinated national
reserve, was initially put forward by the FAO Preparatory Commission
on World Food Proposals as early as 1947. The Rome Conference did
not achieve much on the reserves question; on US insistence it was left
to be discussed in the subsequent intergovernmental consultations. The
outcome to date provides no assurance to the poorer countries that their
emergency needs will be met; they will have to depend upon the 'gener-
osity'[19] of the richer nations. What has gone unnoticed (or at least has
not been fully appreciated) is that if several individual countries maintain national food reserves and use them for stabilisation purposes, then
grain prices will not be allowed to drop substantially from their present
levels — in the current oligopolistic world grain market the US Government can easily see to that. Thus by ensuring the perpetuation of the
present system the US Government has ensured that it can continue
transferring part of the cost of maintaining its food reserves to other
countries, essentially a legitimate objective. But by the same stroke it
can also continue to transfer part of the domestic cost of subsidising
its farmers to foreigners.

4. *An early warning system.* It is hoped that this system will monitor
short-term crop fluctuations and issue timely warnings with regard to
crop failures. In operational terms it does not represent a significant
change except that the effectiveness of the existing system may be
tightened up. The members of the FAO were previously obliged to provide the organisation with information on production, inputs and
prices. Various USDA services have been publishing crop forecasts
for most countries of the world including the communist countries,
for several years. Since membership of the early warning system is
voluntary it represents hardly any improvement on the previous system.

5. *A decision to increase food aid to 10 million tons per annum.*
This is a positive achievement, but it has to be seen in its proper perspective. Food aid was as high as 16 million tons in 1964; even in 1972 it
was 11 million tons. Most food aid will continue to be administered
bilaterally, and there are no safeguards against the use of food aid as a
political weapon.

While the developing countries failed to obtain any substantial con-
cessions from the richer countries as a result of the World Food
Conference, there was a definite psychological boost to their morale.
Kissinger had used the food conference platform in an attempt to split
the poorer countries and to line them up against the OPEC countries.
Obviously, this strategy did not work.

In the course of the Conference of Developing Countries on Raw
Materials held in Dakar in February 1975, the developing countries
gave further proof of their new militancy by adopting a declaration
which came to be known as the Dakar Declaration. This stated that
the present structure and organisation of world commodity trade
was developed by the colonial powers in the nineteenth century and
that it operates largely to the advantage of the richer countries; this
has resulted in a permanent transfer of real resources from the
developing countries because much of the benefits of improvements in
productivity in the production of primary commodities accrue to the
consumer countries.[20] There was a call for a restructuring of the world
economic system.

Subsequently, in April 1975 the initial preparatory meeting for
the International Energy Conference (Paris) collapsed because the
developed countries, under US pressure, refused to include food, raw
materials, resource transfer and world monetary arrangements within
the scope of the discussion. The preparatory meeting was reconvened
in October only when the USA agreed to include these subjects in the
discussion. In the meantime, Kissinger's strategy of creating a united
front of the richer countries through an anti-OPEC consumers' cartel
(the eighteen-nation International Energy Agency) was not making
much progress. It was against this background that the Seventh Special
Session of the UN met in New York in September 1975. Kissinger's
speech, delivered in his absence, laid down several new proposals,[21]
some of which were subsequently withdrawn. At one time the 'Group
of 77', as the poorer countries are nicknamed, met to consider walking
out of the Conference. The day was saved by the last-minute efforts of
the EEC countries who gave an assurance to the developing countries
that they would each aim at a target of giving 0.7 per cent of GNP as
aid by the end of the decade. The USA and Japan reserved their positions on the EEC initiative. In the course of this debate the US attitude
on several other issues was not very encouraging. They bitterly opposed
the provision for the establishment of a link between special drawing
rights and development assistance, although they eventually backed
down. Above all, the US did not agree to use the term 'new economic

order'.

As in the case of the World Food Conference, Kissinger was once again aiming at dividing the Third World. The essence of his message was: '. . . it is ironic also that the most devastating blow to economic development in this decade came not from "imperialist rapacity" but from an arbitrary, monopolistic price increase by the cartel of oil exporters.'[22]

The 'concessions' offered by him were intended to 'buy' time until, 'hopefully', there is a crack in the solidarity of the poorer countries. In his own priorities a 'constructive dialogue' between the richer and poorer countries comes well down the list; this was obvious from his absence from New York on the eve of the Special Session. Many of his 'concessions', if implemented, would by-pass the established UN system. A political settlement in the Middle East will, at least in his calculations, remove the need for Arab solidarity. Similarly, a grain-oil deal with the USSR will reduce US dependence on Arab oil. Furthermore, North Sea and Alaskan oil will further strengthen the western alliance against the OPEC. Given time the additional resources directed towards utilising alternative sources of energy will probably bear fruit. Until then, the best strategy for the richer countries is to keep the developing countries talking, by giving them 'promises', many of which cannot be easily translated into practice.

As has been clearly demonstrated in the Seventh Special Session of the UN the main hope for future international cooperation must lie with the richer countries of Western Europe. Ideologically Japan is a mirror image of the USA and looks to it for inspiration. In terms of economic and military involvement it is too dependent on the USA to be able to take an independent line, even though its interests frequently do not coincide with those of the USA. However, most Western European countries broadly stand between the 'totalitarian' communist countries on the one hand and the monopoly capitalism of the USA and the Japanese on the other. While the USA can plausibly think of being self-reliant in raw materials, the other rich countries are heavily dependent upon the developing countries for their raw materials.[23] Any confrontation between the rich and poor countries would hit the Western European countries hard, and it would be unrealistic for them to go on hoping for a 'split' in the Third World camp.

What is often forgotten is that the desperation resulting from utter frustration may well drive the poorer countries still closer together, with no country coming out better off, least of all the Western

European countries and Japan. The US 'threats' of military action
cannot always be discounted. They certainly have the power to mount
an attack, but sustaining a prolonged wide-ranging military action
would involve a price which many Americans may not be prepared
to pay.[24] Poverty has an uncanny resilience; if this lesson has not yet
dawned on the richer countries, even after the wars in Vietnam and
Cambodia, then there is not much hope for the future of the world.

If the richer countries do not come up with some major concessions
in the next few years, then some form of confrontation with the
poorer countries is inevitable. In the course of international negotiations as well as in any future confrontation increased solidarity among
the developing countries is a precondition for a favourable outcome.
The developed countries are well aware of this and are likely to apply
subtle diplomatic pressures and persuasions in order to divide the
developing countries. It will require a great deal of ingenuity on the
part of the leaders of the developing countries to maintain Third
World unity.

The concessions that the developing countries require have been
highlighted in the Plan of Action for the New International Economic
Order. Since the international agencies are largely dominated by the
rich countries and have not always been 'neutral' between the rich and
the poor, the developing countries must demand an increasing share of
the political power of the international organisations. In practical
terms, this means that many more key posts in the international
agencies must go to nationals of the developing countries.[25] If there is
a shortage of candidates from some developing nations, the UN should
be asked to run crash programmes to train possible candidates to a
suitable standard. A greater population weightage must be given to
regions in the recruitment to senior professional posts. The positions of
heads of the World Bank and the IMF must cease to be the preserve of the
rich and these organisations should be more fully integrated into the
UN system. In any major trade negotiations, UNCTAD must be
accorded the same status as GATT.[26] The recent suggestion of merging
GATT and UNCTAD into an International Trade Organisation (ITO)
is well worth implementing.[27] Above all a permanent Secretariat of
the Third World (as a countervailing force to the OECD) must be
involved in all trade and aid negotiations.

Ultimately, the outcome of the confrontation will depend largely
on how successful the developing countries are in setting their own
house in order, both individually and collectively. So long as mass
misery in the form of hunger, malnutrition and periodic famine,

persists over large areas within any country, that country will be forced
by circumstances to go to the richer countries with a 'begging bowl'.
To talk of confrontation in such a situation will be unrealistic. A
radical 'sharing of poverty' within a country can significantly reduce
the extent of hunger and malnutrition and the worst effects of droughts
and other natural disasters. Of course, some countries will need some
initial support. This can in principle be looked after by what Gamani
Corea, the Director-General of the UNCTAD, calls the 'collective self-
reliance of the developing countries',[28] i.e. greater cooperation with
each other, more exchanges amongst each other and the coordination
of their policies; whether in the field of capital, science, education
or technology there is little (except for advanced space technology)
in which the developing countries as a group cannot, by now, match
the developed countries. Whilst the developing countries may be far
behind with regard to very sophisticated technology, they can easily
do without it. The 'inferiority complex' of the poor countries is
partly the outcome of their colonial past and partly due to the perpetuation of some myths, regarding race, religion and culture. The sooner
they can cast off this complex, the easier it will be for both the rich
and the poorer countries to respect each other. Above all, the most
urgent need for the developing countries is to develop a sense of
mutual self-respect and trust for each other. This has often been lacking.
For instance, an Asian field expert — the Chinese being the only
exception — in Africa exhibits the same colonial traits as the colonial
masters did in the past. The aid missions from one developing country
to another behave no less arrogantly than those from the richer countries. So long as such complexes persist the richer countries will not fail
to take advantage of the resultant weaknesses.

CONCLUSION

In summing up, it must be emphasised that the high incidence of world hunger and malnutrition is largely caused by the unequal distribution of income, wealth and political power between rich and poor, both within and between countries. While it cannot be denied that rapid population growth, particularly in the densely populated countries, constitutes a major obstacle in the path of rapid economic development and greater distributive justice, population programmes often remain ineffective unless they are undertaken as part of an overall socioeconomic trans-formation involving a major redistribution of wealth and power both within and between countries.

All the evidence suggests that even at the current level of technical knowledge the potential exists for feeding much greater numbers of people. However, with present political, economic and social attitudes and institutions, it is doubtful whether the men and materials will be forthcoming in sufficient degree to translate this potential into reality. It is also doubtful whether the fruits of science and technology will be shared more equitably between people. The 'market orientated' materialistic approach to development planning coupled with the current power structure within many developing countries will prevent any meaningful reforms that could guarantee employment and the basic minimum levels of living to the poor. The so-called democratic institutions, rural and urban, will continue to be dominated by the 'elite' unless there is increasingly active participation on the part of the poor and underprivileged. This will require politicising of the masses.

All this can be achieved only through the radical reform of institu-tions and thinking. Whether such a change will require a violent upheaval or not will depend largely upon how soon members of the 'elite' are prepared to accept the change as part of their 'enlightened self-interest', and identify themselves with the masses. Obviously such identification with the masses presupposes a radical change in the elitist bias in the educational systems which make the privileged groups 'alien' to the masses even in their own countries.

On the international level the richer countries have resisted a more equitable distribution of world opportunities and resources as well as political power in much the same way as the rich have within national boundaries. A trickle of aid and trade concessions have been passed on to the developing countries either as a demonstration of the 'charitable' instincts of the rich or as a 'carrot' for toeing the ideological and political line. The international organisations, dominated and manipulated by the richer countries, have, by and large, advocated policies and programmes which do not materially alter the *status quo*. The agencies which do advocate a greater equity in the distribution of economic and political power are immediately suspect in the eyes of the richer countries. Recent experience suggests that only through increased solidarity can the developing countries obtain any meaningful concessions from the developed countries. The military might of the developed countries will continue to be a threat to any united stand by the developing countries to improve their bargaining position. In such an eventuality, taking a clue from Gandhi's message to the poor to wage a non-violent, non-cooperation struggle against the rich (within a country), it may be worthwhile considering the use on a global basis of a collective boycott by the poorer countries of trade and aid from the richer countries. In any case, closer coordination between the developing countries themselves in trade, finance, industrialisation and technical aid programmes can reduce their dependence on the developed countries.

Any scheme of major 'confrontation', however, will necessitate the willingness and ability of the developing countries to suffer increasing deprivation in the face of retaliation from the developed countries. Much will depend on whether the leadership in the developing countries has the moral courage to ask for sacrifices from the people. If the leadership can identify itself with the masses and if the 'elite' are prepared to 'share the poverty' of the masses, then the people will respond positively. They have done so during the fights for national freedom; they will certainly do it again to overthrow the remaining vestiges of colonialism.

APPENDIX 1. ESTIMATING THE AVAILABILITY OF FOOD

It goes without saying that the accuracy of estimates of food deficits or surpluses in a country depends largely on the accuracy of estimates of the availability of food on the one hand and of food requirements on the other. The availability of food in a country or region can be assessed in one of two ways: (i) food balance sheets and (ii) household surveys.

Food balance sheets

A 'food balance sheet presents a comprehensive picture of a country's food supply during a given period, usually a year. It shows the types and quantities of food produced, imported and exported. It allows for movements in stocks and makes appropriate deductions for the amounts used for animal feed, seed, manufacture, and for the amounts wasted during distribution up to the retail level. Taking into account the population figure, it arrives at the estimated quantity and nutritive value of *per capita* supplies of food stuffs available at the retail level.'[1]

These estimates provide an indication of the general pattern of food availability in a country. Food balance sheet data also provide a basis for a comparison of the availability (which is often erroneously referred to as consumption) of food both over time and between countries. However, in making such inter-temporal and inter-country comparisons, the limitations of this approach[2] must be borne in mind, particularly with regard to the data on which the food balance sheets are constructed. For almost all the variables considered in estimating the availability of food (in terms of nutrients *per capita* per day) the current quality of statistics is far from perfect. Even with regard to estimates of gross agricultural production there is a fairly high margin of error, particularly in the developing countries. Even in the developed countries, the statistical services usually concentrate mainly on the collection and verification of production statistics for the principal grain crops; for minor crops or minor producing areas (i.e. kitchen garden) little attempt is made to collect reliable information since the costs of collection are usually thought to exceed the value of the information. In most developing countries, because of the lack of effective statistical organisation, inadequate means of transport and communications, incomplete mapping of the country, as well as predominantly illiterate populations, even the grain statistics do not cover the entire country.

In many countries, particularly in Africa, information on subsistence and semi-subsistence farms is rather limited. Because of communal (or tribal) land holdings, the absence of legal evidence of ownership of land and shifting cultivation, estimation of the area tilled each year is very difficult. Estimating the yield of an individual grain in a mixed cropping system is not always easy. Cropping patterns often vary from region to region and from year to year. Since root crops, such as sweet potatoes, yams, cassava, etc., are continuously harvested or gathered as often as needed, it is difficult to apply normal techniques of estimating production[3] because part of the area is often left unharvested, and also because yields from the harvested area vary a great deal according to the age of the plant.[4] Statistics on vegetables are not available for many countries and statistical coverage differs considerably between countries. The estimates published in the FAO Production Year Book refer to crops grown in fields and market gardens mainly for sale. Crops cultivated in kitchen gardens etc. for family consumption are excluded. Production from family and other small gardens constitute quite a large proportion of the total production of vegetables in many countries. For example, in Austria the figure is around 50 per cent, in West Germany about 45 per cent, while in Italy it is only 8 per cent.[5] The quality of statistics on fruit production[6] may be even poorer than those for vegetables. Generally reported production data for fruits relate to plantation crops or orchard crops grown mainly for sale. Data on production from scattered trees or wild plants are not collected. Even in the case of bananas, which is a major export crop for some countries, comparability of production data between countries is difficult because some countries report production in terms of bunches, which generally means that the stalk is included in the weight.[7] The accuracy of statistics relating to acreage under bananas is far from satisfactory. In many countries bananas are mainly cultivated intercropped with other crops so that a standard per hectare yield estimate cannot be used indiscriminately. Production estimates for livestock products and poultry meat are also highly unreliable. Many countries still do not take a regular livestock census; in those which do livestock kept outside agricultural holdings or on small-holdings, nomadic animals and animals below a certain age are excluded from the figures. In many countries the data for poultry (chickens, ducks and turkeys) do not represent the total number of birds. In the majority of developing countries, large-scale poultry farms are few; birds are kept on widely scattered, individually owned small farms and homes so it is difficult to estimate their total number and egg or meat production. Information on slaughtering rates, average live or carcass weights, and the proportions of reported and unreported production is still very unsatisfactory for many countries. Even milk production data is unavailable in several countries. There is no uniform practice in reporting milk production; in some countries total production consists of whole fresh milk, excluding milk sucked by young animals but including amounts fed to livestock, while in some other countries, particularly in Europe, reported milk production includes milk sucked by young animals.[8]

Thus it is often difficult to derive a sufficiently reliable estimate of gross availability of various foods, particularly of different types of meat, milk, eggs, fruit and vegetables, and especially those produced in home gardens or slaughtered in the homes, a common practice in rural areas in most developing countries.

The conversion of gross into net estimates of the availability of food encounters further problems due to the lack of reliable information necessary for estimating the allowances to be made for seed, animal feed, wastage or stock adjustment. In so far as the export and import of food, particularly grains, is mainly conducted by large private or public enterprises the statistics on foreign trade in agricultural products are usually fairly reliable, but there may still be considerable under-reporting of trade across the borders of countries having land frontiers. Reliable information on farm and commercial stocks is often non-existent in developing countries for government holdings of grain. Estimates of the quantities utilised for feed, seed, industrial purposes and wastage as well as the related technical conversion factors (e.g. flour extraction rate from wheat or conversion rate of paddy into rice) are little more than intelligent guesses. It is well known that in most developing countries a substantial part of production is processed by rural households often using rudimentary methods, and the extraction rate under such conditions varies significantly between different methods of processing. Similarly the seed rate (seed required per acre of land being planted) depends on methods of tilling, the type of soil and various other topographical and ecological factors on which information is sparse. This is also true for food (e.g. grains) used as animal feed especially when livestock or birds are kept on a small scale, often as part of the family. In the absence of adequate storage facilities, losses in storage are often higher in the case of rural households than in commercial warehouses. In the absence of sufficient cold storage facilities and quick transport the rate of spoilage of fruits, vegetables, livestock products and fish is very high, particularly in tropical countries. Again information on the extent of such losses is poor.

The estimation of nutritional content is also open to serious margins of error. Most food composition tables, which provide information on the nutritional content of foods, are based on limited local information and are not always representative of the whole country, especially in larger countries, since significant ecological and cultural differences lead to differences in food preparation. Differences in conditions of storage, temperature and maturity often alter the nutritive contents of foods such as fruits, vegetables and livestock products. The situation is still worse where national figures on food composition are not available and international data have to be used for calculating the nutritional value of a diet.[9] The data on which food balance sheets are based refer to the availability of food at the retail level and not the amount of food actually consumed by the population. The latter is often lower because of the losses of food and nutrients in the course of food preparation and cooking, as well as plate-waste and the quantities fed to domestic animals or pets. Further error is introduced into the estimated net availability of food for human consumption by the uncertainty about population totals themselves. For a number of countries there is no proper statistical basis for population figures as yet.[10] Even in those countries where regular censuses or population surveys are taken, the estimation of population for post-census years may sometimes introduce appreciable error.

Thus the resulting figures for net *per capita* food availability in any country should not be taken as anything more than an approximate picture of the food situation. Food balance sheet data, being very aggregative in nature, do not give any indication of the differences in food consumption levels between different socioeconomic groups or regions, nor do they give any information on seasonal variations, even at the national level.

Household surveys

Any assessment of the nutritional deficiencies of the most vulnerable sections of the population, of 'hungry' seasons and of regional variations must be based upon food consumption surveys.[11] These surveys can be conducted for the whole population either by complete enumeration or using randomly selected samples of households. In view of the time and costs involved the latter is more common. In order to obtain a fair representation of the various strata of society, a stratified random sample is often taken. Information on family income and other socioeconomic characteristics of the household, total expenditure and expenditures on various items of food consumption are collected by one of the following three methods:

(1)   interviewing with a 'food recall list';
(2)   food accounts;
(3)   actual measurement of food.

With the first method the investigator interviews the householder and obtains information on quantities consumed and expenditure on various items of food during the reporting period, often the week preceding the interview. Sometimes the investigator supplies the householder with a list of likely items of consumption (called a 'food recall list') to help him 'recall' his or her expenditure. With the food accounts method the householder agrees to keep a detailed account of both quantities consumed and actual expenditure on various items purchased and the imputed values of home-produced food and items otherwise procured, as well as a detailed inventory of such items at the beginning and end of the period under investigation. With the third type of household survey the investigator stays with a family or visits it several times a day and weighs various food stuffs before they are cooked or eaten. Sometimes food is weighed only at the beginning or at the end of the period under investigation.

Each of the three techniques has serious limitations. The interview method is the simplest and least expensive and is perhaps the most appropriate in countries with predominantly illiterate populations. As this method involves only one or two visits by the investigator, the risk of causing annoyance to the respondent is rather low and the chances of a response relatively high. Since the interviewer records the *ex-post* quantities of expenditures on food his presence does not usually influence or distort the pattern of food consumption of the household. It is possible, however, that a householder of moderate means will try to avoid revealing the real financial state of his family and will therefore give an exaggerated account of the quantities of food, particularly 'status' foods, consumed. A more common problem, of course, is memory lapses on the part of the householder who may not be able to recollect the precise quantities and expenditure on

various items. This risk is much greater in the case of families with low
levels of literacy or families which do not keep regular records of
purchases etc.

With the food accounting technique the respondent is expected to
record the quantities of and expenditures on foods immediately after
purchase. Since this is rather inconvenient there is a high rate of non-
response or alternatively the respondents complete the entire form
at the end of the period largely by memory. Thus the risk of memory
lapses is not completely eliminated. There is also a risk of 'prestige'
bias. Since the technique requires a certain level of education on the
part of the householder it is not always appropriate for those developing countries where a high percentage of the population is illiterate.

The technique which involves the actual measurement of food
purchases by the investigator is the most reliable, but, at the same
time, the most expensive. Therefore, the sample is usually kept very
small and is used mainly for nutritional studies termed *diet surveys*.
Since the respondents are conscious of being constantly under
observation there is a high risk of their temporarily changing the
pattern of food consumption by including more 'prestige' foods for
the period under investigation. Obviously, the accuracy of the data
obtained by household surveys depends largely on the cooperation of
the respondents which in turn depends on the skill of the investigator
in gaining the confidence of the householder. Such a degree of skill
is rather scarce in most developing countries.

Increasing emphasis is being placed by both national and international agencies on the collection and analysis of household surveys.
So far such surveys have only been conducted in a few countries.
Since many of these surveys have been limited to urban areas or to
special population groups they are not representative of the country
as a whole. Often the sample selected is too small and the period
of enumeration too short to take account of seasonal variations in
food consumption which may be of special significance for solving
the problem of hunger and malnutrition among landless labour
and very small farmers, because of the seasonal nature of their
employment. Generalisations based on such short-term surveys may not
be valid for longer periods, especially in rural areas with their greater
dependence on locally or home-produced food. This limitation can
be corrected by conducting surveys during the different seasons. With
a view to keeping the cost of surveys low and to reduce the risk of
annoyance to the respondents under observation, sometimes the total
period of a survey is split into a number of smaller periods and in each

period only a sub-sample is surveyed.

One of the most serious limitations of most available food consumption surveys is that they provide an estimate of the *average* level and pattern of family food consumption ignoring the distribution of food among the various members of the family. They are inappropriate, therefore, for estimating hunger and malnutrition among women and children.

If sufficiently reliable and representative (of the national level and pattern of food consumption) data were made available by food consumption surveys, which is certainly not the case in most developing countries, they could serve as a cross-check for the food balance sheet data. For the present, the data from both sources have high margins of error and, as such, they should only be used for policy formulation and/or international comparisons of food consumption with a great deal of caution.

APPENDIX 2. ENERGY AND PROTEIN REQUIREMENTS

To assess the adequacy of an average diet for a country or population group the general practice is to compare the *per capita* availability of food against a scale of requirements recommended by nutrition experts. These requirements are usually expressed in terms of energy (calories[1]), proteins, fats and vitamins. Several groups of experts[2] under the auspices of the FAO and the World Health Organisation (WHO) have deliberated on energy and protein requirements as well as on other nutritional elements. The *energy requirement* is defined by the FAO/WHO Joint Ad Hoc Expert Committee (1971) as 'the energy intake that is considered adequate to meet the energy needs of the average healthy person in a specified age/sex category'.[3] Similarly, the safe level of protein intake is 'the amount of protein considered necessary to meet the physiological needs and maintain the health of *nearly all* persons in a specified group'.[4]

The energy requirement is conventionally estimated on the basis of an arbitrarily defined *reference man* who is between 20 and 39 years of age, weighs 65 kg., enjoys good health and is fit for active work. Similarly a reference woman belongs to the same age group, is healthy and fit for active work. Both *reference* man and woman are assumed to be engaged for 8 hours a day in a moderately active occupation. When not working they are supposed to spend 4-6 hours sitting or moving around in only very light activity, 2 hours in walking, active recreation or housework and the remaining 8 hours in bed.[5]

According to the nutrition experts the energy requirement depends largely on four interdependent variables: (1) physical activity,[6] (2) body size and composition, (3) age and (4) climate and other ecological factors. Therefore adjustments in the energy requirement are made for differences in these variables. Additional energy is needed for growth in childhood and adolescence as well as among women during pregnancy and lactation. Ethnic origin or climatic variables (except in the case of extreme and unusual environments and that too probably because of differences in the activity rates) do not directly affect the energy requirement. The Committee felt that 'individuals of the same size living in the same environment and with the same mode of life have a similar energy requirement whatever their ethnic origin'.[7] They also considered that the 'energy expended in standard tasks is the same in different climates, except possibly in extreme and unusual environments'.[8]

The energy requirement varies significantly between activities. For instance, the average energy requirement for a reference man engaged in light activity is around 2,700 calories per day, whereas for exceptionally active work it can be as high as 4,000 calories. Similarly, the energy requirement varies with body weight. For an average male in light activity with a body weight of 50 kg. the per day energy requirement is only 2,100 calories; this goes up to 3,360 calories for someone with a body weight of 80 kg. The age of the person concerned may also have some effect on the energy requirement. With children the energy requirement per unit of body weight decreases with age until adulthood is reached. For male children the Committee estimated the energy requirement at 112 calories per kg. of body weight before the child is one year old; up to 4 years it is around 100, after which it declines fairly rapidly, reaching 50 calories by the age of 17 years. The scale is similar for female children. The Committee felt that the average energy requirement of men and women between 20 and 39 years of age remains almost unchanged, while there is some decline between the ages of 40 and 59 years. A faster decline in the energy requirement sets in from the age of about 60.[9]

For obvious reasons these recommendations are only broad approximations. While there is some information on the age and sex structure as well as broad occupational structure in many countries, little is known about the distribution of body weight in population groups or the way people distribute their time between various activities. Even in the same occupational groups within a country individual differences in activity rates are very common. This kind of information is lacking even in the developed countries.[10] It is not yet certain whether the four major variables mentioned earlier are the only main variables determining energy requirements. Widdowson in her study of the variations in calorie intake of children found that even after allowing for sex, age, body weight, height and surface area, large unexplained residuals were left. She concluded that 'much more research lies ahead before we can begin to understand why one person can live on half the calories of another and yet remain a perfectly efficient physical machine'.[11] Other research workers have come to similar conclusions.

The estimation of protein requirement has proved to be more difficult and controversial. Nutrition experts use two methods of estimating nitrogen requirements. In the first method, called the factorial method, the protein requirement is derived from the estimate of loss of nitrogen through urine, faeces, sweat, etc. in a situation when the diet does not contain any protein. In the case of the adult man, the average nitrogen loss is estimated at 54 mg. per kg. of body weight.[12] There is some additional loss of nitrogen due to minor infections and other sources of stress in daily life. To compensate for such losses the Joint FAO/WHO Expert Group on Protein Requirement recommended an addition of 10 per cent to the above bringing the total to 59 mg. of N per kg. of body weight. A further addition of 20 per cent was made to arrive at the *safe level*. An estimation of requirement for children must include additional nitrogen for the deposition of new tissues which is reflected in gains in weight as well as for the nitrogen concentration in the body, which is often termed maturation.[13] For instance obligatory losses for a child at one year are estimated at roughly 104 mg. per kg. of body weight to which another 16 mg. is added for growth. This brings the total requirement to around 120 mg. per kg. of body weight. Gradually this declines to about 80 mg. at the age of 9. This decline continues until adulthood when it stabilises in the case of men at around 54 mg. and in women at around 49 mg. Since pregnant women have to meet the nitrogen requirement of the foetus and foetal membranes, etc. their requirement of nitrogen per kg. of body weight is much higher and generally varies with the size of the baby. Similarly, additional protein is needed by lactating women.

In the second method of estimating protein requirements, several levels of protein are fed to a subject and the results are analysed to see whether differing doses of protein intake maintain N equilibrium in the subject under study. It has been generally found that the amount of nitrogen required per unit of body weight to maintain N equilibrium is not substantially different in men and women.[14] It is estimated that the average N intake required to maintain balance, allowing 5 mg. of N per kg. for cutaneous and miscellaneous losses, is 77 mg. of N per kg. per day when the nitrogen is derived from milk, egg, casein or mixed diets containing animal protein.[15] In the case of cereals or vegetable diets the nitrogen requirement rises to 93 mg. per kg. of body weight.

In recommending a scale of protein requirements[16] the FAO/WHO Committee started by estimating the factorial values and then increased them by 30 per cent; this was because even with excellent protein sources such as milk or eggs[17] larger amounts of nitrogen are needed to secure N equilibrium and to maintain growth than those indicated by the factorial method. The resulting estimate is considered the average physiological requirement. To allow for individual variations the Committee increased the average requirement by a further 30 per cent. This was thought to represent a *safe level* which would be adequate to meet the protein requirement of all but 2.5 per cent of the population. The *safe level* of protein requirement for a child of one year is around 1.27 gr. protein per kg. of body weight per day. This comes down to only 0.85 gr. per kg. per day at nine years. The requirement for an adult male works out at 0.57 gr. per kg. per day and for an adult female at 0.52 gr. per kg. per day. Thus for the *reference* man the protein requirement (in terms of high quality protein) would be only about 37 gr. per day. If the diet consists of inferior quality proteins[18] the recommended intake of protein has to be higher.[19] These recommendations are much lower than the previous set of recommendations[20] which were seriously challenged by many scholars.[21]

   The interrelationship between calories and protein has been increasingly stressed in recent years. It is now generally agreed that when the diet is inadequate in calories the protein in the diet is partly diverted from its primary function to the provision of energy.[22] In experiments on nitrogen balance in adults it has been shown that when the total daily calorie intake is around 900, protein intake in excess of 10 grams is not retained by the body, and is therefore wasted. When the calorie intake is increased to 1,600, protein retention increases but there is still some loss, but this decreases progressively with increases in calorie intake. It is only when the calorie intake is adequate and above the critical limit that the body can fully utilise the protein consumed. Therefore, in any assessment of the incidence of protein deficiency in a country, one cannot consider protein intake in isolation; account must be taken of calorie intake.[23] As the Joint FAO/WHO Committee rightly stresses, 'the adequacy of energy intakes must receive first consideration, so that any additional protein supplied to meet the estimated protein needs will be efficiently utilized for this purpose'.[24]

   In view of the importance of the calorie-protein interaction many scholars have been trying to estimate the optimum protein/energy ratio. Some nutritionists suggest that in national planning the aim should be to attain a level of food supply in which at least 10 per cent of the energy is provided by protein foods.[25]

   Among other nutrients, the FAO Committee on Calcium Requirement (1962) recommended a calcium intake of between 400 and 500 mg. per day for adults, with higher figures for children and pregnant and lactating women.[26] Though there is no unanimity of views on fat requirements, it is suggested that if 20 per cent of the calories are provided by fats the diet should be adequate in this regard.

So far estimated food requirements for different regions and populations have been largely rough approximations. The Joint FAO/WHO Committee clearly stated that 'while it can offer guidelines for the estimation of target *per caput* energy intakes' the data available to the Committee did not 'permit it to translate the prediction of individual protein requirements into meaningful guidelines for population feeding'.[27] There was even less information on carbohydrates, fat, alcohol, etc. It stressed that 'while there is a clearly definable minimum intake of protein that is consistent with health, the precise limits over which the proportions of energy from carbohydrate, fat, and alcohol may vary without harm to health are very poorly defined'.[28]

NOTES

INTRODUCTION

1.   McNamara, R. (1973), *One Hundred Countries, Two Billion People: The Dimensions of Development*, pp. 106-7.
2.   Lord Boyd Orr's proposals for a World Food Board in 1946. For a detailed discussion of the problem see Sinha, R. P. (1976), 'World Food Security', *Journal of Agricultural Economics*, vol. XXVII, no. 1, Jan.
3.   Boerma, A. H. (1975), 'The Thirty Years War Against World Hunger', Inaugural Lecture of the Boyd Orr Memorial Trust (mimeo.), p. 13.
4.   McNamara, Robert S. (1971), *Address to the Board of Governors*, p. 28.

CHAPTER 1

1.   It is customary to define 'hunger' as a situation in which there is an inadequate quantity of food (energy) available while malnutrition refers to an unbalanced diet. According to the current thinking on nutrition it is felt that if the energy requirement is met mainly by cereals, protein malnutrition will not arise. However, if the energy requirement is met largely by starchy roots then the diet may still be deficient in proteins (see Gopalan, C. (1968), 'Kwashiorkor and Marasmus: Evolution and Distinguishing Features' in McCance, R. A. and Widdowson, E. M. (eds.), *Calorie Deficiencies and Protein Deficiencies*; Miller, D. S. and Payne, P. R. (1969), 'Assessment of Protein Requirements by Nitrogen Balance', *Proceedings, Nutrition Society*, vol. 28, no. 2; Sukhatme, P. V. (1969), 'The Protein Gap – Its Size and Nature', *Proceedings Nutrition Society of India*, no. 8; Joy, L. (1973), 'Food and Nutrition Planning', *Journal of Agricultural Economics*, vol. XXIV, no. 1).
2.   This view is now being widely accepted. See for instance Sukhatme (1969), *op. cit.*, p. 5; and Joy (1973), *op. cit.*, p. 182.
3.   These rates must be used with caution. Even with the improvements that are being introduced in the collection of agricultural and population statistics in the developing countries there is still a wide margin of error. For many developing countries there is a complete absence of 'Time series of population and food statistics'. Population censuses in many African countries have only been undertaken fairly recently. Under the circumstances, no firm conclusions as to either past or future trends can be drawn.
4.   Some of this high rate of increase in agricultural output between 1952 and 1962 may well be *statistical*, resulting partly from improved methods of crop estimation and partly from extended geographical coverage. Besides, the 1950s were a period of post-war recovery in several parts of Asia and Europe. In view of this it is not possible to assert that *per capita* availability of food has in fact declined in subsequent periods.
5.   A more recent UN Publication estimates the rates of population growth in less developed areas at only 2.3 per cent between 1960 and 1970. (UN (1975), *Selected World Demographic Indicators by Countries, 1950-2000*, prepared by the Population Division, Department of Economic and Social Affairs (mimeo.).)

6.   For an interesting account of these problems and the efforts made to ameliorate the situation see Moraes, D. (1974), *A Matter of People*.

7.   For a review of the controversy see Sinha, R. P. (1969), 'Unresolved Issues in Japan's Early Economic Development', *Scottish Journal of Political Economy*, vol. XVI, no. 2; see also Nakamura, James I. (1968), *Agricultural Production and the Economic Development of Japan, 1873-1922*; Ohkawa, K. and Rosovsky, H. (1960), 'The Role of Agriculture in Modern Japanese Economic Development', *Economic Development and Cultural Change*, vol. 9, no. 1, Part II, October.

8.   Increases in grain imports are not *always* the result of population growth outstripping food supply, as can be seen from a simple example: if it is assumed that a country's population and food supply are increasing by 2.5 per cent each, and its *per capita* income by 2 per cent, then the demand for food will approximately increase (assuming an income elasticity of 0.8, which is not uncommon for developing countries) by 2.5 + (2 x 0.8) = 4.1 per cent. Therefore, imports will have to rise by just over 1 per cent if this demand is to be met at current prices.

9.   In the case of Japan annual net imports constituted 39 per cent of the total supply of cereals between 1966 and 1970. Corresponding figures were for the UK 38 per cent, Italy 30 per cent, West Germany 23 per cent, and the Netherlands 66 per cent. Corresponding figures for India and China were 6 and 2 per cent respectively.

10.   Japan, though the largest net importer of cereals, also paid its farmers to reduce the acreage under rice because of a growing surplus of rice.

11.   'Requirement' can broadly be taken to mean adequate for health and efficiency. For the method of calculation see Appendix 2.

12.   See Appendix 2.

13.   United States Department of Agriculture (henceforth USDA) (1974), *The World Food Situation and Prospects to 1985*, p. 51. According to this estimate 0.15 kg. of cereal can provide 500 calories.

14.   *Ibid.*, p. 51.

15.   *Ibid.*, p. 48.

16.   *Ibid.*, p. 50, Table 22. However, a survey conducted by the Public Health Service in the USA in 1969 indicated that between 10 and 15 million people were constantly and chronically hungry and had nutritional levels as low as those in developing countries. (See Ehrlich, Paul R. and Ehrlich, Anne H. (1972), *Population Resources Environment: Issues in Human Ecology*, p. 94.)

17.   The predominance of foods of animal origin in their diets has meant that the richer countries use up much more energy to produce food than the developing countries. It has been estimated that the developing countries are able to produce from 5 to 50 calories for each calorie they invest through their agricultural systems. The richer countries invest 10 calories to get one in return. (See UNICEF (1975), *Priorities in Child Nutrition in Developing Countries*, vol. V. Annex, p. 11 (mimeo).)

18.   FAO/WHO (1973), *Energy and Protein Requirements: Report of a Joint FAO/WHO Ad Hoc Expert Committee*, p. 19.

19.   Jean Mayer (1974) has argued that: 'If Americans would decrease the meat they eat by 10 per cent, it would release enough grain to feed 60 million people.' (*Newsweek*, 11 Nov. 1974.)

20.   Brown, Lester R. and Eckholm, Erik P. (1974), 'Food and Hunger: The Balance Sheet', *Challenge*, Sept.-Oct.

21.   McNamara, Robert S. (1970), *Address to the Board of Governors*, p. 23.

22.   For some of the major limitations of food statistics see Appendix 1.

23.   UN World Food Conference (1974), *Assessment of the World Food*

Situation (henceforth *Assessment*), p. 66 (mimeo.).

24.   National Institute of Nutrition, *Diet Atlas of India* (1971), Table XVI. Another recent nutrition survey suggests that, on average, only 58 per cent of the calorie needs of pregnant and lactating women between the ages of 15 and 19 years are met. In higher age groups the percentage varies between 73 and 84 per cent. Similarly, the protein intake in the cases of mothers between 15 and 19 years of age meets only 78 per cent of the requirement. In the higher age groups, it is around 90 per cent. (See US AID (1975), *The Tamil Nadu Nutrition Study*, vol. 1, Tables 11 and 12, pp. 81-2 (mimeo).)

25.   It must, however, be pointed out that the prevalence of breast feeding itself may lead to inadequate nutrition. In the Tamil Nadu nutrition study it was found that for weaned children in the 7 to 18 months age group 65 per cent of calorie needs were met, while in the case of non-weaned children depending solely on breast feeding only 52 per cent of the nutritional requirements were met. (*Ibid.*, p. 92.)

26.   For instance nearly 57 per cent of the deaths of children under 5 years of age are caused by gastro-enteritis in Egypt as against only 0.7 per cent in Sweden. (See, UNICEF (1975), *op. cit.*, p. 16, Table 6.)

27.   FAO (1974), *The State of Food and Agriculture*, p. 152.

28.   National Institute of Nutrition (1971), *op. cit.*, Table XVI.

29.   Some experts feel that prolonged poor diets during the first six years when the brain development is highly sensitive to amino acids, will lead to permanent impairment of brain function. (See UNICEF, *op. cit.*, p. 17.)

30.   FAO (1975), *Population, Food Supply and Agricultural Development*, p. 17.

31.   *Ibid.*, p. 17.

32.   UNICEF (1975), *op. cit.*, p. 17.

33.   Casley, D. J., Simaika, J. B. and Sinha, R. P. (1974), 'Instability of Production and its Impact on Stock Requirements', *Monthly Bulletin of Agricultural Economics and Statistics*, vol. 23, no. 5, p. 3. An instability index is a statistical measure of fluctuations around a trend growth line. There are several ways of measuring such fluctuations. One of the simplest methods is to calculate the standard deviation (or coefficient of variation) of the annual growth rate from the trend growth rate. A similar result can be obtained by calculating the 'logarithmic variance' using the following formula:

$$\text{Log (var)} = \frac{1}{N-2} \Sigma [\log x_{t+1} - \log x_t \frac{1}{N-1} \Sigma(\log x_{t+1} - \log x_t)]^2$$

where N = number of years, x_t = index of production in year t. The instability index is the antilog of the log (var) multiplied by 100.

34.   Quoted in Dutt, R. P. (1947), *India To-Day*, pp. 106-7 (my italics).

CHAPTER 2

1.   The White House (1967), *The World Food Problem: A Report of the President's Science Advisory Committee* (henceforth the White House Study), vol. II, p. 434. Another recent study suggests a total area of 3,419 million hectares. (See Buringh, P., Van Heemsb, H. D. J. and Staring, G. J. (1975), *Computation of the Absolute Maximum Food Production of the World*, p. 1.) Some Russian soil scientists believe that the total potentially cultivable land is around 5,000 million hectares. (See Kovda, V. A. (1974), *Biosphere, Soils and their Utilization*, quoted in Buringh *et al.*, p. 4.) See also Norse, D. (1976), 'Development Strategies

and the World Food Problem', *Journal of Agricultural Economics*, vol. XXVII, no. 1, Jan. This study estimates the total potentially cultivable area at 3,139 million hectares.

2.   This has been confirmed by a more recent study by Iowa State University. (See Blakeslee, Leroy L., Heady, Earl O. and Framingham, Charles F. (1973), *World Food Production, Demand and Trade*.)

3.   The 'potentially cultivable area' is that which can be brought under cultivation with the currently known technology of land development. In the estimation procedure, the physical, chemical and biological properties of soil, the annual range and seasonality of temperature and the annual amount of seasonal distribution of precipitation relative to potential evapotranspiration are taken into account. For details of the method see the White House Study (1967), pp. 411-35, see also Buringh *et al.* (1975), *op. cit.*

4.   The scope for extension of the area under double cropping is also more limited in Asia than in other developing countries. The cropping intensity (which is obtained by dividing the harvested area by the total arable area and is used as an index of double cropping) is already equal to 1.0 in Asia, as against 0.50 for all other developing countries, which means that while an average unit of land in Asia produces one crop each year, in all other countries it produces one crop every two years (see FAO (1970), *Provisional Indicative World Plan for Agricultural Development* (henceforth IWP), vol. 1, Table 3, p. 44).

5.   Buringh *et al.* (1975), p. 32. The White House Study puts the proportion at only 11 per cent (p. 440).

6.   The FAO estimate of 76 million hectares (*Production Year Book*, 1972) seems to be a gross over-estimate. (See Sinha, R. P. (1975), 'Chinese Agriculture: A Quantitative Look', *Journal of Development Studies*, vol. 11, no. 3, April.)

7.   USDA (1974), *op. cit.*, p. 69.

8.   White House Study (1967), p. 447.

9.   Buringh *et al.* (1975), p. 32.

10.   Nitrogen (N), Phosphates (P) and Potash (K).

11.   UN World Food Conference (1974), *The World Food Problem: Proposals for National and International Action* (henceforth *Proposals*) (mimeo.), p. 49.

12.   Government of India, Directorate of Plant Protection, Quantity and Storage, quoted in IWP (1970), vol. 1, pp. 206-7.

13.   Cramer, H. H. quoted in IWP (1970), p. 207.

14.   IWP (1970), pp. 208-9.

15.   *Ibid.*, p. 209.

16.   According to the USDA estimate referred to above, 0.15 kg. of cereals can provide 500 calories. If the 460 million malnourished people in the world were each provided with additional grain equal to 500 calories daily, the total requirement comes to only 25 million tons per annum. (pp. 50-51)

17.   IWP (1970), p. 209.

18.   *Ibid.*, p. 211.

19.   *Ibid.*, p. 186.

20.   In a recent study it has been shown that 'Taking into account the possibilities of irrigation and the limitations of crop production caused by local soil and climatic conditions, the absolute maximum production expressed in grain equivalents of standard cereal crop is computed as 49,830 million tons per year, that is almost 40 times the present cereal crop production. As at present approximately 65 per cent of the cultivated land is used for cereal production, the maximum production of that area could be 32,390 million tons of grain equivalents or 30 [26] times the present production.' (See Buringh *et al.* (1975), *op. cit.*, p. 1.) To the authors themselves this is a rather 'optimistic view of the food production capacity of the world'. (p. 50.)

21.   Joy (1973), *op. cit.*, p. 185.
22.   Sukhatme, P. V. (1969), *op. cit.*, p. 8.
23.   US AID (1975), *op. cit.*, vol. 1, p. 3.
24.   This figure is based on the estimates of the Kano Irrigation Project from the preliminary draft of Kano Plain Reconnaissance Study, US Bureau of Reclamation April and May 1966 quoted in White House Study (1967), p. 436. The costs referred to here are in mid-1960 prices.
25.   White House Study, *op. cit.*, p. 438.
26.   *Ibid.*, pp. 460-9.
27.   UN World Food Conference (1974), *Proposals*, p. 2.
28.   *Ibid.*, p. 8.
29.   As a result of the Seventh Special Session of the UN General Assembly there is some hope that the transfer of real resources to developing countries will increase in the foreseeable future. The EEC countries have given a fresh assurance that they intend to reach the target of transferring 0.7 per cent of GNP annually by the end of this decade. (See UN General Assembly Ad Hoc Committee of the Seventh Special Session, Agenda Item 7, A/AC 176/L 3 Add. 2, 14 Sept. 1975.)

CHAPTER 3

1.   Voelcker, J. A. (1893), *Report on the Improvement of Indian Agriculture*, pp. 10-11.
2.   Elvin, M. (1973), *The Pattern of the Chinese Past*, pp. 113-30.
3.   Rangnekar, D. K. (1959), *Poverty and Capital Development in India*, p. 17.
4.   Yanaga, C. (1966), *Japan Since Perry*, pp. 96-7.
5.   *Ibid.*, p. 97.
6.   A system in which a portion of a farm is 'laid down' to grass.
7.   [British] Ministry of Agriculture, Fisheries and Food (1970), *Modern Farming and the Soil: Report of the Agricultural Advisory Council on Soil Structure and Soil Fertility* (henceforth *Modern Farming*).
8.   *Ibid.*, p. 1.
9.   How futile such generalisations can be is illustrated by the following example. According to the Council, soils differ from each other in many ways that are important to farming. They can differ in altitude, aspect, slope, parent material, amount of stone, amount of chalk, organic matter, depth, texture, structure, permeability, consistency, drainage, weather and the treatment they receive. If there were only two variants of each of these fifteen factors, there would be over 32,000 different soils. If there were three variants the number of different soils would rise to 14 million. (*Ibid.*, p. 5.)
10.   Continuous planting of crops, often the same crop, without the grass break or leguminous crops in the rotation.
11.   *Modern Farming* (1970), p. 3.
12.   *Ibid.*, p. 55.
13.   United Nations Economic and Social Council (1971), *Development and Coordination of the Activities of the Organisations within the United Nations System; Thirty-Seventh Report of the Administrative Committee on Coordination*, p. 25.
14.   Billings, M. and Singh, A. (1970), 'Mechanization and Rural Employment with some Implications for Rural Income Distribution', *Economic and Political*

Weekly, 27 June; also Inukai, I. (1970), 'Farm Mechanization, Output and Labour Input: A Case Study in Thailand', *International Labour Review*, vol. 101, no. 5, May.

15.　Indian Famine Commission (1881), *Report* (C.3086 British Parliamentary Papers), vol. IV, Appendix, p. 101.

16.　Ishikawa, S. (1967), *Economic Development in Asian Perspective*, p. 245.

17.　Griffin, K. (1974), *The Political Economy of Agrarian Change*, p. 52.

18.　Hanumantha Rao in a study of tractorisation in the Punjab (India) suggests that 'the incentive for tractorisation among large farms arises owing to the increasing requirements of bullock and human labour with the rise in the scale of operations as well as the rise in the costs of bullock and human labour'. (See Rao, C. H. H. (1973), *Investment in Farm Tractors in Punjab (India): Private versus Social Costs and Benefits* (mimeographed).) Other researchers have questioned Rao's findings. For an excellent review of the economics of tractorisation in India see Sen, A. (1975), *Employment Technology and Development*, Appendix D.

cultural Economics', *Indian Journal of Agricultural Economics*, vol. 24, no. 4, Oct.-Dec.

20.　Yudelman, M., Butler, G. and Banerjee, R. (1971), *Technological Change in Agriculture and Employment in Developing Countries*, p. 78.

21.　Griffin (1974), *op. cit.*, p. 66.

22.　According to a Government of India estimate farms of less than 0.20 hectares provide only about 5 per cent of their output as marketed surplus as against 41 per cent for farms above 6 hectares.

CHAPTER 4

1.　Government of India, Planning Commission (1954), *The Problem of Economic Development*, p. 23.

2.　Government of India, Planning Commission (1956), *The Second Five Year Plan*, p. 26.

3.　*Ibid.*, p. 26.

4.　*Ibid.*, p. 124.

5.　As early as 1955 the (UN) *Economic Bulletin for Asia and the Far East*, vol. VI, no. 3, reported that in 'all countries of the ECAFE region, the objectives of development programmes go beyond the simple maximizing of the long-term rate of growth of output and income. In most countries – and especially in Japan, India and Indonesia – either the creation of employment opportunities is a major objective, or the full-employment level of national income is considered as the major determinant of the development programme . . . In India and in some other countries of the region where raising the level of employment has recently become an increasingly important objective, efforts are being made to increase labour-intensive investment in village industry and in community development projects.' (p. 5.)

6.　ILO (1961), *Employment Objectives in Economic Development*.

7.　FAO, *The State of Food and Agriculture, 1973*, p. 137. The IWP assumed a rate of growth of GDP of 4 to 6 per cent per annum between 1962 and 1985. The required rates of growth of agricultural production were estimated at between 3.4 and 3.9 per cent per annum. (See IWP (1970), *Summary and Main Conclusions*, p. 3.) These rates would require a considerable improvement over past performances.

8.　See Chapter 2, Table 3.

9.   United Nations Industrial Development Organisation (henceforth UNIDO) (1974), *Industrial Development Survey*, p. 97.

10.   According to the UNIDO study, in the first half of the Second Development Decade employment in manufacturing in the developing countries increased by nearly 4 per cent per annum. (*Ibid*., p. 97.)

11.   In another UNIDO study prepared by Raj Krishna it was found that in India the ratio of total employment generated to direct employment was 1.60 for industry. (*Ibid*., p. 98.)

12.   In many countries for which the relevant information is available employment in the factory organised part of the manufacturing sector in the 1960s absorbed less than 10 per cent of the labour force, while in several it was less than 5 per cent and in a few as low as 3 per cent. (*Ibid*., p. 90n.)

13.   *Ibid*., p. 89.

14.   This seems to have happened in textiles as well, probably as a result of the recent rationalisation and modernisation of the textile industry in many countries. In both Latin America and Asia, value-added increased by 4 per cent per annum, while employment grew at only 0.8 per cent in Latin America and only 0.4 per cent in Asia. (*Ibid*., p. 93.)

15.   It is estimated that in those countries with an average annual growth of manufacturing output of 11 per cent the import of capital goods increased by nearly 12 per cent; in countries with an annual growth rate of manufacturing output of 5 per cent imports of capital goods increased by 4.5 per cent. (*Ibid*., p. 169.)

16.   *Ibid*., p. 169.

17.   Helleiner, G. K. (1973), 'Manufactured Exports from Less Developed Countries and Multinational Firms', *The Economic Journal*, vol. 83, 329, pp. 29, March.

18.   *Ibid*., p. 35.

19.   Some of these issues will be discussed in a subsequent section.

20.   Streeten, P. (1975), 'Industrialisation in a Unified Development Strategy', *World Development*, vol. 3, no. 1, p. 4.

21.   Fei, John C. H. and Ranis, G. (1964), *Development of the Labour Surplus Economy, Theory and Policy*, p. 43.

22.   Sen, A. (1975), *op. cit*., p. 85. See also Rao, V. K. R. V. (1956), 'Investment, Employment and the Multiplier' in Singh, V. B. (ed.), *Keynesian Economics*, and Das-Gupta, A. K. (1954), 'Keynesian Economics and Underdeveloped Countries', *Economic Weekly*, 26 Jan.

23.   Much the same kinds of problems arise if new employment is created largely by the establishment of heavy industries. Since the gestation lag between the intial investments in heavy industries and the commencement of production is very long, there is a gap between the increase in the effective demand for and the supply of goods, particularly consumer goods, which leads to an inflationary situation. The degree of the inflationary pressures will vary between different industries, according to the length of the gestation period.

24.   The Chinese leadership, while giving enough emphasis to the production of steel and other capital goods, did not neglect consumer goods.

25.   In fact the method of payment for employment on public works (e.g. irrigation projects) is devised so as to prevent inflationary pressures. The people who are 'drafted' for working on public works projects receive only a token additional payment; they continue to earn work-points which entitle them to a share in the total agricultural output of their commune.

26.   In fact this statement applies equally to other sectors of an economy. For example, one of the main reasons for low productivity in the modern industrial sector is the lack of understanding between the management and employees with

regard to goals and aspirations and the inequalities in the distribution of power
in industrial management. In public administration, nepotism, bureaucratic
practices and the social distance between the top and bottom of the hierarchy
are the main causes of inefficiency.

CHAPTER 5

1.   These terms do not always denote similar groups of people. Doreen Warriner rightly warns against the indiscriminate use of such terms:

> . . . the indiscriminate use of the term suggests that the agrarian structures
> in underdeveloped countries are all of the same kind. This is not true. The
> ex-*Zamindar* in an Indian village is a small squire-farmer, not in the least
> resembling the flying magnates of Peru or the coffee speculators of Brazil.
> The sophisticated cotton pashas of Egypt were big capitalistic farmers,
> centuries removed from the tribal sheikhs or city merchants of Iraq – al-
> though in both countries the stock phrase was used to define the purpose of
> reform. In the economic sense, the concept loses its meaning when broadened
> to include so much.

(See Warriner, D. (1969), *Land Reform in Principle and Practice*, p. 9.)
2.   *Ibid*., p. xiv. See also Lipton, M. (1974), 'Towards a Theory of Land
Reform' in Lehmann, D. (ed.), *Agrarian Reform and Agrarian Reformism*.
According to Lipton land reform 'comprises (1) compulsory take-over of
land, usually (a) by the state, (b) from the biggest landowners, and (c) with
partial compensation; and (2) the farming of that land in such a way as to spread
the benefits of the man-land relationship more widely than before the take-
over.' (p. 270.)
3.   Lipton argues that the primary motivation of land reform, as defined by
him, is not the growth of agricultural output, but the reduction of poverty by
reducing inequality. (*Ibid*., p. 270.)
4.   See Warriner (1969), *op. cit*., pp. 57-8. The idealisation of the small
family farm has been taken to fanatical lengths only in France and the USA.
In the latter family farmers were the 'most precious part of a state'. (See
Griswold, A. W. (1952), *Farming and Democracy*, p. 45.) It may, however, be
noted that in America the Jeffersonian tradition towards family farms has
remained mainly an ideal; in actual fact, 'Large-scale farming and tenancy have
characterized the trend in America for a long time, contrary to the dictates of
of the ideals.' (See Tuma, Elias H. (1965), *Twenty Six Centuries of Agrarian
Reform*, p. 10.)
5.   Dore, R. P. (1959), *Land Reform in Japan*, pp. 49-50.
6.   Rawski, E. S. (1972), *Agricultural Change and the Peasant Economy of
South China*, p. 12.
7.   This does not apply to share-cropping tenancies.
8.   As early as 1810 the Acting Judge of Morshidabad had drawn attention to
this phenomenon.

> . . . Another class of zemindars are men of wealth, whose sole object is to add
> daily to their store; they are resident in other parts and draw from hence their
> lacks (Lakh of rupees) annually, to the impoverishment of the district . . . what
> is the natural effect? . . . A general system of rack-renting, hard-heartedness,
> and exactions, through . . . the whole host of Zemindari Amla [officers] and
> their dependents . . . Even this rack-renting is unfairly managed. We have no

regular leases executed between the Zemindar and his tenants. We do not find a mutual consent and unrestrained negotiations in their bargains; but, instead, we hear of nothing but arbitrary demands, enforced by stocks, duress of all sorts, and battery of their persons . . . There is also an intermediate class, the moneyman [country banker], in every village, who first relieves, then aggravates the evil by his own usurious practices, and enforces them by like means. The general consequence is general poverty.

(See Briggs, J. (1830), *Land Tax in India*, pp. 205-6.
9.   Warriner (1969), *op. cit.*, p. 239.
10.   *Ibid.*, p. 241.
11.   Myrdal, G. (1968), *Asian Drama*, pp. 1318-19.
12.   *Ibid.*, p. 1319.
13.   Warriner (1969), *op. cit.*, p. 59, and also xiv.
14.   *Ibid.*, p. 60.
15.   *Ibid.*, p. 73. See also Weitz, R. (1971), *From Peasant to Farmer*:

The Indian farmer, the settler in Ceylon, the South American campesino, and others like them throughout the developing countries are unable to cope singly with a service system based on large-scale operations and with no provision for their personal and direct contact with those who provide the services. Therefore, there must be an intermediate organizational structure in developing countries between the individual farmer and the service system that will enable the small producer to utilize the services available for the development of his farm. This can best be achieved by united action of the producers through cooperative associations formed for the purpose of obtaining services. (pp. 95-6.)

16.   -Warriner (1969), *op. cit.*, p. 73. Another species of the same genus is the Polish agricultural circles which were a traditional form of mutual aid founded in the second half of the nineteenth century by enlightened estate owners and church dignitaries. They were revived when the collectivisation of agriculture did not work and the government decided to establish family farm units. The agricultural circles provide agricultural extension services, farm machinery, fertilisers and improved seeds to the peasants, and are financed by the state through an Agricultural Development Fund. (See Jacoby, Erich H. and Jacoby, Charlotte F. (1971), *Man and Land*, p. 233.)
17.   Myrdal (1968), *op. cit.*, p. 1244.
18.   *Ibid.*, pp. 1377-84.
19.   *Ibid.*, p. 1380. On the face of it, Myrdal suggests this alternative because of the absence of the political will or administrative ability to introduce radical reforms. But in the discussion which follows his bias towards capitalist farming is quite clear. For instance, he suggests that: 'An honest attempt – even if only imperfectly implemented – to imitate the controlled and restrained pattern of capitalist practice that has gradually evolved in Western Countries would offer some considerable advantages over the policies and practices now prevailing.' (p. 1381.) To Myrdal 'a policy . . . aimed at developing a genuinely capitalist system of production does not imply the preservation of the *status quo* but is to be recognized as a quite radical "land reform" . . . It must be designed in such a way that the land owners are encouraged to become cultivators, at least in the sense of being genuine agricultural entrepreneurs.' (pp. 1381-2.)
20.   *Ibid.*, p. 1381.
21.   *Ibid.*
22.   *Ibid.*, p. 1382.

23. *Ibid.*, p. 1382.
24. *Ibid.*, p. 1383. See also Bell, C. L. G. and Duloy, John H. (1974), 'Rural Target Groups' in Chenery, H. *et al., Redistribution With Growth*. These authors talk of three options for densely populated countries: (1) to accommodate a great many families on smaller holdings; (2) a smaller number on larger holdings and (3) the Chinese type of communal land ownership. True to the tradition of western 'liberal' thinking, the authors exclude the third alternative outright, whilst the first is ruled out on the grounds of the inefficiencies involved in a large number of holdings of marginal size. What they have to offer landless labour turns out to be even less significant than Myrdal — 'house-plots which are large enough to support some horticultural and animal husbandry operations'. (p. 122.) The summary rejection of the Chinese-type communal ownership of land alternative, which typifies the approach of the entire book, makes nonsense of the subject matter to which the book addresses itself. If 'The bulk of developing countries have mixed economic systems combining elements of public and private ownership as well as mixed political systems combining democratic and authoritarian features' (p. xvii) there is all the more reason to have a more informed discussion on the abolition of private property in land, particularly in countries like India where the Communist Party operates legally alongside the other political parties.
25. Myrdal (1968), *op. cit.*, p. 1375.
26. I owe the entire description of the Gezira Scheme to S. A. Tyfour's Ph. D. thesis 'The Economics of Cotton in Sudan with special reference to Sudan Gezira Scheme' submitted to Glasgow University in 1969 (unpublished).
27. *Ibid.*, p. 15.
28. Jacoby and Jacoby (1971), *op. cit*, p. 294.
29. Myrdal (1968), *op. cit.*, p. 1376.
30. Jacoby and Jacoby (1971), *op. cit.*, p. 232.
31. Myrdal (1968), *op. cit.*, p. 1376.
32. The tradition among 'liberal' social scientists to take a stand on ideological grounds, even if it runs counter to their own considered intellectual judgement, is a long-standing one. Malthus is a classic case of such schizophrenia. In *The Principles of Political Economy* he argued that a more equal distribution of land than the one that prevailed in Europe during his time would increase effective demand [and therefore employment]. He emphasised that a 'very large proprietor surrounded by very poor peasants, presents a distribution of property most unfavourable to effectual demand' (p. 373). 'Thirty or forty proprietors, with incomes answering to between one thousand and five thousand a year, would create a much more effectual demand for necessities, conveniences, and luxuries of life, than a single proprietor possessing a hundred thousand a year.' (p. 374.) However, in his policy recommendations he did not support a more egalitarian distribution of land because he was committed to the maintenance of the British landed aristocracy — in his view the champion of British values. He himself confessed that:

> Although therefore it be true that a better distribution of landed property might exist than that which actually prevails in this country at present; and although it also be true, that to make it better, the distribution should be more equal; yet it may by no means be wise to abolish the law of primogeniture which would be likely to lead to a sub-division of land greater probably than would be favourable even to the wealth of the country; and greater certainly than would be consistent with those higher interests, which relate to the protection of a people equally from the tyranny of despotic rulers and the fury of despotic mobs. (pp. 381-2.)

33.   Myrdal (1968), *op. cit.*, pp. 1376-7.
34.   Chao, K. (1970), *Agricultural Production in Communist China*, p. 52.
35.   Pelzel, J. (1972), 'Economic Management of a Production Brigade in post-leap China' in Willmott, W. E. (ed.), *Economic Organisation in Chinese Society*, pp. 387-404.
36.   *Ibid.*, p. 389.
37.   Myrdal (1968), *op. cit.*, p. 1376.
38.   'Resolution on Some Questions Concerning the People's Communes' adopted by the Eighth Central Committee of the Chinese Communist Party at its Sixth Plenary Session, 10 Dec. 1958, reproduced in Chao, Kuo-chun (1960), *Agrarian Policy of the Chinese Communist Party*, Appendix III.
39.   The above figures are based on figures the author collected during his visit to five communes. Since there are local variations it is difficult to generalise for the country as a whole. Sartaj Aziz, who was on the staff of the Pakistan Planning Commission from 1961 to 1971 and is currently Director of the Commodities and Trade Division of the FAO, has visited China several times. He gives the following figures:

> Only about 50 to 55 per cent of the total gross revenue of the Commune is distributed among the Commune members . . . About 20-25 per cent of the gross revenue of the Commune is set apart for current production and operational costs (including 2 to 3 per cent for administrative expenses) and about 15-20 per cent of the gross income of the Commune is transferred to the Accumulation Fund . . . The Social Fund, which supports welfare and cultural activities receives 2-3 per cent and the rest (about 6 per cent) is paid as unified agricultural tax.

(Aziz, S. (1974), 'The Chinese Approach to Rural Development' in *World Development*, vol. 2, no. 2, Feb., p. 89. (See also Watson, A. (1975), *Life in China*, pp. 66-80.
40.   It is not an 'election' in the formal sense as it is known in western democracies, or some developing countries modelled on western lines. But the role of consultation in deciding the final list is quite significant. It must be remembered that the selection of a candidate for a constituency or, for that matter, until recently, the 'election' of the leader of the Conservative Party in this country was based on consultation among the upper echelons of the Party.
41.   Skinner, G. W. (1964-5), 'Marketing and Social Structures in Rural China', *Journal of Asian Studies*, vol. 24, nos. 1-3, p. 394.
42.   *Ibid.*, pp. 397-8.
43.   Chao (1970), *op. cit.*, p. 62.
44.   Warriner (1969), *op. cit.*, p. 72.
45.   Perkins, Dwight H. (1966), *Market Control and Planning in Communist China*, ch. IV, and Schran, P. (1969), *The Development of Chinese Agriculture 1950-59*, p. 77.
46.   This is being done in Tanzania which is experimenting with Ujamaa villages. The experiment retains the traditional principles of the extended African family but establishes collective cultivation. Under the new system introduced in 1970 all land in Tanzania is public property and the tenants are given the rights of occupation. In the Ujamaa villages distribution of income is based on both the work done by the members and the needs of their families. (See FAO (1971), *Report of the Special Committee on Agrarian Reform*, p. 22.) This idea that indigenous communal tenures predispose peasants towards collective farming has been seriously questioned by Warriner. She says that several African countries have found communal tenure unworkable (p. 70). But even she is prepared to concede that: 'All this experience of failure does not prove that genuine

cooperative farming or voluntary collective farming is impossible: in exceptional circumstances it can be done.' (p. 72.) The question remains whether the 'exceptional' can be made more 'general'.

47.   Largely because of their preoccupation with the Russian type of collectivisation western liberal social scientists seem so allergic to the idea of collective social forms that even in serious academic writings they tend to verge on irrationality. One example is the following statement by Warriner in her book, which is a major contribution to the literature on land reform: 'By contrast with integral reform [the American approach], which is advice given in good faith, the co-operative farming band-wagon is dishonest: it suppresses the truth and suggests the false, by playing up the advantages of large scale, while playing down compulsion and the extraction of grain surpluses from recalcitrant peasants.' (p. 69.)

48.   Jacoby and Jacoby (1971), *op. cit.*, p. 295.

49.   Brandt, W. (1973), in a speech before the UN General Assembly quoted in Mesarovic, M. and Pestel, E. (1975), *Mankind at the Turning Point*, p. 115.

CHAPTER 6

1.   It is not unusual, even in developed countries, to find that institutional credit is not available to the poor, so that they end up borrowing from money-lenders and pawnbrokers who charge very high interest rates.

2.   Long, Millard F. (1973), 'Conditions for Success of Public Credit Programs for Small Farmers', *A.I.D Small Farmers Credit: Analytical Papers* (mimeo.), p. 84.

3.   Carroll, Thomas F. (1973), 'Group Credit for Small Farmers', *A.I.D., op. cit.*, p. 280.

4.   Abott, J. C. and Creupelandt, H. C. (1966), *Agricultural Marketing Boards, Their Establishment and Operation*, p. 188.

5.   *Ibid.*, p. 190.

6.   *Ibid.*, p. 191.

7.   FAO (1967), *Incentives and Disincentives for Farmers in Developing Countries*, p. 4.

8.   *Ibid.*, p. 9.

9.   Habakkuk, H. J. (1956), 'Essays in Bibliography and Criticism: The Eighteenth Century', *Economic History Review*, second series, vol. VII, pp. 437-8.

10.   Olson, M. and Harris, Curtis C. (1959), 'Free Trade in Corn', *Quarterly Journal of Economics*, p. 162.

11.   Chambers, J. D. and Mingay, G. E. (1966), *The Agricultural Revolution 1750-1880*, p. 150.

12.   Ricardo, David (1822), *On Protection to Agriculture*, 4th ed., p. 44. It is interesting to note that a similar controversy between Lipton and Byres is going on under a more modern garb. Lipton advocates high prices for farmers and regards any attempt to keep down grain prices as 'urban-biased' while Byres is critical of high prices because they hinder industrialisation. (See Byres, T. J. (1974), 'Land Reform, Industralization and the Marketed Surplus in India: An Essay on the Power of Rural Bias', in Lehmann, D. (1974), *op. cit.*; see also Lipton (1974), *op. cit.*)

13.   Chambers and Mingay (1966), *op. cit.*, p. 159.

14.   *Ibid.*, p. 159.

15.   *Ibid.*, p. 159.

16.   IBRD (1975), *Rural Development*, p. 30 (my italics).

17.   Sen (1975), *op. cit.*, p. 143.

18.   For a detailed appraisal of such schemes see Sen (1975), *op. cit.* Commenting on India's small and marginal farmers' schemes which aim at raising the level

of living of the very poor through provision of credit and marketing facilities and crash programmes of employment creation Sen points out that: 'Through significant loopholes in the conception of the programmes, it has turned out that many among the poorest cannot benefit at all from these programmes, while some of the relatively better-off can be covered by them. The institutional framework of rural India makes these problems extremely real.' (p. 144.)

CHAPTER 7

1.   For lack of sufficient knowledge on the part of the author some of the important religious ideologies are not being included in the discussion.
2.   Self-rule.
3.   Since Marxism itself is basically 'materialistic' Mao's mass line may also be regarded as 'modified' materialism.
4.   Meadows, Donella H., Meadows, Dennis L., Randers, Jorgen and Behrens III, William W. (1972), *The Limits to Growth*, p. 23.
5.   *Ibid.*, p. 24.
6.   *Ibid.*, pp. 175-6.
7.   It seems clear that Malthus recognised the virtues of a more egalitarian distribution of land but did not recommend it as a policy measure (see p. 67, n.32).
8.   Meadows *et al.* (1972), *op. cit.*, p. 191.
9.   *Ibid.*, p. 194.
10.   *Ibid.*, p. 195.
11.   *Ibid.*, p. 193.
12.   *Ibid.*, p. 193-4.
13.   Mesarovic and Pestel (1975), *op. cit.*
14.   *Ibid.*, p. 147.
15.   *Ibid.*, p. 154.
16.   *Ibid.*, p. 40.
17.   *Ibid.*, p. 155.
18.   *Harijan*, 1 June 1974, quoted in Rao, U. S. Mohan (ed.) (1970), *The Message of Mahatma Gandhi* (henceforth *Message*), p. 47.
19.   *Young India*, 10 October 1921, quoted in *Message*, p. 46.
20.   *Message*, pp. 46-7.
21.   *Message*, p. 48.
22.   Rao, V. K. R. V. (1970), *The Gandhian Alternative to Western Socialism*, p. 6.
23.   It can, however, be argued that even this *minimum* amount of private property cannot be made available to everyone in a densely populated country like India. There does not seem to be a clear answer to this problem in the Gandhian scheme of thinking.
24.   Rao (1970), *op. cit.*, p. 25.
25.   *Message*, pp. 48-9.
26.   Myrdal (1968), *op. cit.*, p. 755.
27.   *Message*, p. 59.
28.   *Ibid.*, p. 49.
29.   *Ibid.*, pp. 52-3.
30.   *Ibid.*, p. 54.
31.   Cannabis.
32.   *Message.*, p. 80.
33.   *Ibid.*, p. 76.
34.   After Tolstoy he calls it Bread Labour.
35.   *Message*, p. 83.

36.   *Ibid.*, p. 84.
37.   *Ibid.*, p. 83.
38.   In his *Report on an Investigation of the Peasant Movement in Hunan* written in March 1927 he highlighted the considerable inequality in the distribution of income and land ownership. For example, in Changsha County, poor peasants comprised 70 per cent of the rural population. He subdivided them into the utterly destitute and the less destitute.

> The utterly destitute, comprising 20 per cent, are the completely dispossessed, that is, people who have neither land nor money, are without any means of livelihood, and are forced to leave home and become mercenaries or hired labourers or wandering beggars. The less destitute, the other 50 per cent, are the partially dispossessed, that is, people with just a little land or a little money who eat up more than they earn and live in toil and distress the year round . . .'

(See *Selected Works of Mao Tse-tung*, vol. I, p. 32.)

39.   Mao Tse-tung quoted in Winberg, Chai (ed.), *Essential Works of Chinese Communism*, p. 156.
40.   'Land Gift' movement.
41.   Robinson, Joan (1973), *The Cultural Revolution in China*, p. 12.
42.   The difference, however, is that with Gandhi changes in attitudes are a pre-condition for social change, which makes the latter a distant goal, given the socioeconomic and political powers of the vested interests. With Mao 'rectification' of the individual follows the destruction of such vested interests.
43.   Gray, J. (1974), *Mao Tse-tung*, p. 69. Gandhi's concept of progress did not coincide with economic progress. He stresses that:

> I do not believe that multiplication of wants and machinery contrived to supply them is taking the world a single step nearer its goal . . . I wholeheartedly detest this mad desire to destroy distance and time, to increase animal appetites and go to the ends of the earth in search of their satisfaction. If modern civilisation stands for all this, and I have understood it to do so, I call it satanic.

(Quoted in Rao, V. K. R. V. (1970), *op. cit.*, p. 5.) He is more emphatic in the following statement:

> An economics that inculcates Mammon worship, and enables the strong to amass wealth at the expense of the weak, is a false and dismal science. It spells death. True economics, on the other hand, stands for social justice, it promotes the good of all equally, including the weakest, and is indispensable for decent life. (*Ibid.*, p. 4.)

44.   D'Aeth, R. (1974), 'Changing Perspective in Educational Planning and Cooperation between countries of the Third World and Western Europe', *World Development*, vol. 2, no. 2, Feb., pp. 34-5.
45.   Tawney, R. H. (1964), *Equality* (with a new introduction by R. M. Titmuss), p. 129.
46.   Bhagwati, J. (1973), 'Education, Class Structure and Income Equality', *World Development*, vol. 1, no. 5, May, p. 25.
47.   There are some constitutional provisions in India for reservations in schools, universities, jobs, legislatures, etc., for the so-called backward classes, backward tribes and the *Harijans* (untouchables) but the traditional imbalance has yet to be redressed.

48.   Similar arguments have been put forward by Sher, G. (1975), 'Justifying Reverse Discrimination in Employment', *Philosophy and Public Affairs*, vol. 4, no. 2, p. 165.
49.   Bhagwati (1973), *op. cit.*, p. 36.
50.   Balogh, T. (1974), *The Economics of Poverty*, p. 152.
51.   This phenomenon has been noticed by social scientists in most developing countries. See for instance Frantz Fanon in *Black Skin, White Masks*:

> The Negro of the Antilles will be proportionately whiter — that is, he will come closer to being a real human being — in direct ratio to his mastery of the French language . . . Every colonized people — in other words, every people in whose soul an inferiority complex has been created by the death and burial of its local cultural originality — finds itself face to face with the language of the civilizing nation; that is, with the culture of the mother country. The colonized is elevated above his jungle status in proportion to his adoption of the mother country's cultural standards. He becomes whiter as he renounces his blackness, his jungle. (p. 18.)

Fanon mentions how the middle class in the Antilles never speak Creole except to their servants. Some families completely forbid the use of Creole and mothers scorn their children for speaking it (p. 20). Such instances are not uncommon among the upper middle class in some parts of India. Parents take great pride in their children's ability to speak 'pukka' English even though they may not be able to speak their own mother tongue.
52.   Students of social sciences, particularly economic development, could learn a great deal from the economic and social history of the developed countries during their early stages. But such courses are rarely given in connection with development economics, while there is an abundance of mathematical macro-models, with their restrictive and often unrealistic assumptions, which have little relevance for developing countries.
53.   One or two examples may suffice. An educationalist has this to say about the main features of education in Western Europe: 'It comprises a highly developed system . . . to prepare them [young people] for growing to maturity in a rich and deeply-rooted culture; to enable them to enjoy responsibly the freedom of individual thought and expression characteristic of Western democracies . . .' (D'Aeth (1974), *op. cit.*, p. 34.) Even after a long spell in the UK it is difficult to convince oneself that such privileges are accessible to the masses in general. Similarly see Myrdal on the 'general level of corruption' in Asia. He stresses that 'it is unquestionably much higher than in the Western developed countries (even including the United States) . . . ' (p. 942). On the face of it the statement is probably right but an unqualified statement like this is misleading. Firstly, the two groups of countries, Asian on the one hand and Western European on the other are at two different stages of development — while it may be true that the level of corruption in Asian developing countries is higher today than in the developed countries of Western Europe, the same thing cannot be said with any degree of confidence of the Western European countries of the late nineteenth and early twentieth century. Besides, there is a conceptual problem involved. For instance, in Britain, a significant proportion of appointments and promotions in business, public utilities, local government and even in the universities are made by 'back-door' methods; advertisements of vacancies are often inserted and applications called for mainly to regularise the decisions already made. Much of this is accepted in Britain without protest. In India it would be branded as 'nepotism'.
54.   Though, of course, the developing countries will face many additional

problems due to the constantly changing world environment.

55.   Streeten, P. (1974), 'The Limits to Development Research', *World Development*, vol. 2, nos. 10-12, Oct.-Dec., p. 21.

56.   *Ibid*.

57.   This applies equally to technically trained people such as doctors. If the majority of doctors refuse to work in the villages where three-quarters or more of the people live, it makes little difference to a country's welfare whether an Indian doctor (for example) works in Delhi or in London.

CHAPTER 8

1.   Wilson, H. (1975), 'World Trade in Commodities'. Speech delivered to the Commonwealth Heads of Government Meeting in Kingston, Jamaica on1 May 1975 (mimeographed). In fact, in the Seventh Special Session of the UN General Assembly (September 1975), in spite of the US reservations on the use of the term 'new economic order', the developing countries gained, at least, a moral victory on the question of reorganisation of the world economic system.

2.   In 1973 the total net flow of resources, including private capital flows, from the Development Assistance Committee (DAC) (which includes all Western European countries, USA, Canada, Australia, New Zealand and Japan) to developing countries was less than a third of total exports from developing countries to the non-Communist richer countries. Net official development assistance (ODA) was only about one-eighth of the exports.

3.   Dell, S. (1973), 'An Appraisal of UNCTAD III', *World Development*, vol. 1, no. 5, May, p. 11.

4.   United Nations Conference on Trade and Development (UNCTAD), *An Integrated Programme for Commodities: trade measures to expand processing of primary commodities in developing countries: Report by the Secretary General* (mimeo.) TD/B/C.1/166/Suppl. 5, 18 Dec. 1974.

5.   Effective Protection is calculated by relating tariffs not to the value of imports but to the value added at various stages.

6.   Wipf, Larry J. (1971), 'Tariffs, Non-Tariff Distortions and Effective Protection in US Agriculture', *American Journal of Agricultural Economics*, vol. 53, no. 3, August, p. 428.

7.   *Ibid*., p. 429.

8.   According to the FAO estimates the rates of growth of agricultural exports of the developing countries between 1959-61 and 1967-69 was only 2.8 per cent against 5.7 per cent for the developed countries. (See FAO, *Commodity Review and Outlook*, 1972-3, Table 11, p. 35.)

9.   General Agreement on Tariffs and Trade (GATT) (1974), *International Trade 1973/74*, p. 105.

10.   According to the UNIDO (1974), *Industrial Development Survey*:

... the average rate of effective tariff placed on manufactured exports from developing countries to the developed market economies was over 33 per cent prior to the Kennedy Round. The comparable figure was 19.2 per cent for the manufactured trade from the world. The negotiations resulted in substantial reduction in both averages. However, the relative tariff burden placed on the manufacturing sectors of the developing countries was still double the world average (22. 6 per cent compared with 11.1 per cent) ... The Kennedy Round negotiations actually increased the degree of tariff bias against the developing countries by comparison with the developed countries. (p. 60.)

11.   Kissinger, Henry A. (1975), 'Global Consensus and Economic Development'. Address before the Seventh Special Session of the UN General Assembly, N.Y., 1 Sept. 1975 (mimeo.).
12.   UNCTAD (TD/B/C.1/166 Suppl. 5), p. 7.
13.   *The Economist* (London), 28 Dec. 1974.
14.   The ceiling for the aggregate value of all GSP sensitive product groups under the 1972 EEC Scheme was fixed at $354 million. The beneficiary countries exports of these products to the EEC were already $470 million in 1970. See Murray, T. (1973), 'How Helpful is the Generalised System of Preferences to Developing Countries?', *The Economic Journal*, vol. 83, no. 330, p. 453n. See also Iqbal, Z. (1975), 'The Generalised System of Preferences Examined', *Finance and Development*, vol. 12, no. 3.
15.   Elliot, C. (1973), *Fair Chance For All*, p. 31.
16.   The variable levy system of the EEC is aimed at raising the price of imported food to the levels of community prices which have invariably been higher than world prices. For cereals the levy is calculated daily in Brussels, taking account of any changes in the world market. The levy is imposed so as to bring cereal prices up to the desired level. (See Commission of the European Communities, *The Common Agricultural Policy*, July 1974.)
17.   Public procurement is a major bone of contention between the EEC and the US Government. The US Government provides a clear margin of preference for domestic traders; 6 per cent usually, 12 per cent when jobs in depressed areas are at stake and up to 50 per cent on defence contracts; defence includes such items as boots, sailors' bell bottoms and airmen's goggles. Europeans complain that most of the contracts in the USA are awarded by the States and not by the federal government and that the States treat European tenders shabbily. (See *The Economist*, 26 Oct. 1974.)
18.   According to GATT classifications these include Albania, Bulgaria, Czechoslovakia, German Democratic Republic, Hungary, Poland, Romania, USSR, China, Mongolia, North Korea and North Vietnam. Thus this is not the same as the Soviet Bloc countries.
19.   Kidron, M. (1972). *Pakistan's Trade With Eastern Bloc Countries*, p. 9. Writing about Tanzania Bienefeld suggests that:

> Trade with the socialist countries has strongly reinforced the old 'colonial' specialization in cotton, coffee, sisal . . . these three commodities earned roughly between 40 and 60 per cent of total export earnings in each year since independence. By contrast, until 1969, these three commodities accounted for between 90 and 100 per cent of export earnings from socialist countries. Since 1970 this proportion has fallen, but only to remain at between 80 and 90 per cent.

(See Bienefeld, M. A. (1975), 'Special Gains from Trade with Socialist Countries: The Case of Tanzania', *World Development*, vol. 3, no. 5, May, p. 265.)
20.   Datar, Asha L. (1972), *India's Economic Relations with the USSR and Eastern Europe, 1953-1969*, p. 182.
21.   Kidron (1972), *op. cit.*, p. 53.
22.   The Chinese have paid a small premium on primary commodity exports from Tanzania. (See Bienefeld (1975), *op. cit.*, p. 270.) Similarly Nayyar feels that the 'terms of trade under bilateral agreements were, on balance, probably favourable to India and, at any rate, no worse than those obtained from other countries.' (See Nayyar, D. (1975), *World Development*, vol. 3, no. 5, May, p. 298.) It is suggested that the USSR buys Egyptian cotton at prices which are generally higher than unit values realized from other countries. (See Mabro, R. (1975),

'Egypt's Economic Relations with the Socialist Countries', *World Development*, vol. 3, no. 5, May, p. 308.)

23.   GATT (1974), p. 4.

24.   *Ibid.*, p. 2.

25.   *Ibid.*

26.   *Ibid.*, p. 106.

27.   *Ibid.*

28.   *Ibid.*, pp. 111-12.

29.   *Ibid.*, p. 113.

30.   *Ibid.*, p. 114.

31.   Wilson, T., Sinha, R. P. and Castree, J. R. (1969), 'The Income Terms of Trade of Developed and Developing Countries', *The Economic Journal*, vol. 79, no. 316, Dec.

32.   GATT (1974), Table 6, p. 24.

33.   Bergsten, C. Fred (1974), 'The New Era in World Commodity Markets', *Challenge*, Sept.-Oct.

34.   FAO (1974), *Monthly Bulletin of Agricultural Economics and Statistics*, vol. 23, Oct./Nov., p. 2.

35.   Labys, W. C. (1974), *Speculation and Price Instability on International Commodity Futures Markets*, UNCTAD, TD/B/C.1/171 10 Dec. 1974 (mimeo.), p. 2.

36.   The US Congress is considering reforming the regulations of the Commodity Exchange Authority (CEA) so as to include commodities produced in developing countries, the CEA itself being replaced by an independent 'Commodity Futures Trading Commission'. UNCTAD also has commissioned special studies.

37.   Macbean, A. I. (1968), *Export Instability and Economic Development*, p. 43.

38.   *Ibid.*, pp. 53-4.

39.   *Ibid.*, p. 127.

40.   In 1973/74 85 per cent of the soya bean, 60 per cent of feed grain, 45 per cent of wheat, 30 per cent of cotton and 25 per cent of rice traded on world markets were of US origin. On the consumption side the USA is the world's largest buyer of coffee, cocoa beans and sugar.

41.   Elliot (1973), *op. cit.*, p. 45.

42.   William Eberle quoted in Wingarten, A. (1975), 'Developments in Agricultural Trade Policy', *Journal of Agricultural Economics*, vol. XXVI, no. 1, Jan, p. 134.

43.   Kissinger (1975), *op. cit.*, pp. 19-20.

44.   UN (1974), *Commodity Trade and Economic Development*, Appendix D; see also Macbean (1968), *op. cit.*, p. 303.

45.   UN (1961), *International Compensation for Fluctuations in Commodity Trade*.

46.   IBRD (1965), *Supplementary Financial Measures*.

47.   *Ibid.*, p. 7.

48.   For details see IMF (1966), *Compensatory Financing of Export Fluctuations: A Second Report by the International Monetary Fund*; see for a summary UNCTAD (1974), *An Integrated Program for Commodities: Compensatory Financing of Export Fluctuations in Commodity Trade: Report by the Secretary General of UNCTAD* (mimeo.), TD/B/C.1/166 Suppl. 4, 13 Dec.

49.   UNCTAD (1974), TD/B/C.1/166 Suppl. 13 Dec., p. 11.

50.   *Ibid.*, pp. 13-14. In the Seventh Special Session of the UN General Assembly it was decided to 'expand and liberalize' the compensatory financing facilities.

51.   UNCTAD (1974), *op. cit.*, pp. 4-5, 9. Dec. This kind of multi-commodity

approach was suggested by an FAO expert as early as 1949 in the FAO proposals for the establishment of an International Commodity Clearing House which was to be constituted as a public corporation with an authorised capital fund of five billion dollars. (See FAO (1956), *Functions of a World Food Reserve*, p. 50.)

52.   Wheat, maize, rice, sugar, coffee (raw), cocoa beans, tea, cotton, jute and jute manufactures, wool, hard fibres, rubber, copper, lead, zinc, tin, bauxite, aluminium and iron ore.

53.   UNCTAD (1974), *op. cit.*, 9 Dec., p. 14.

54.   *Ibid.*, p. 16.

55.   The UNCTAD Scheme could, in fact, be launched without US participation if the OPEC members were prepared to underwrite the scheme. However, the US Government could, if it wished, undermine the working of the scheme, at least in the short run, by prohibiting its dealers in grain (and other agricultural commodities) from doing business with the international authority handling the scheme. In the long run such action would be counterproductive, since the US Government would have to spend enormous sums on income/price maintenance schemes for American farmers. There would also be the risk of losing some world markets because the international agencies running the UNCTAD scheme could, by investing in potential grain exporters, increase the world supply of grain.

56.   The ACP countries had insisted that they were not interested so much in *association* as in a convention of partnership.

CHAPTER 9

1.   OECD (1974), *Development Cooperation Review*, p. 14.

2.   *Ibid.*, p. 117.

3.   *Ibid.*, p. 135.

4.   *Ibid.*

5.   Datar, Asha L. (1972), *op. cit.*, p. 11.

6.   *Ibid.*, pp. 11-12.

7.   *Ibid.*, p. 12.

8.   Aziz, S. (1975), *The Lean Years* (mimeo.), p. 21e.

9.   OECD (1974), *op. cit.*, p. 136.

10.   The most important of these were: The FAO Committee on Surplus Disposal to watch over the FAO Principles of Surplus Disposal, the Food Aid Conventions and the Wheat Trade Convention.

11.   OECD (1974), *op. cit.*, p. 88.

12.   FAO (1975), *Commodity Review and Outlook 1974-75*, pp. 31-32.

13.   OECD (1974), p. 16.

14.   *Ibid.*, p. 164.

15.   *Ibid.*, pp. 171-2.

16.   FAO (1975), *Review of Field Programmes 1974-75*, p. 67.

17.   Except the USA for which the details are not provided in OECD (1974), *op. cit.*

18.   It is estimated that if the aid from socialist countries, OPEC and the other non-DAC donor countries were added together, the value of official development assistance commitment to agriculture would be about US $2,500 million in 1973 and US $3,600 in 1974. (See FAO (1975), *Review of Field Programmes*, p. 67.)

19.   IBRD (1975), *op. cit.*, p. 11 and p. 58.

20.   *Ibid.*, p. 11.

21.   McNamara, Robert S. (1974), *Address to the Board of Governors*, p. 3.

22.   Some of the statements regarding the number of people benefitting from such projects have to be taken with a pinch of salt. In absolute terms they sound impressive, but their true nature becomes apparent only when they are translated into *per capita* terms. For instance, let us examine the following statement of the World Bank President regarding a project in India's drought-prone areas which cover 250,000 square miles, and in which 66 million people live.

It aims to diversify their production into activities less dependent on rainfall. The project includes minor irrigation works, watershed management, improved crop production methods, sheep and dairy development, credit facilities (especially to small-holders), applied research and farmer training programmes. A population of over one million will have their incomes increased as a direct result of the project. *One hundred thousand man years of additional employment will be generated.* [My italics.]

(McNamara (1974), *Address to the Board of Governors*, p. 6.) The total employment created, if evenly distributed over the 1 million people who are supposed to benefit from the project, will provide each of them 36.5 days of additional employment per year, which is reasonably significant. However, if it is spread over the entire working population (assumed to be 40 per cent of the total population) it will provide only 1.5 days of additional employment per worker per year.

23.   IBRD (1975), *op. cit.*, p. 69.
24.   *Ibid.*, p. 29.
25.   In his 1972 speech he had emphatically stated that 'there is no rational alternative to moving towards policies of greater social equity', (*Address to the Board of Governors, 1972*, p. 15.) and that: 'The problems of poverty are rooted deeply in the institutional frameworks, particularly in the distribution of economic and political power within the system. Outside agencies can assist but cannot solve such problems. It is governments that have the responsibility of essential domestic reform, and there is no way they can escape that responsibility. To postpone reform on the grounds of political expediency is to invite political extremism. To remain indifferent to social frustration is to foster its growth.' (p. 15.)
26.   McNamara, Robert S. (1974), *Address to the Board of Governors*, pp. 2-3.
27.   *Europa*, March 1975.
28.   For a very comprehensive review of the discussion see Lall, S. (1974), 'Less-Developed Countries and Private Foreign Direct Investment: A Review Article', *World Development*, vol. 2, nos. 4 and 5, April-May.
29.   Streeten, P. (1971), 'New Approaches to Private Overseas Investment' in Ady, P. (ed.), *Private Foreign Investment and the Developing World*, p. 59.
30.   Lall (1974), *op. cit.*, p. 44. See also Stewart, F. (1974), 'Technology and Employment in L.D.C.s', *World Development*, vol. 2, no. 3, March, pp. 38-9. Also Stewart, F. in Ady, P. (ed.), *op. cit.*, pp. 69-70.
31.   Lall (1974), *op. cit.*, p. 45. See also Stewart, F. in Ady (ed.), *op. cit.*, p. 73; Streeten, P. (1973), 'The Multinational Enterprise and The Theory of Development Policy', *World Development*, vol. 1, no. 10, October.
32.   Quoted in Stamp, M. (1974), 'Has Foreign Capital Still a Role to Play in Development', *World Development*, vol. 2, no. 2, Feb., p. 124.
33.   Streeten in Ady (ed.), *op. cit.*, p. 53.
34.   OECD (1974), *op. cit.*, p. 141.
35.   Streeten (1973), *op. cit.*, p. 5.
36.   OECD (1974), *op. cit.*, p. 145.
37.   *Ibid.*, p. 144.

38.   Neerso, P. (1974), 'Selected Aspects of Tanzania's Policies on Foreign Investment', *World Development*, vol. 2, no. 2, Feb., p. 144.
39.   Stamp (1974), *op. cit.*, p. 128.
40.   *Ibid.*, p. 127.
41.   OECD (1974), *op. cit.*, p. 139.
42.   Stamp (1974), *op. cit.*, p. 129.

CHAPTER 10

1.   For a critical appraisal of the working of GATT see UN (1964), *Towards a New Trade Policy for Development: A Report by the Secretary General of UNCTAD*, pp. 27, 99-103. See also Sydney Dell who stressed a similar point: 'Countries that would not dream of abandoning their domestic agricultural support policies, involving quantitative regulations of production and price determination, are quite prepared to argue in UNCTAD that the frustration of free market forces is a dangerous thing . . .' (*World Development*, vol. 1, no. 5, May 1973, p. 10).
2.   Dell, *op. cit.*, p. 7.
3.   Based on 'Background Material in the Field of Trade, International Monetary Reform and Development Financing', Annex II of the UN (1975), *A New United Nations Structure for Global Economic Cooperation* (mimeographed).
4.   Elliot (1973), *op. cit.*, p. 24.
5.   Press Communique issued 18 Dec. 1971; quoted in Meier, G. M. (1974), *Problems of a World Monetary Order*, p. 181.
6.   In recent conferences it has been difficult to find out what exactly the US Government's attitude is on certain problems. For example, at UNCTAD III in Santiago, the USA was the only major abstention on the question of the 'link'. But during the conference John Hannah, the Head of AID indicated that the USA was in favour of the proposed 'link'. A spokesman for the US Treasury immediately issued a statement saying that this was not the view of the US Government (see Dell, *op. cit.*, p. 5). Similarly, just before the Rome Food Conference, President Ford while addressing the UN General Assembly categorically denied that the US Government had ever used food as a political weapon. However, during the Conference the US Secretary of State for Agriculture confessed that the US Government had used food aid as a political weapon and defended its possible use as such in future.
7.   Similarly, in recent months the World Bank's 'soft-line' in relation to the OPEC countries has been resented by the US Government.
8.   Even the allies of the USA find it difficult to defend some of the US actions:

> The Government of a country which has intervened in Chile or Cuba cannot effectively denounce the Russians for intervening in Hungary or Czechoslovakia. The Russians may have been brutal but this is not the point. By intervening in other country's affairs the CIA has twice betrayed the principle of self determination which the Atlantic Alliance and the United Nations exist to defend.

(The Editorial of *The Guardian*, 9 April 1975.)
9.   Some developing countries are also open to such criticism. One obvious example is the treatment of Asians in some African countries. Those countries which practice racial discrimination themselves can hardly pass judgement on the racialism of the whites in South Africa or the discrimination against the blacks in the USA.

10.   If in the eyes of the richer countries it was wrong to provide red-carpet treatment to Arafat, it is probably still less defensible to afford VIP treatment to US dignitories in the light of continuous US – particularly CIA – involvement in the internal affairs of other countries because it goes directly against the UN principle of non-interference in the domestic matters of other member countries. It is ironic that one of the highest officials of a founder member of the UN is on record as saying that the US should not stand by and watch a country go communist 'because of the irresponsibility of its own people', an opinion not necessarily shared by many in the USA. Such statements reflect an utter contempt for the developing countries – in fact a contempt for democracy itself – and do not augur well for a meaningful dialogue between the rich and poor nations.

11.   The minority view held by North America, Western Europe, parts of Asia (excluding China, and India) and Latin America was that 'where trends of population growth, distribution and structure are out of balance with social, economic and environmental factors, they can constitute serious barriers to the achievement of sustained development'. This group therefore advocated population planning as an integral part of any effective development strategy. (See Mauldin, W. P., Choucri, N., Notesstein, F. W. and Teitelbaum, M. (1974), 'A Report on Bucharest', *Studies in Family Planning*, vol. 5, no. 12, Dec., pp. 362-3.)

12.   *Ibid.*, p. 372. In a Forum discussion in Rome at the time of the Food Conference some members from developing countries reportedly dramatised this statement by suggesting that a reduction in the total population of the richer countries by one person would save enough resources to support five persons in the developing countries.

13.   Harris, A. (1975), 'Now Where Were We?', *PAN*, January. Most of the details on the Food Conference quoted here are taken from this source. The concrete expression of this policy was reflected in the US Trade Act passed in December 1974, which debars countries from GSP treatment if they join any cartels.

14.   Aziz, S. in an interview with CERES, Feb. 1975, p. 25.

15.   A remnant of the British imperialistic wisdom which claimed yo rule the colonies in their (the colonies) own interests.

16.   *PAN* (1975), *op. cit.*, p. 6.

17.   *Ibid.*, p. 7.

18.   Boerma, A. H. (1975), 'The Thirty Years' War Against World Hunger'. Inaugural Lecture of the Boyd Orr Memorial Trust on 10 April 1975 (mimeographed), p. 21.

19.   This is at a time when some people in the USA are advocating 'triage' – the idea of 'ditching' some people on the high seas so as to reduce the burden of a sinking boat. It is being suggested that 'spaceship' earth has now reached its full carrying capacity so that perhaps some countries like Bangladesh and India should be left to die. Garret Harden, as reported in the London *Sunday Times*, 26 Jan. 1975, p. 7. The tremendous leverage of 'food' in political decisions has also been highlighted by a CIA Study. Unfortunately the analogy of 'triage' is more than just a fiction for many developing countries. Bangladesh (then a part of India) has once before been a victim of 'triage' during the Second World War. One of the main reasons for several million famine deaths in Bengal in 1943 was that the British Cabinet turned down the Indian Viceroy's request for ships to carry the grains the Canadian Government was offering India, on the grounds that the war effort on the Western Front had priority. (See Mansergh, N. (ed.) (1970), *The Tranfer of Power in India*, vol. IV, p. 741.

20.   It is estimated that because of the concentration of processing, marketing and transport of primary commodities in the hands of the richer countries only

about 20 per cent of the price paid by the consumers in the richer countries, ever reaches the producers in the poorer countries.

21.   The original proposals included the creation within the IMF of a financing agency which would lend developing countries up to $10 billion, at a rate of $2.5 billion or more a year, to sustain their development programmes in the face of fluctuations in export earnings; the establishment of an International Investment Trust under the IFC to attract private capital for investment in developing countries by safeguarding against major losses; the creation of an international energy institute to develop alternative sources of energy; the establishment of an international industrialisation institute to aid the developing countries with research on industrial technology, and the establishment of an international centre for the exchange of technological information.

22.   Kissinger's speech to the Seventh Special Session, p. 2 (mimeo).

23.   For a discussion of resource self-sufficiency see Connelly, P. and Perlman, R. (1975), *The Politics of Scarcity*, pp. 97-8.

24.   It is necessary, however, that the American people be made aware of the other side of the story. Developing countries have no so far made any major effort to present their own case. The US 'development' lobby is much weaker than those in Western Europe. Ordinary people in America must be made aware that just a small reduction in military expenditure could make a big difference in the lives of millions in the Third World. In 1973 total US military expenditure was $78 billion as against net official development assistance of $3 billion. If just 5 per cent of the current military expenditure were diverted to the developing countries it would mean a doubling of official development assistance. A reasonably well-fed population in the developing countries is probably a better guarantee against 'communism' than all that military might which failed to prevent many South-East Asia countries from turning communist.

25.   In a recent report, *What Now*, prepared by the Dag Hammarskjöld Foundation for the Seventh Special Session of the UN General Assembly a strong case has been made out for the decolonisation of the Secretariat and the opening of it to qualified Third World candidates 'so as to promote the new concepts of self-reliant pluristic development, as opposed to the mimetic integration into the still-dominant one-dimensional system' (p. 119). The Report argues in favour of early retirement for 'serious rejuvenation of the Secretariat, at all levels'. The question of early 'voluntary' retirement is a debatable issue; it might lead to 'witch-hunt' but at the same time there is certainly a need for retiring people with colonial mentality and people (from both developed and developing countries) who harbour a distinct feeling of contempt for their colleagues, experts and delegates from developing countries. Such people are not rare in the UN agencies. There is also a need for proper scrutiny of the method of appointment of consultants, which has become the greatest source of patronage in the system. Some people prefer to resign from regular appointments but continue to reap rich dividends because of their past connections.

26.   UN General Assembly in its 29th Session has asked for the representation of the Director General of the UNCTAD in all GATT negotiations. An interesting thing about this decision was that the EEC, USA and Japan had opposed this move and the Scandinavians had abstained. (Ref. UN General Assembly, 29th Session, 22nd Committee, Agenda Item No. 42.)

27.   UN (1975), *A New United Nations Structure for Global Economic Co-operation: Report of the Group of Experts on the Structure of the United Nations System* (mimeographed), Annex. III, p. 23.

28.   Dag Hammarskjöld Report, *op. cit.*, outlines five broad areas within which such a 'collective self-reliance' is feasible:

(1)   'Coordination of industrial and agricultural development aimed at securing greater collective economic balance and productive efficiency, with trade among members as a necessary supporting means to achieving these gains. Directly linked to production and trade is the creation of joint or co-ordinated institutions in such fields as transport, marketing and consultancy to facilitate coordinated development of production and to reduce dependence on transnational corporations in trade, transport and knowledge provision.'
(2)   'Reinforcement of autonomous financial capacity in Third World countries through the building up of Third World controlled and funded channels for financial flows.'
(3)   'Movement towards a Third World monetary system.'
(4)   'Strengthening technological capacity through innovation and internalizing the process of knowledge creation, adaptation and use. This is needed to reduce the very heavy and pervasive dependence on foreign created and owned knowledge.'
(5)   'Strengthening autonomous channels of communication among Third World countries and between them and industrial countries to exchange specific information and to help create new patterns of communication, life-style goals and cultural cooperation.' (pp. 78-9.)

There is an urgent need for establishing a permanent Secretariat of the Third World, with its own 'think-tank' to devise ways and means for such cooperation and also to devise strategy and tactics for confronting the richer countries.

APPENDIX 1

1. FAO (1972), *Production Year Book*, p. 718. Sukhatme supplies the following formula for estimating the *per caput* calorie supply per day at retail level:

$$C = \sum (P + I + J_1 - E - J_2 - S - F - W - M) \frac{RN}{Pop} \cdot \frac{1}{365}$$

where summation is over commodities. For any commodity P represents the gross output, I and E represent imports and exports, J_1 and J_2 represent the stocks at beginning and at the end of the year; S stands for seed; F for feeds; W for wastage; M for industrial uses; R represents extraction factor and N is the nutrition coefficient. (See Sakhatme, P. V. (1961), 'The World's Hunger and Future Needs in Food Supplies', *JRSS*, Part IV, pp. 463-508.)
2.   One of the earliest attempts at highlighting the limitations of Food Balance Sheet Sata was an article be Helen Farmsworth (1961), 'Defects, Uses and Abuses of National food supply and Consumption Data', *Food Research Institute Studies*, no. 2, pp. 179-201. There has been some improvement in the collection of agricultural statistics in recent years but Farnsworth's criticisms would still apply to many countries. For a more recent assessment of Food Balance Sheets see Schulte, W., Becker, K. and Naiken, L. (forthcoming), 'Food Consumption, Food Balance Sheets, Food Supplies', *International Encyclopedia of Food and Nutrition*, vol. 5, ch. I.
3.   FAO (1962), *Africa Survey*, p. 126.
4.   Royer, J. (1959), 'Note on Rural Surveys Covering Food Consumption and Household Expenditure in Tropical West Africa', *Monthly Bulletin of Agricultural Economics and Statistics*, vol. VIII, no. 1, Jan.
5.   FAO (1973), *Production Year Book 1972*, p. 415.
6.   *Ibid*., p. 416.
7.   *Ibid*., p. 417.

8.   *Ibid.*, p. 420.
9.   Smit, C. P. G. T. (1962), 'International Comparison of Food Consumption Data', *Monthly Bulletin Agricultural Economics and Statistics*, vol. 11, no. 12.
10.   FAO (1972), *Production Year Book 1971*, p. 718.
11.   A distinction is often made between household budget surveys which include other items of consumption in addition to food and food consumption surveys.

APPENDIX 2

1.   Traditionally energy was expressed in terms of kilocalories but now it is expressed in Joules (KJ), one K Cal is equal to 4.184 KJ.
2.   The FAO convened groups of experts on energy requirements in 1949 and 1956 and on protein requirements in 1953. Another expert group on protein requirements was convened jointly by the FAO and the WHO in 1963 and yet another on energy and protein requirements in 1971. Other groups of experts have dealt with other nutritional elements, i.e. calcium, iron, and vitamins, etc.
3.   FAO/WHO (1973), *Energy and Protein Requirements: Report of a Joint FAO/WHO Ad Hoc Expert Committee*, p. 11. What follows here is largely based on this report.
4.   *Ibid.*, p. 10 (my italics). Since the safe level of protein intake takes into account *nearly all* people this requirement is higher than the *average* requirement.
5.   *Ibid.*, p. 28.
6.   The Joint FAO/WHO expert committee broadly classifies the activities as light (e.g. office workers, professionals, shop workers, unemployed, housewives with mechanical household appliances, etc.); moderately active (e.g. light industry, students, fishermen, soldiers not on active service, housewives without mechanical household appliances); very active (e.g. some agricultural workers, unskilled labourers, forestry workers, soldiers on active service, mine workers, steel workers, etc.); and exceptionally active (e.g. lumberjacks, blacksmiths, rickshaw-pullers, women construction workers). (*Ibid.*, p. 25.) The Committee warns that these categories may have to be modified in view of the peculiar circumstances of a particular country.
7.   *Ibid.*, p. 22.
8.   *Ibid.*, p. 27.
9.   *Ibid.*, p. 32.
10.   Clark, Colin and Haswell, M. (1970), *The Economics of Subsistence Agriculture*, 4th ed., p. 9.
11.   Quoted in Harries, J. M., Hobson, E. A. and Hollingsworth, D. F. (1962), 'Variations in Energy Expenditure and Intake', *Proceedings of the Nutrition Society*, vol. 21, no. 2. p.167
12.   FAO/WHO (1973), *op. cit.*, p. 44.
13.   *Ibid.*
14.   *Ibid.*, p. 48.
15.   *Ibid.*, p. 49.
16.   In estimating protein requirement both protein quality, which depends mainly on the pattern of amino-acids, and the efficiency of utilisation are taken into account. The latter depends on the quality and the quantity of protein in the diet, the adequacy of the diet, environmental conditions and the physiological condition of the person concerned. (*Ibid.*, p. 65.)
17.   The relative concentration of amino-acids in eggs and milk resembles closely the amino-acid requirements of both children and adults. (*Ibid.*, p. 58.) The Committee assumed that pregnant and lactating women and children require

a higher concentration of essential amino-acids than the average adult. (*Ibid.*, p. 61.)

18.   The Committee felt that the quality of protein in the diets of rich countries have an approximate value of nearly 80 per cent of that of milk or eggs (assuming their quality as 100), while those of poor countries are about 70 per cent. But in diets consisting mainly of cassava and maize and little animal food, the relative quality may be as low as 60 per cent. (*Ibid.*, p. 73.)

19.   For instance if protein quality is assumed at 60 per cent level the intake of protein for adult male has to be 62 gr. per day.

20.   For example the Technical Commission of the Health Committee of the League of Nations (1936) and the United States Food and Nutrition Board (1945) recommend a level of 1 gr. of protein per kg. of body weight. (FAO/WHO *op. cit.* (1973), p. 18.) The FAO Committee on Protein in 1957 recommended a safe practical allowance of 0.66 gr. per kg. of body weight in a country with a high standard of living and 0.84 gr. per kg. of body weight in countries where the diet consisted mainly of vegetables. (*Ibid.*, p. 18.) But an expert group of the FAO/WHO (1963) recommended an intake of 1.01 gr. of protein per kg. of body weight. (*Ibid.*, p. 18.)

21.   Clark and Haswell (1970), *op. cit.*, pp. 6-7.

22.   Sukhatme, P. V. (1971), *Summation and Findings of The Protein Problem* (mimeo.) (ESS MSSC/71/6).

23.   *Ibid.*, p. 2.

24.   FAO/WHO (1973), *op. cit.*, p. 19.

25.   *Ibid.*, p. 77n.

26.   FAO (1962), *Report of the Committee on Calcium Requirement*, p. 30.

27.   FAO/WHO (1973), *op. cit.*, p. 77.

28.   *Ibid.*, p. 93.

SELECTED BIBLIOGRAPHY

Abbott, J. C. and Creupelandt, H. C. (1966), *Agricultural Marketing Boards, Their Establishment and Operations*, Food and Agricultural Organisation of the United Nations, Rome.

Ady, P. (ed.) (1971), *Private Foreign Investment and the Developing World*, Praeger Publishers, N.Y.

Aziz, S. (1974), 'The Chinese Approach to Rural Development', *World Development*, Vol. 2, No. 2, Feb.

Balogh, T. (1974), *The Economics of Poverty*, Weidenfeld and Nicolson, London.

Bhagwati, J. (1973), 'Education, Class Structure and Income Equality', *World Development,* Vol. 1, No. 5, May.

Blakeslee, Leroy L., Heady, Earl O. and Framingham, Charles F. (1973), *World Food Production, Demand and Trade,* Iowa State University Press, Ames.

Briggs, J. (1830), *The Present Land-Tax in India: Considered as a Measure of Finance*, Longman, Rees, Orme, Brown and Green, London.

Buringh, P., van Heemst, H.D.J. and Staring, G.J. (1975), *Computation of the Absolute Maximum Food Production of the World*, Agricultural University, Wageningen.

Byres, T.J. (1974), 'Land Reform, Industrialisation and Marketed Surplus in India: An Essay on the Power of Rural Bias', in Lehmann, D. (ed.), *Agrarian Reform and Agrarian Reformism,* Faber and Faber, London.

Casely, D.J., Simaika, J.B. and Sinha, R.P. (1974), 'Instability of Production and its Impact on Stock Requirement', *Monthly Bulletin of Agricultural Economics and Statistics,* Vol. 23, No. 5, May.

Chambers, J.D. and Mingay, G.E. (1966), *The Agricultural Revolution 1750-1880,* Batsford, London.

Chai, W. (1969), *Essential Works of Chinese Communism,* Bantam Books Inc., N.Y.

Chao, kuo-Chun (1960), *Agrarian Policy of the Chinese Communist Party, 1921-1959*, Asia Publishing House, London.

Chao, K. (1970), *Agricultural Production in Communist China, 1949-1965*, The University of Wisconsin Press, Madison.

Chenery, H., Ahluwalia, M., Bell, C.L.G., Duloy, J.H. and Jolly, R.

(1974), *Redistribution with Growth*, Oxford University Press, London.

Clark, C. and Haswell, M. (1970), *The Economics of Subsistence Agriculture*, Macmillan and Co. Ltd., London.

Connelly, P. and Perlman, R. (1975), *The Politics of Scarcity; Resource Conflicts in International Relations*, Oxford University Press, London.

Datar, Asha L. (1972), *India's Economic Relations with the USSR and Eastern Europe 1953-1969*, Cambridge University Press, London.

Dell, S. (1973), 'An Appraisal of UNCTAD III', *World Development*, Vol. 1, No. 5, May.

Dore, Ronald P. (1959), *Land Reform in Japan*, Oxford University Press, London.

Dutta, R. Palme (1947), *India Today*, People's Publishing House, Bombay.

Elliott, C. (1973), *Fair Chance For All: Money and Trade Between Unequal Partners*, United Nations, N.Y.

Ehrlich, Paul R. and Ehrlich, Anne H. (1972), *Population Resource Environment: Issues in Human Ecology*, W. H. Freeman and Company, San Francisco.

Fanon, F. (1967), *Black Skin, White Masks*, Grove Press Inc., N.Y.

Fei, John C. H. and Ranis, G. (1964), *Development of the Labour Surplus Economy, Theory and Policy*.

Food and Agricultural Organisation of the United Nations (1967), *Incentives and Disincentives for Farmers in Developing Countries*, Rome.

Food and Agriculture Organisation of the United Nations (1970), *Provisional Indicative World Plan for Agricultural Development*, Rome.

— (1973), *Production Year Book 1972*, Rome.

— (1973), *Annual Fertiliser Review 1972*, Rome.

— (1973), *Commodity Review and Outlook 1972-73*, Rome.

— (1973), *State of Food and Agriculture 1973*, Rome.

— (1975), *Review of Field Programmes 1974-75*, Rome.

— (1975), *Population, Food Supply and Agricultural Development*, Rome.

Food and Agricultural Organisation of the United Nations and the World Health Organisation (1973), *Energy and Protein Requirements: Report of a Joint FAO/WHO Ad Hoc Expert Committee*, Rome.

General Agreement on Tariffs and Trade (1974), *International Trade*

1973-74, Geneva.

Gray, J. (1974), *Mao Tse-tung*, Lutterworth Press, London.

Griffin, B. K. (1974), *The Political Economy of Agrarian Change: An Essay on Green Revolution*, Macmillan, London.

Griswold, A. W. (1952), *Farming and Democracy*, Yale University Press, New Haven.

Habakkuk, H. J. (1956), 'Essays in Bibliography and Criticism: The Eighteenth Century', *Economic History Review*, Second Series, Vol. VIII, No. 3.

Helleiner, G. K. (1973), 'Manufactured Exports from Less Developed Countries and Multinational Firms', *The Economic Journal*, Vol. 83, No. 329, March.

International Bank of Reconstruction and Development (1975), *Rural Development: Sector Policy Paper*, Washington D.C.

International Labour Organisation (1961), *Employment Objectives in Economic Development*, Geneva.

Ishikawa, S. (1967), *Economic Development in Asian Perspective*, Kinokuniya Bookstore Co. Ltd., Tokyo.

Jacoby, Erich H. and Jacoby, Charlotte F. (1971), *Man and Land: The Fundamental Issue in Development*, Andre Deutsch Ltd., London.

Joy, L. (1973), 'Food and Nutrition Planning', *Journal of Agricultural Economics*, Vol. XXIV, No. 1, Jan.

Kidron, M. (1972), *Pakistan's Trade with Eastern Bloc Countries*, Praeger Publishers, N.Y.

Lall, S. (1974), 'Less Developed Countries and Private Foreign Direct Investment: A Review Article', *World Development*, Vol. 2, No. 3, March.

Lehmann, D. (ed.), *Agrarian Reform and Agrarian Reformism*, Faber and Faber, London.

Lipton, M. (1974), 'Towards a Theory of Land Reform', in Lehmann (ed.), *op. cit.*

Long, Millard F. (1973), 'Conditions for Success of Public Credit Program' in United States Agency for International Development, *Small Farmers Credit: Analytical Papers*, (mimeo.).

Macbean, Alasdair I. (1966), *Export Instability and Economic Development*, George Allen & Unwin Ltd., London.

McNamara, Robert S. (1973), *One Hundred Countries, Two Billion People: The Dimensions of Development*, Praeger Publishers, N.Y.

McCance, R. A. and Widdowson, Elsie M. (1968), *Calorie Deficiencies and Protein Deficiencies*, J. & A. Churchill Ltd., London.

Mansergh, N. (ed.) (1970), *The Transfer of Power in India 1942-47*, HMSO, London.

Meadows, Donella H., Meadows, Denis L., Randers, Jorgen and Behrens, William W. (1972), *The Limits to Growth: A Report for the Club of Rome's Project on the Predicament of Mankind*, Potomac Associates Book, London.

Meier, Gerald M. (1974), *Problems of a World Monetary Order*, Oxford University Press, N.Y.

Mesarovic, M. and Pestel, E. (1975), *Mankind at the Turning Point: The Second Report to The Club of Rome*, Hutchinson & Co. (Pub.) Ltd., London.

Miller, D. S. and Payne, P. R. (1969), 'Assessment of Protein Requirements and Nitrogen Balance', *Proceedings Nutrition Society*, Vol. 28, No. 2, March.

Ministry of Agriculture, Fisheries and Food (1970), *Modern Farming and the Soil: Report of the Agricultural Advisory Council on Soil Structure and Soil Fertility*, HMSO, London.

Moraes, D. (1974), *A Matter of People*, Andre Deutsch Ltd., London.

Murray, T. (1973), 'How Helpful is the Generalized System of Preferences to Developing Countries', *The Economic Journal*, Vol. 83, No. 330, June.

Myrdal, G. (1968), *Asian Drama: An Inquiry into the Poverty of Nations*, Allen Lane, The Penguin Press, G.B.

Nakamura, James I. (1968), *Agricultural Production and Economic Development of Japan 1873-1922*, Princeton University Press, Princeton.

Ohkawa, K. and Rosovsky, H. (1960), 'The Role of Agriculture in Modern Japanese Economic Development', *Economic Development and Cultural Change*, Vol. 9, No. 1, part II Oct.

Organisation for Economic Cooperation and Development (1974), *Development Cooperation 1974 Review*, Paris.

Pelzel, J. (1972), 'Economic Management of a Production Brigade in post-leap China', in Willmott, W. E. (ed.), *Economic Organisation in Chinese Society*, Stanford University, Stanford.

Perkins, Dwight H. (1966), *Market Control and Planning in Communist China*, Harvard University Press, Cambridge, Mass.

Rangnekar, D. K. (1959), *Poverty and Capital Development in India: Contemporary Investment Patterns, Problems and Planning*, Oxford University Press, London.

Rao, C. H. H. (1973), *Investment in Farm Tractors in Punjab (India): Private versus Social Costs and Benefits*, (mimeo.), Institute of

Economic Growth, Delhi.

Rao, V. K. R. V. (1956), 'Investment, Employment and the Multiplier' in Singh, V. B. (ed.), *Keynesian Economics*, People's Publishing House Ltd., Delhi.

— (1970), *The Gandhian Alternative to Western Socialism*, Bhartiya Vidyabhawan, Bombay.

Rawski, E. S. (1972), *Agricultural Change and the Peasant Economy of South China*, Harvard University Press, Cambridge, Mass.

Robinson, Joan (1973), *The Cultural Revolution in China*, Penguin Books Ltd., Harmondsworth.

Schran, P. (1969), *The Development of Chinese Agriculture 1950-59*, University of Illinois Press, Urbana.

Sen, A. (1975), *Employment Technology and Development*, Clarendon Press, Oxford.

Sinha, R. P. (1969), 'Unresolved Issues in Japan's Early Economic Development', *Scottish Journal of Political Economy*, Vol. XVI, No. 2, June.

— (1974), 'Chinese Agriculture: Past Performance and Future Outlook', *Journal of Agricultural Economics*, Vol. XXV, No. 1, Jan.

— (1975), 'Chinese Agriculture: A Quantitative Look', *Journal of Development Studies*, Vol. 11, No. 3, April.

— (1975), 'World Food Security', *Journal of Agricultural Economics*, Vol. XXVII, No. 1, Jan.

Skinner, G. W. (1964-5), 'Marketing and Social Structures in Rural China', *Journal of Asian Studies*, Vol. 24, Nos. 1-3, Nov.-May.

Streeten, P. (1971), 'New Approaches to Private Overseas Investment', in Ady, P. (ed.), *op. cit.*

— (1973), 'The Multinational Enterprise and The Theory of Development Policy', *World Development*, Vol. 1, No. 10, Oct.

— (1974), 'The Limits to Development Research', *World Development*, Vol. 2, No. 10-12, Oct.-Dec.

— (1975), 'Industrialisation in a Unified Strategy', *World Development*, Vol. 3, No. 1, Jan.

Stewart, F. (1974), 'Technology and Employment in LDC's', *World Development*, Vol. 2, No. 3, March.

Sukhatme, P. V. (1969), 'The Protein Gap — Its Size and Nature', *Proceedings Nutrition Society of India*, No. 8, (reprinted by the FAO).

Tawney, R. H. (1964), *Equality* (with a new introduction by Richard M. Titmuss), George Allen & Unwin Ltd., London.

Tuma, Elais H. (1965), *Twenty Six Centuries of Agrarian Reform:*

A Comparative Analysis, University of California Press, Berkeley.

Tyfour, S. A. (1969), 'The Economics of Cotton in Sudan with Special Reference to Sudan Gezira Scheme', unpublished Ph.D. Thesis submitted to Glasgow University.

United Nations Children's Emergency Fund (1975), *Priorities in Child Nutrition in Developing Countries* (mimeo.), (prepared by the Harvard University School of Public Health), N.Y.

United Nations Conference on Trade and Development (1974), *An Integrated Programme for Commodities: Report by the Secretary General of UNCTAD* (mimeo.) TD/B/C.1/166 9 Dec. and supplements: *The Role of International Commodity Stocks*, Suppl. 1, 12 Dec.; *A Common Fund for Financing of Commodity Stocks*, Suppl. 2, 12 Dec.; *The Role of Multilateral Commitments in Commodity Trade*, Suppl. 3, 13 Dec.; *Compensatory Financing of Export Fluctuations in Commodity Trade*, Suppl. 4, 13 Dec.; and *Trade Measures to Expand Processing of Primary Commodities in Developing Countries*, Suppl. 5, 18 Dec.

— (1974), 'Speculation and Price Instability on International Commodity Futures Markets', TD/B/C.1/171, 10 Dec.; Study prepared by W. C. Labys.

United Nations Industrial Development Organisation (1974), *Industrial Development Survey*, N.Y.

United Nations World Food Conference (1974), *Assessment of the World Food Situation* (mimeo.), Rome.

— (1974), *The World Food Problem: Proposals for National and International Action* (mimeo.), Rome.

United States Agency for International Development (1973), *Small Farmer Credit: Analytical Papers* (mimeo.), Washington D.C.

— (1975), *The Tamil Nadu Nutrition Study* (mimeo.), (prepared by Sydney M. Cantor Associates Incorporated, Haverford, Penn.), Washington D.C.

United States Department of Agriculture (1974), *The World Food Situation and Prospects to 1985*, Washington D.C.

United States White House (1967), *The World Food Problem: A Report of The President's Science Advisory Committee*, Washington D.C.

Voelcker, J. A. (1893), *Report on the Improvement of Indian Agriculture*, Eyre and Spottiswoode, London.

Warriner, D. (1969), *Land Reform in Principle and Practice*, Clarendon Press, Oxford.

Watson, A. (1975), *Living in China*, Batsford Ltd., London.

Weitz, R. (1971), *From Peasant to Farmer: A Revolutionary Strategy for Development*, Columbia University Press, N.Y.

Wiff, Larry J. (1971), 'Tariffs, Non-Tariff Distortions and Effective Protection in U.S. Agriculture', *American Journal of Agricultural Economics*, Vol. 53, No. 2, May.

Willmott, W. E. (ed.) (1972), *Economic Organisation in Chinese Society*, Stanford University Press, Stanford.

Wilson, T., Sinha, R. P. and Castree, J. R. (1969), 'The Income Terms of Trade of Developed and Developing Countries', *The Economic Journal*, Vol. 79, No. 316, Dec.

Yanaga, C. (1966), *Japan Since Perry*, Archon Books, Hamden, Connecticut.

Yudelman, M., Butler, G. and Banerjee, R. (1971), *Technological Change in Agriculture and Employment in Developing Countries*, OECD, Paris.

INDEX

Abbott, J. C. 169
Abu Dhabi 129
Ady, P. 177
Agriculture 14-16, 18, 26-7, 31, 33,
    36-8, 48, 71, 73, 75, 104, 108,
    124-6, 137, 159, 161-3, 166, 168,
    173, 178, 182
aid (also development assistance)
    16, 24, 41, 106, 115, 117-31,
    140, 143-5
Albania 174
Arafat, Y. 135
Argentina 41, 101
Australia 8, 18, 20, 76, 103, 137,
    138
Austria 96, 98, 147
Aziz, S. 168, 176, 179

Balogh, T. 88, 172
Banerjee, R. 163
Bangladesh 6, 23, 97, 106, 124,
    179
Becker, K. 181
Behrens, W.W. 170
Belgium 117
Bell, C.L.G. 167
Bergsten, C.F. 175
Bhagwati, J. 87-8, 171, 172
Bhave, V. 85
Bhoodan Movement 85
Bhutan 124
Bienefeld, M. A. 174
Billings, M. 162
Blakeslee, L. R. 161
Boerma, A. H. 3, 158, 179
Bolivia 106, 129
Botswana 124
brain drain 91
Brandt, W. 169
Brazil 23, 41, 101, 165
Briggs, J. 166
Britain (United Kingdom) 8, 15, 28,
    74, 90, 97, 103, 107, 116-17, 124,
    137, 159
(British) Ministry of Agriculture,
    Fisheries and Food 28, 162
Brown, L. R. 159

buffer stock 107, 110-11, 114
Bulgaria 96
Buringh, P. 160-1
Burma 37
Butler, G. 163
Byres, T. 169

cadre 62, 84, 88
calorie 10, 13, 22, 153-7, 159-61,
    182
Cambodia 142
Canada 8, 10, 18, 20, 96, 103, 117,
    124, 138
capitalist farming 52-4
Carroll, T. F. 169
Caseley, D. J. 160
Castree, J. R. 175
Central African Republic 124
cereal 8, 10-11, 14, 20-2, 30, 101-3,
    121-2, 155, 158-9, 161, 174
Chambers, J. D. 75, 169
Chambers, P. 128
Chao, K. 168
Chao, Kuo-chun 168
chemicals 19-21, 41, 95, 102, 161
Chenery, H. 167
Chile 123
China 6-8, 10, 12, 16, 19, 25-6, 31-3,
    44-6, 49-51, 56, 58-65, 68-9,
    85-6, 88, 119, 127, 135, 159,
    164-5, 168, 174, 179
Choucri, N. 179
Clark, C. 182-3
Club of Rome 78-80
collectivisation (also collective
    enterprise) 45, 51, 56-66, 166
    169
Colombia 23, 35
commodity prices 101-4
Common Agricultural Policy (CAP)
    115, 174
commune 56, 59-65, 68, 85, 168
communication 15, 44, 72, 147, 181
community development 45, 59, 163
compensatory financing 109-11
confrontation 4, 90, 132, 141-5
Connally, J. B. 134

191